Eugene J. Molessa

A THEOLOGY OF MARY

A THEOLOGY OF MARY

CYRIL VOLLERT S.J.

HERDER AND HERDER

1965
HERDER AND HERDER NEW YORK
232 Madison Avenue, New York 10016

SAINT MARY'S THEOLOGY SERIES, 3

Library of Congress Catalog Card Number: 64–19740
© 1965 by Herder and Herder, Incorporated
Printed in the United States of America

This book is dedicated to my many friends and associates in the Mariological Society of America, particularly to Juniper B. Carol O.F.M., and Philip J. Donnelly S.J., theologians of depth and originality.

Contents

7

Foreword

Mariology today is a field for the specialist. Father Vollert has long since qualified himself in it, and I have not. Hence, I took up his work with the interest of a disciple, and my expectations, created by years of admiration for his attainments as a theologian, were not disappointed. The work is solid, instructive, satisfying. It reveals at every turn the qualities of theological inquiry commended by the canon of St. Vincent of Lérins—the qualities of sustained, reverent, and temperate thought, which is able to situate a mystery of faith in its right relation to the order of reason, to the mysterious order of the economy of salvation, and to pilgrim-life of the people of God in history.

Father Vollert is rightly concerned with theological clarification of popular marian piety, which often remains, he says, "on a sub-theological level." The faithful "understand that their spiritual life requires filial love of the Mother of God, who is also their mother. But their theological knowledge is likely to be unequal to their piety and apostolic activity. They rightly regard Mary as the ideal of purity, humility, and union with God. They are also aware that her matchless prerogatives flow from her divine maternity. But what is sensed obscurely by all Christians ought to be brought out clearly by theologians" (p. 174).

This is the aim that the author sets for himself. His basic concern is with the organic structure of mariology, with the organization of all the marian dogmatic themes in their relation to one another and to what he calls the fundamental principle of marian theology. Chapter 2, which is the quest for this fundamental principle, is a model of thoroughness, revealing the author's command of the extensive literature. One is reminded of Suarez, "*in quo auditor tota schola.*" No serious voice is left unheard; what each has to say is sifted with serene critical acumen; and the author's own view is stated with modesty and conviction.

The same qualities of wide learning and personal judgment are visible also in the treatment of the co-redemptive mission of Mary, her relation to the work of her Son and of the Church. The situation of this controversial issue, not in a place apart, but in the chapter on Mary and the Church, is witness to the author's delicate theological sense. These pages will command attention, if not agreement, as a contribution to the "growing end" of mariology.

The bulk of the book is given over to the construction of a synthesis of marian dogma and to an orchestration of its constituent themes. The synthesis is firm, and in the orchestration chords of considerable beauty are often struck. In the end, the author comes, as he must, to the underlying theological issue, the development of marian dogma. The issue is of paramount importance today, both from a theological and also from an ecumenical viewpoint. Some theologians, like myself, may find Father Vollert's solution somewhat less than satisfactory, both in its premise —a conception of revelation that seems excessively propositional —and in certain of its dynamic elements, for instance, the appeal to a "higher methodology" (p. 233) available to the magistery of the Church, and to a "divine logic that elevates and perfects our human logic by supplying for its shortcomings" (p. 245). On the other hand, if Father Vollert has fallen short here, he is in good company; no one else has yet found an adequate solution. In fact, as he notes, the materials for a solution have not yet been assembled in the necessary form of detailed historical studies of the actual movement of marian thought within the changing contexts of the Church's life and piety.

There is, I might add, a more disabling deficiency. We do not yet possess an adequate theory of the new world of interiority

which the grace of faith creates within the Christian subject—
and the believing community—who are the historical bearers of
the Church's life of growth in understanding of "the gifts bestowed on us by God" (1 Cor 2:12), whose primary inner principle is the Gift himself, the Holy Spirit given to us. In the absence of this theory, history itself is not intelligible. It may be
that Father Vollert is pointing to this new interior world by
certain of his suggestions. For the moment, however, the suggestions seem not to go beyond an unexplained illuminism. In
any case, Father Vollert has mustered his not inconsiderable
powers of clarity in the statement of a theory of development. It
should be helpful in the ongoing enterprise.

JOHN COURTNEY MURRAY S.J.

Introduction

ON November 21, 1964, Paul VI promulgated the Constitution *De Ecclesia* (On the Church), decreed by the Second Vatican Council. Chapter 8 of the Constitution treats of "The Blessed Virgin Mary, Mother of God, in the Mystery of Christ and the Church." On adjourning the council that same day, the Pope proclaimed Mary Mother of the Church.

Debates during the first two sessions of the council on the schema *De Beata Virgine* had brought to light two apparently opposing trends among the bishops and their theologians. What is the correct place to be assigned to Mary in Christian doctrine and life? This became known as "the marian question."[1] One trend seeks to exalt Mary more and more, to emphasize her privileges and functions; in certain of its representatives it is exposed to the danger of cultivating an independent mariology that obscures relations with the rest of theology. The other trend fears exaggerations and insists on leaving to Mary her place as a creature, a redeemed daughter of Adam, a member of the Church; it desires a better understanding of marian doctrine by relocating it in the whole of theology around the central theme "Mary and the Church." The labels employed to describe the two tendencies, "maximalist" and "minimalist," "christotypical" and "ecclesiotypical," are not very satisfactory. A theologian may be a "maximalist" in one phase of mariology, a "minimalist" in another. He may be a progressive in all the other theological

[1] See R. Laurentin, *La question mariale,* Paris 1963; J. A. de Aldama S.J., *De quaestione mariali in hodierna vita Ecclesiae,* Rome 1964.

13

disciplines, but quite conservative and reserved in marian teaching, particularly if he lives in a Protestant environment and is eager to promote ecumenical fellowship.

The difference between these mentalities is illustrated by their attitudes toward the authority of the ordinary magisterium, especially the great abundance of papal pronouncements about Mary and her offices in salvation history. One side insists on the importance of attending seriously to teachings which the Church has approved for many centuries, which have been preached to the Christian people, which are inculcated by the liturgy, and which popes, one after another for more than a hundred years, have explicitly proclaimed. The other side, while acknowledging the authority of pronouncements emanating from Rome, stresses the necessity of correctly interpreting papal addresses and encyclicals. Most of them are laudatory and hortatory; their purpose is to foster piety rather than to teach definitive truths about Mary. With rare exceptions, the literary form of the documents indicates that they were not designed primarily to propose doctrinal standards.

At any rate, the literary form of the eighth chapter of the new Constitution raises no special problem. The council expressly intends to describe the role of the Blessed Virgin in the mystery of the incarnate Word and the mystical body, as well as the relations of redeemed mankind toward the Mother of God who is also the mother of men. It does not, however, intend to give a complete doctrine on Mary, nor does it wish to settle questions which theologians have not yet fully clarified. Therefore, opinions propounded in Catholic schools concerning her may be retained (54).

Mary's place in the mystery of Christ is clearly set forth. She is the Mother of God, of Christ the Redeemer. Hence she far surpasses all other creatures in heaven and on earth. At the same time, she belongs to the offspring of Adam and so is one with all who are to be saved. She is the mother of the members of Christ, for she cooperated by charity that the faithful might

14

be born in the Church. Accordingly, she is the most eminent member of the Church, and its type and model in faith and love (53).

In consequence of her unique position in the mystery of Christ, Mary has a providentially assigned function in the economy of salvation. The woman who was to be mother of the Redeemer is prophetically foreshadowed in the promise of victory over the serpent which was given to our first parents after their fall into sin (55). As a woman contributed to death, so a woman was to contribute to life. Mary, daughter of Adam, consenting to the divine Word, became the mother of Jesus, the one and only mediator. She devoted herself totally to the person and work of her Son and, by divine grace, served the mystery of redemption under him and with him. "Rightly the holy Fathers see her employed by God not merely in a passive way, but as freely cooperating in the work of human salvation through faith and obedience" (56).

The union of the Mother with the Son in the work of salvation continued from the time of the virginal conception of Christ to his death (57). Mary faithfully persevered in her collaboration with her Son all the way to the cross, where she stood in keeping with the divine plan. Uniting herself with his sacrifice, she lovingly consented "to the immolation of this Victim which she herself had brought forth" (58).

Assuredly, there is but "one mediator of God and men, the man Jesus Christ, who gave himself a redemption for all." Mary's maternal activity in our behalf does not in any way detract from Christ's unique mediation; her salvific influence on men flows from his mediation, depends entirely on it, and draws all its power from it (60). The Mother of the Redeemer, who was also his associate, "conceived, brought forth, and nourished Christ; she presented him to the Father in the temple, and was united with him by suffering with him as he died on the cross. In this singular way, she cooperated by her obedience, faith, hope, and burning love in the work of the Savior in restoring supernatural life to souls. Therefore, she is our mother in the order of grace" (61). Rightly she is invoked by the Church under such titles as advocate and mediatress (62). The source of her mediation is the unique mediation of the Redeemer; and yet, "placed by the grace of God, as God's Mother, next to her Son, Mary intervened in the mysteries of Christ" (66).

The divine maternity, which unites the Blessed Virgin to her Son the Redeemer, is the basic reason why she is also united with the Church. The Mother of God is the type of the Church in the order of faith, love, and perfect union with Christ. The Son whom she brought forth is the first-born among many brethren, in whose birth and education she cooperates with maternal love (63).

The Constitution throughout emphasizes the truth that Mary is a sign of unity in Christ; her salvific activity is wholly oriented toward procuring the union of men with God. Chapter 8 goes far in its effort to synthesize the complementary values of the two trends that have divided theologians.

My purpose in writing this book is not to compose a complete theology about the Mother of God; perhaps such an undertaking is at present impossible. I seek to propose what I regard as reasonable solutions to some problems that have not yet received a wholly satisfactory clarification. Among such problems are the basic principle of marian theology, its scientific structure, the place and function of Mary in the mystical body of Christ, the relationship of Mary to the Church, and the development of marian dogma.

To achieve this aim, I outline an account of contemporary thinking about such controverted themes, discuss the strong and weak points of proposals made by many theologians writing in the main European languages, and finally state my own position. Definitive answers to some questions in this area are hardly forthcoming at the present time. Yet I cherish the hope that I have made a modest contribution toward the progress of marian theology, which has prospered so notably in our day.

For gracious permission to republish, in modified form, sections of this book that have already appeared elsewhere, grateful acknowledgment is hereby expressed to the Bruce Publishing Company of Milwaukee, publishers of the three-volume set, *Mariology;* to J. B. Carol O.F.M., editor of *Marian Studies;* to Joseph C. Fenton, former editor of *The American Ecclesiastical Review;* and to the Catholic Theological Society of America, which issues an annual volume of *Proceedings.*

CYRIL VOLLERT S.J.

I

The Structure of Marian Theology

THE mystery and career of Christ cannot be understood without Mary, for the incarnation took place through her. The theologian cannot reflect on the Word of God or elaborate his science without including the Blessed Virgin. Mary, of all the countless beings that have issued from God's creative hand, has been placed by revelation on an eminence not to be attained by other creatures, and theology signalizes her with a title never before or since accorded to any member of the human race. Around the person of God's Mother and her unique function in the economy of salvation many truths and thoughts of Christian tradition converge. These elements, scientifically explored and organized, combine to form mariology, a part of theology which must be inserted and articulated into this latter discipline and which, in turn, is called on to further theological progress by contributing to the realization of theology's high aim: the clearer, the more certain, the more abundant knowledge of God through a study of his words, his actions and his works. Therefore, theology is necessarily about Mary.

Around the time of the fiftieth anniversary of the definition of the immaculate conception, that is, toward the beginning of the twentieth century, an advance in marian theology was gaining momentum. By 1930 the movement had become truly impressive and in many respects, particularly in precision and

19

fruitfulness of discussion, surpassed all previous endeavors. The goal of this new movement, which shows no sign of abating but on the contrary is steadily accelerating, is no less than the achieving of a thoroughly scientific marian theology.

1. Is Mariology a Science?

The theologian's objective is *intellectus fidei,* an understanding of the faith. Quite naturally, Christ and the mystery of his person were the first truths that had to be clarified; theology started as christology. Pressing hard in the steps of St. Paul and St. John, the two apostles who were also great theologians, the early Fathers triumphantly vindicated the divinity of Jesus Christ.

Soon thereafter the Fathers turned to Mary, and the foundation stone of marian theology was laid: Mary is the Mother of God. Other stones were set in place on this foundation. One had been prepared by St. Paul, who drew out the antithesis between Christ and Adam; extension of this parallel led to the perception that Mary is the new Eve. Furthermore, although Mary was literally the Mother of God, she conceived and gave birth to Jesus without diminishing her virginity, a perfection she never lost. Again, the angel had proclaimed that she was full of grace and that God was with her in a special way. The profound implications of Gabriel's announcement only gradually came to be understood. In contemplating Mary's holiness, theologians saw more and more clearly that she was free from original sin, and that at the close of her earthly life the Mother of God was assumed, body and soul, into heaven.

Theological reflection continued and, as the centuries rolled on, an extensive teaching about the Blessed Virgin was progressively accumulated. Like other theological disciplines, an organized mariology could not appear except at the end of long ages of investigation, formulation, inference and speculation. At the culmination of such a process, the need for systematic organization becomes imperative.

When St. Thomas replies affirmatively to the question whether Christian teaching verifies the notion of science, he understands science in the Aristotelian sense, to the extent that this concept is applicable to theology. According to Aristotle, science is knowledge of one reality in another that accounts for it; science is knowledge of a thing in its cause or principle. Furthermore, such knowledge is discursive, not intuitive. The purpose of science, thus conceived, is to reconstruct the ontological connections whereby that which is derived or subsequent in things is based on and accounted for by that which is primary.

St. Thomas did not think that he had to change this concept of science radically when he transferred it to the domain of supernatural cognition. In this order, too, science is knowledge through causes that explain why things are as they are and cannot be otherwise.[1] The great difficulty that, despite the infused light of faith, the principles of theology or articles of faith are not evident to us was satisfactorily solved by the observation that theology is a subalternate science which accepts its principles from a superior science. Since theology is a science that is subalternate to the science of God and the blessed in heaven, it receives its principles from this higher science in which the principles are intrinsically evident.[2]

Rightly, then, St. Thomas does not simply identify theology with science as described by Aristotle. His question is: does Christian teaching verify the notion and function of science? He finds that theology meets the two requirements of any science. First, Christian teaching furnishes us with truths, intrinsically evident to God and the beatified, that are the sources of other truths. Faith adheres unquestioningly to both kinds of truths. Secondly, when we discover the values of and relations between the truths of Christian teaching, we find that these truths fall into place according to an intelligible pattern in which those

---

[1] See *Posteriora Analytica* 1, lect. 4.
[2] See *Summa Theol.* I, q. 1, a. 2; *In Boetium de Trinitate,* q. 2, a. 2 ad 5.

that express secondary and derived realities are joined, as conclusions to principles or as effects to causes or as properties to essences, to truths that express primary and principal realities.[3]

Accordingly, we have a science when, starting with known truths in any area open to our cognition, we advance to a knowledge of things we had not understood before. Our grasp of Christian teaching takes on the form of science when, beginning with the primary truths we know by faith in consequence of our assent to the First Truth,[4] we come to a knowledge of all reality as God knows it, not on the level of the simple assent of faith, but on the level of our discursive reason, utilizing all the resources and procedures of scientific investigation.[5]

Since the theologian's procedure is scientific, he necessarily employs syllogistic reasoning that leads to conclusions. Yet, since his goal is an understanding of the faith, a grasp of the revealed mysteries in their relations with one another and with man's last end,[6] his main purpose in drawing conclusions is not the uncovering of remote implications of revealed truths, but an intelligent apprehension of the revealed truths themselves. The notion of a theology that strays from the truths of faith deeper and deeper into alien regions the farther it advances has given way again to the Thomistic conception of a theology that leads to an understanding of God.[7]

Deduction is, of course, an indispensable operation in theology, and theologians rightly infer conclusions that have not been revealed. Yet the chief function of deduction in theology is not the derivation of new truths, but an ascent to a more perfect intelligence of truths that are already possessed with the certi-

[3] See M. J. Congar O.P., "Théologie," *Dictionnaire de Théologie Catholique* 15, col. 459f.

[4] *In Boetium de Trinitate*, q. 2, a. 2.

[5] Congar, *art. cit.*, col. 460.

[6] See First Vatican Council, *Constitutio de fide catholica*, chapter 4, Denz. 3016.

[7] See B. Lonergan S.J., "Theology and Understanding," *Gregorianum* 35, 1954, 630–648.

tude of faith. The theologian reasons and he understands; and his very reasoning is understanding, for he moves from principles to conclusions in order to embrace both principles and conclusions in one comprehensive view.[8]

To the mind of St. Thomas, at any rate, the scientific character of theology is not gauged by the deduction of new, unrevealed truths; theology as science is the rational organization of Christian teaching, effected by joining truths that are conclusions to truths that are principles.[9] From the argument of appropriateness to the derivation of consequences, St. Thomas engages in the contemplation of revealed truth. His aim is to know and elaborate, through the complicated processes of discursive reasoning, what God knows in the absolute simplicity of intuition.[10] The final objective of theological study is not the knowledge of conclusions, but the knowledge of God such as he has revealed himself to us.

Accordingly, theology, so far as it can within the limits of human, rational activity, imitates and tries to reproduce the knowledge God has of himself. As St. Thomas says, it is a sort of impress of God's own knowledge, *impressio divinae scientiae*, which is one and simple, yet reaches out to everything.[11]

The general effort at self-examination made by theology is particularly significant when applied to mariology. The twentieth century is active in perfecting a special treatise on the Blessed Virgin; marian theology is in full course of progress. Although the content of revelation about Mary is restricted to a few sentences in the Bible and to brief passages in the ancient Fathers concerning the woman who is the Mother of God and the new Eve, under the guidance of the Holy Spirit immense wealth has been mined from these sources.

[8] *Ibid.* See also *Summa Theol.* I, q. 14, a. 7; II–II, q. 8, a. 1 ad 2.
[9] M. J. Congar, *Bulletin Thomiste* 5, 1938, 500.
[10] M. D. Chenu O.P., *La théologie comme science au XIIIe siècle*, 2nd. ed., Paris 1943, 98.
[11] *Summa Theol.* I, q. 1, a. 3 ad 2.

However, despite the advances that have been made, marian theology has not yet acquired its full development. Theological endeavor has ample opportunity to exert itself in order to construct by research, reflection and discursive reasoning an ordered and coherent corpus of marian doctrine which is capable and worthy of occupying a distinctive place among the treatises of theological science and which, thus articulated as a part in the whole, may in turn contribute to the end of theological study— the more certain and perfect knowledge of God in himself, in his actions and in his effects.

When theologians ask whether mariology may rightfully be regarded as a special treatise in theology, their inquiry is theoretical and methodological. Practically considered, the question has long been answered in the affirmative. Theologians coming after Suarez have actually constructed such a treatise, as their predecessors had erected treatises on the Trinity, christology and the sacraments. They had every right to proceed as they did, for they possessed copious materials to classify and principles that permitted a synthesis.

Yet the methodological question has been repeated. Do we have good reasons and sufficient means for achieving, on the basis of Catholic teaching about the Blessed Virgin, a discipline that will be truly theological and that will constitute a special part of sacred doctrine?[12] Is mariology rightly a distinct treatise in dogmatic theology? Can or ought the study of what revelation discloses on the subject of the Blessed Virgin result in a series of questions organically connected so as to form a doctrinal whole that exposes the value of a vital element of our faith, irreducible to any other class of revealed truths?[13]

The response to such queries depends on the place and function that are to be assigned to Mary, according to God's plan, in

[12] J. Lebon, "L'élaboration d'un traité de mariologie est-elle possible?" *Journees Sacerdotales Mariales* (*JSM*), Dinant 1952, 15.

[13] E. Druwé S.J., "Position et structure du traité mariale," *Bulletin de la Société Française d'Études Mariales* (*BSFEM*) 2, Paris 1936, 11.

the economy of salvation. The reason for a distinct treatise on mariology as an integral part of theology can be discerned only in this perspective, in which Mary is the Savior's Mother who takes her stand at the side of her Son with a personal role in the accomplishment of our salvation. Although a grasp of the details of Mary's cooperation is the fruit of centuries of contemplation and has not yet been completely elucidated, a substratum of doctrine was possessed by the Fathers in common with later theologians. The Fathers beheld in Mary not only the Mother of Christ, but also an associate who shared in the redemptive activity of the Savior. From early times Mary was recognized, though not with the clearer insight of contemporary theologians, as mediatress of salvation. In this general sense, at least, her mediatory office is a truth taught by the Church. Thus, theologians can assert the right of mariology to be a theological treatise.

Not every exposition of marian doctrine is a treatise in mariology. In some manuals written a generation ago, we are likely to find a number of pages about the Blessed Virgin that complement a discussion of christology and soteriology. But mariology is not a mere appendix to the incarnation or a collection of scattered truths about Mary in conjunction with the birth of Christ. Other textbooks reveal a situation that is still less satisfactory. In various parts of the courses on dogmatic theology and even in different volumes, truths about the Blessed Virgin are introduced as exceptions to the common designs of divine providence. The immaculate conception is viewed as an exemption from the universal law of original sin, the assumption is taken to be an anticipation of the general resurrection, and so on. Even if such dispersed theses were brought together in one book bearing a distinctive title, they would not constitute a true treatise of mariology because they would not be a systematic exposition of questions organically linked and stressing a vital factor in the economy of salvation.

A treatise is not a simple series of chapters or theses referring to a single subject. In a treatise all the truths knowable about

NB !

25

the subject are reduced to unity through a consolidating principle that will dominate the entire development and will enable us to appreciate, in due perspective, the importance of every aspect that has a bearing on the intelligibility of the whole. The deepest foundation on which the structure stands must be reached, and it must support the complete edifice as a unit and in all its parts. In short, the treatise must be scientific. And a treatise in theology has the function and verifies the notion of science.

No one would maintain that every book written about the Blessed Virgin is scientific; far from it. But that marian theology is, or can be, scientific is the conviction of all theologians. It is undoubtedly capable of being formed into an organic system of truths logically articulated in the light of principles received from God. It is a part of the science of theology and, like all theology, is originally taught by God through revelation. It also teaches about God, as all theology does; no creature can equal the Blessed Virgin, the Mother of God, in making God known to us. Finally, it leads to God, for Mary, in subordination to her Son from whom she is inseparable, is the way to God for us all.

NB

Repeated pronouncements by the Holy See in recent times, the discussion of Mary's role in redemption by the fathers of the Second Vatican Council, and intensified study by theologians have opened up vast areas of knowledge about the Mother of God. Her unique mission in the economy of redemption is being more clearly discerned. Grave questions remain to be solved; various aspects of Mary's association with the Savior demand clarification; the need of the mind for understanding has to be satisfied. The task of theology is to supply answers that will enable us to know better the perfection of God through the work he accomplishes in the greatest of his creatures. Subject matter for a special treatise in mariology is at hand in rich abundance. Moreover, the many truths relative to the Blessed Virgin are known by God and are knowable by us, not in isolation or without connection, but unified in a logically ordered synthesis. Therefore, the special treatise can be scientific.

To realize fully the potentialities of his science the mariologist has to meet certain requirements.[14] Remarkable progress has been made. Yet theology has never entertained the thought that further improvement is impossible. Mariology must continue to interrogate itself, verify its bases, examine its sources, test the quality of the arguments it uses to develop these sources, and explore the avenues of future advance. The mariologist may not lose sight of the fact that his profession is closely linked with the mission he has received from the magisterium and involves responsibilities to the Christian populace.

The true task of mariology is the scientific study of revelation concerning the Blessed Virgin. God has disclosed to us the necessary mystery of his trinitarian life and the free mystery of man's salvation that is effected through the redemptive incarnation. The main quest in marian theology is the discovery of Mary's place and function in the divine program of redemption, an undertaking that safeguards its theological character, that is, its constant reference to God. The theologian's proper business is the investigation of facts, not of possibilities; and in the domain of mariology these facts originate in God's wise and freely devised plan, which is not known to man except by divine revelation. Consequently, this plan cannot be fabricated by us through a process of logical deduction, as in the science of geometry.[15]

Therefore, the mariologist "must always go back to the sources of divine revelation," and these sources "contain treasures of truth so numerous and rich that they will never be exhausted."[16] Scripture and tradition are the remote sources, for the teaching Church is the proximate source. Hence the mariologist must first interrogate the magisterium, with the purpose of making a methodical inventory of its teachings, properly evaluating

[14] See A. Mouroux, "Quelles sont les conditions de la valeur d'un traité théologique de mariologie?" *JSM*, 1952, 31–76.
[15] *Ibid.* 45.
[16] *Humani generis*, *AAS* 42, 1950, 568.

their sense and their degree of certitude. Since the liturgy is one of the organs of the magisterium, it can furnish testimonies and proofs that are valuable to mariology.[17]

The teaching of the magisterium is the point of departure and the guide for further researches into Scripture and tradition. Even after a doctrine has been defined, such researches are necessary to contribute precision and enhance understanding. They are strongly encouraged by the Church, which assigns to theology the duty of showing how the defined dogma is contained in the deposit of revelation.[18] Pius XII sets an example in his apostolic constitution on the assumption. After affirming that the actual unanimity of the teaching Church is a sufficient criterion, he summons the witnesses of tradition to give their deposition. Their testimonies occupy an important part in the document.

The speculation that takes up where positive theology leaves off must proceed with incisive acumen, yet at the same time with care and prudence. The speculative theologian must maintain contact with the sources. His work may not anticipate the research of the positive theologian, but must follow it and find support in it; revealed truth regulates every phase of theological activity. The procedures to be employed by speculative theology have been indicated by the First Vatican Council.[19] To arrive at a more perfect understanding of revelation, reason should seek clarity from similarities it apprehends between naturally known things and the supernatural world. Knowledge of relations between human beings, such as the relations existing between a son and his mother, between a mediator and the people he is trying to reconcile, can direct the mind to a better grasp of relations in the supernatural order. Ideas gained from a consideration of secular royalty can aid in a description of the regal dignity of Christ and Mary. Other comparisons brought out by positive

---

[17] *Munificentissimus Deus, AAS* 42, 1950, 758ff.
[18] *Humani generis.*
[19] *Const. de fide catholica,* chapter 4, Denz. 3016.

theology or presented by the liturgy yield illuminating insights. The parallel between Eve and Mary is particularly fruitful; as Eve contributed to our fall, so Mary has cooperated in our redemption. The striking points of likeness between Mary and the Church are being intensively studied by mariologists of our time.

The First Vatican Council further directs the theologian to promote understanding by searching out the connections that exist between the mysteries of revelation, particularly the connection with man's last end. Such bonds are real, for God's plan is unified. They are especially important in mariology, as *Munificentissimus Deus* points out in passages that stress the harmony which, by God's will, prevails among Mary's privileges and functions.[20]

A marian theology that is constructed in accord with these ideals is truly scientific. It is a subalternate science which receives its principles, the articles of faith, from the higher science of God. It fulfills the two requisites of science, for it possesses truths that are sources of other truths and joins derived truths or conclusions to primary truths or principles, relating what is less clearly perceived to what is more clearly perceived, and eventually to God, the First Truth. It is knowledge of realities in other realities that account for them, grasping both principles and conclusions in a unified, comprehensive view. Its final end is the reproduction in ourselves of God's own knowledge of himself and his works, faint though that reflection may be, for it is but discursive science as compared with God's infinitely perfect intuition.

Accordingly, mariology may be defined as a distinct, though by no means separate or isolated, part of the science of theology which treats of the Blessed Virgin Mary, Mother of God, from the viewpoint of her position and function in the divine economy of salvation.

[20] *AAS* 42, 1950, 754, 758–761.

2. THE INTERNAL STRUCTURE OF THE TREATISE

Contemporary mariologists are devoting much thought to the problem of the structure of their science. Progress has been made and will continue; yet a thoroughly satisfactory treatise has still to be written. Two tendencies are current and have been succinctly described by M. J. Congar. Of the two ways of constructing a theological treatise about the Blessed Virgin, the one that has been too often adopted proceeds according to the following scheme. Having learned once and for all that Mary is the Mother of the incarnate Word and that she thus enjoys exceptional privileges, theologians of the first persuasion consider her as she is in herself, elaborate a sort of metaphysics concerning her by deducing a series of timeless attributes, and draw out more and more consequences of these privileges. Their procedure is like that of the philosopher or theologian who, in the treatise on God, deduces his attributes from the principle of his absolute perfection. Use is made of principles that are disputable, such as the axiom: "Mary has by grace all that God has by nature and that is compatible with the condition of a creature." Congar thinks that this is a poor method of working out a theology on the subject of Mary, and does not see how mariologists who limit themselves to it can reconcile their procedure with God's absolute freedom in dispensing grace.

Fortunately, this tendency is on the wane. Other theologians are much more intent on investigating biblical sources and on developing a theology that is more solidly rooted in tradition. Mariologists of this second kind, whose number is likely to increase, view marian theology in the light of the economy of salvation, of the free designs of God's grace, as made known by the witness of Scripture interpreted according to the tradition of the Church.[21] A sign of the shift in attitude is the favorable reception accorded to R. Laurentin's aphorism: "Everything can

[21] M. J. Congar, "Notes théologiques à propos de l'Assomption," *Dieu Vivant* 18, 1951, 109f.

be connected with the mystery of the Blessed Virgin's maternity; practically nothing can be deduced from it."[22] This is perhaps an exaggeration, but it points in the right direction.

In any case, the necessity of erecting mariology on the rock of faith must be emphasized; theology has to rest on revelation. Speculative theology may not be separated from positive theology. The passages of the New Testament that formally teach us about Mary must be thoroughly exploited by all the resources of exegesis. Other biblical texts in which Mary is not expressly named, from the third chapter of Genesis, through the Psalms, the sapiential books, the prophets, and up to the Apocalypse with its vision of the woman clothed with the sun, must be probed, sifted, interpreted and applied. Tradition is likewise indispensable. It is needed as a guide toward an understanding of Scripture and as a witness to the unceasing growth of comprehension in the mind of the Church concerning the Blessed Virgin's place in the economy of salvation.[23] Studies of the sources must be conducted in the full light of the teachings of the magisterium. If all this is done, then the fecundity of theological speculation is assured.[24] Piloted by the magisterium, the theologian can decide what ought to be kept or abandoned in the mariological efforts of the past and can prepare the way for mariological progress in the future.

Such progress will be fostered if the mariologist constantly keeps before his eyes several norms that ought to regulate the structure of the treatise. In the first place, unity is essential. The basic principle of the treatise must control its entire development, provide the standard for an accurate appreciation of the relative importance of its various parts and direct the organization of all the truths about Mary into a well-integrated science. Furthermore, mariology must be closely linked to christology. Mary exists for Christ. Christology and mariology must be

NBB!

---

[22] "Le movement mariologique à travers le monde," *La Vie Spirituelle* (*VS*) 86, 1952, 183.

[23] See E. Druwé, *art. cit.* 33.   [24] *Humani generis* 568.

joined in our knowledge because Christ and Mary are joined in reality. Lastly, the true place of mariology in the whole of theology must be clearly discerned and correctly assigned. Its due prominence must be recognized and its full value must be safeguarded. It may not be omitted from the theological synthesis or allotted the status of a poor relation.

Some authors, aware of the necessity of associating Mary with Christ in the enterprise that is common to both of them, wish to develop christology and mariology in parallel lines and to model the latter on the former. Abbé Bonnichon goes so far as to suggest a "reform" that consists in breaking up the course that deals with the Blessed Virgin Mary and distributing its theses among the other treatises of theology. Since the mystery of Jesus and the mystery of Mary illuminate each other, why not join them step by step throughout? The thesis on the immaculate conception is inserted into the treatise on sin. Study of the divine maternity forms part of the course on the incarnate Word and is followed by the thesis on Mary's perpetual virginity. Consideration of Christ's grace is followed by the corresponding thesis on Mary's sanctity. Our Lady's spiritual motherhood complements the theses on Christ's capital grace. The section on Mary as coredemptress is attached to the treatise on Christ the Redeemer, and the assumption is added at this point. Room is found in the treatise on the Church for Mary's queenship; the course on grace is the place for her universal mediation.[25]

Abbé Bonnichon thinks that this scheme has the advantage of displaying the close union between the mystery of Jesus and that of Mary; it sets forth the divine plan in all its beauty, of which the Blessed Virgin's constant collaboration is not the least cause. He sees only one real disadvantage: the unity of

[25] Bonnichon, "Rapport sur la pratique de l'enseignement de la théologie mariale," *BSFEM* 2, 1936, 61f.

marian theology would be impaired and the strong coherence of the treatise would be weakened. In reply to this objection, he asserts that his proposal of integrating most of mariology into christology assures rather than imperils its unity.

In the discussion that followed the reading of Bonnichon's paper at the 1936 meeting of the French Mariological Society, the Abbé Petit mentioned that over the years he had taught mariology ten times. He had employed both methods, that of fusing mariology with other treatises and that of presenting it as a distinct discipline. His experimentation had convinced him that the advantages of the second method were far superior.[26] Agreement with this criticism is expressed by F. J. Connell. Presentation of the theology of our Lady as a separate treatise stresses its importance and brings out the momentous fact that Mary's part in the divine plan of salvation was far greater than merely providing the incarnate Word with a body in which he was to endure suffering.[27]

Notwithstanding Bonnichon's assurances, J. Thomas fears the threat to the very existence of mariology that is inherent in the suggested reform. He admits that, since Jesus and Mary, constituting a single principle of supernatural life for humanity, are joined to the point of being but one, the ideal would be that the two sciences, christology and mariology, should also be but one. However, their fusion would be fatal to clarity of ideas. In his view the best structure of the mariological treatise would be based on a plan that groups together all the truths about the Blessed Virgin, but at the same time connects them with Christ. He likens his own formula to a great christological fresco exhibiting the realization of God's design for salvation and devised as a diptych, in which Christ occupies the primary place and Mary takes her subordinate place. Such a fresco would

[26] *Ibid.* 82.
[27] "Toward a Systematic Treatment of Mariology," *Marian Studies* (*MS*) 1, 1950, 57; see 58ff.

show forth the unity of mediation in the duality of the mediators.[28]

To secure this unity in duality, a preliminary chapter on the predestination of Christ and Mary is set at the head of the two divisions of the single treatise. Such a chapter will show that Mary is willed by God along with Christ to be comediatress with the Mediator. The treatise itself will unfold in a sort of diptych in which Christ and Mary are studied in parallel fashion. There will be three parts to the treatise and each will include two sections. The first part treats of the person of the Mediator and is followed by a study of the person of the mediatress. The second part takes up the work of the Mediator and then the work of the mediatress. Finally, the third part considers the glory of the Mediator and is completed by a consideration of the glory of the mediatress.[29]

This contrivance preserves mariology as a distinct division of theology, but one that is not studied for itself alone. The difficulties are solved by treating Christ and Mary together in the preliminary chapter and by subsequently developing christology and mariology in a fresco with two panels. Thomas believes that his proposal discloses the true sense of Mary's mediation, which, though subordinate, is essential and is modeled on that of Christ because in reality the two are one. There is a single mediation, but it is carried out by two agents who are associated by God's eternal will.[30]

A previous attempt to match christology and mariology had been made by R. Bernard O.P., who wished to derive an entire theology of the Blessed Virgin from the theology of the incarnate Word in such a way as to pattern the former exactly, step by step, on the latter.[31] The idea did not arouse enthusiasm.

---

[28] J. Thomas, "Quelle est la meilleure structure interne d'un traité théologique de mariologie?" *JSM*, 1952, 108f.

[29] *Ibid.* 109–118.   [30] *Ibid.* 124.

[31] "La maternité spirituelle de Marie et la pensée de Saint-Thomas," *BSFEM* 1, 1935, 105–114.

M. Becqué C.SS.R. thought that the endeavor to harmonize the ⑤ two treatises in every detail would turn out quite defective.[32] In all such projects, the treatise on the incarnate Word, which is usually divided into two parts, christology and soteriology, is followed by a bad copy, mariology and marian soteriology. The chapters written about Christ, his mediatorial work and his glorification are reëdited under a marian label. The clarity produced by such iteration is illusory. We have not been redeemed twice, first by Christ and then by Mary. No one even thinks that we have, but the appearance of caricature ought to be shunned.[33] Mary is not a simple replica of Christ. The respective missions of both would be falsified if they were forcibly compressed into a single scheme. A rigid system may not be substituted for the living reality of the mystery.[34]

The light of experience gained from teaching mariology guides M. M. Philipon in drawing up the broad outlines of the ⑥ plan he prefers. In mariological science the divine motherhood has the same pivotal role as the hypostatic union in christology. The treatise is divided into two major parts, following the distinction between the order of being and the order of operation, as in the treatise on the mystery of Christ.

The first part is a scientific study based on causes. Mary's divine motherhood, viewed against the background of the redemptive incarnation, is the constantly recurring theme. The essential nature of the divine maternity and its connection with the hypostatic order must be determined. Then the consequences of the divine motherhood are to be drawn out. These are: in regard to God, special relationships with the Blessed Trinity; in regard to Christ, Mary's association with Christ as the new Eve, coredemptress of the world; in regard to mankind, the

[32] "Que penser des essais modernes de réalization d'un traité de mariologie?" *JSM*, 1952, 102.

[33] See G. Philips, "Lugar de la mariología en la teología católica," *Estudios Marianos (EM)* 10, 1950, 9.

[34] See R. Laurentin, "Marie et l'Église," *VS* 86, 1952, 304.

spiritual motherhood; in itself, Mary's fullness of grace and all her personal privileges. The first part is concluded by a study of Mary as universal mediatress, which sums up the whole mystery as the name "Mediator" sums up the whole mystery of Christ.

In the second part, the great acts of mediation in Mary's life are investigated. Mention of the prophecies of the Old Testament bearing on Mary is followed by a consideration of the acts of God's Mother in behalf of mankind: her cooperation at the incarnation, her coredemptive compassion at the foot of the cross, and her mediatory activity in heaven. By way of general conclusion the cult of Mary is studied; it comprises the cult of hyperdulia and the marian devotions practiced in the Church.[35]

Construction of a truly organic treatise of the theology of Mary requires a thorough analysis of the Blessed Virgin's divine maternity and its illustration by the analogy of human maternity, considered in all the wealth of its spiritual elements.[36] The divine motherhood, root of all the supernatural prerogatives of Mary, perfectly explains her collaboration in the work of our redemption on earth and our sanctification in heaven, as well as her own glorification. Analysis of the divine maternity suffices to account for all her gifts, which are the principles enabling her to perform her mission.[37]

The disruptive effects of Bonnichon's suggestion, which proposes a fusion of christology and mariology, and the element of artificiality discerned in Thomas' "fresco" which envisions mariology as a parallel to christology or its minor counterpart, can be avoided without in any way impairing the structure of marian theology. In fact, the integrity of both treatises requires the

[35] M. M. Philipon O.P., *The Mother of God,* Westminster 1953, 132ff.

[36] This analysis has been competently undertaken by M. J. Nicolas O.P., "Le concept integral de maternité divine," *Revue Thomiste* 42, 1937, 58–93, 230–272. See also the article by G. Van Ackeren S.J., "Mary's Divine Motherhood," *Mariology,* ed. J. B. Carol O.F.M., Milwaukee 1957, vol. 2, 177–227.

[37] M. R. Gagnebet O.P., "Questions mariales," *Angelicum* 22, 1945, 167.

preservation of the unity of each as a distinct part of theology.

The divine maternity is the bond forever uniting Mary with Christ, and therefore mariology with christology.[38] Likewise, the divine maternity, not as viewed by us "in the abstract" but as viewed by God in his infinite wisdom, is the basis of Mary's enduring union with her Son in life, her mediatorial activity on earth and in heaven, and her eternal glorification. At the head of all Catholic beliefs about Mary stands the truth that she is the Mother of Jesus, and therefore the Mother of God. Her motherhood engages her in the mystery of the incarnation; therefore, she is associated with Christ in his mission and his work.

To understand the divine maternity, we must recall that the universe of creatures is divided into three great orders, according to their relationship with God.[39] If creatures are simply effects of God, made to his image and gathered together in an orderly world the better to resemble him, we have the order of nature. If, in addition, we are united to God by supernatural knowledge and love, we are raised to the order of grace, which all spiritual creatures are invited to enter. If a created nature is taken into a personal union with God, it is engaged in the hypostatic order, which the incarnate Word occupies and which draws to itself the orders of nature and of grace. Mary belongs to this hypostatic order because she is the Mother of God. She is not substantially united to God, but has nonetheless a unique relation of real affinity[40] with the second person of the Trinity. Her divine motherhood elevates her above every creature; inseparable from her Son, she is, in the hypostatic order, along with the human nature of the Word, above the entire universe and the

---

[38] From all eternity the Mother of God is united with the incarnate Word in one and the same mysterious decree of predestination. See *Munificentissimus Deus* 768.

[39] See M. J. Nicolas, "Essai de synthèse mariale," *Maria: Études sur la Sainte Vierge*, ed. H. du Manoir S.J., Paris 1949, vol. 1, 707–741. The sketch of the internal structure of mariology attempted in the following pages utilizes some of the ideas expressed in this excellent article.

[40] *Summa Theol.* III, q. 27, a. 4.

37

world of grace. This does not imply that Mary is "thereby snatched away from us," as A. Müller objects.[41] On the contrary, it is the reason why she is so close to us in the order of grace, and especially why she is our mother, as will be seen.

Since the order of grace is wholly orientated to the hypostatic order, which is its foundation, exemplary cause and end, it must find its summit and fullness in those who occupy the hypostatic order, that is, in the human soul of Christ and in the soul of his Mother. The person who stands closest to Christ, the source of grace, receives grace in plenitude from that source. This person is his Mother for from her he received his human nature. Therefore, the Blessed Virgin is the "one full of grace."[42] Mary's fullness of grace involves, in turn, her immaculate conception, her freedom from personal sin throughout her life, and her complete consecration to God. These great gifts are all revealed and are entirely intelligible in the light of the divine motherhood.

The same is true of Mary's perpetual virginity. Her maternity, regarded "in the abstract," can be thought of without this prerogative. In the physical order, it is true, a certain repugnance between maternity and virginity is encountered.[43] Yet, with revelation before us, we can readily comprehend why God's Mother, made fruitful by the action of the Holy Spirit, should preserve an intact virginity at the birth of Christ and ever afterward.[44]

Our Lady's mediatorial office is likewise intelligible. Her divine motherhood locates her in the hypostatic order, in closest proximity to God, who employs the most perfect beings, the ones nearest to him, as intermediaries between him and less perfect beings. Consequently, the Mother of God, along with the man Christ and in total dependence on him, is called on to

[41] *Divus Thomas,* Freiburg, 29, 1951, 398. A summary of this article appears in *Theology Digest (TD)* under title of "The Basic Principles of Mariology," 1, 1953, 139–144.

[42] *Summa Theol.* III, q. 27, a. 5; see q. 7, aa. 1, 9, 13.

[43] See Elias de la Dolorosa, *EM* 3, 1944, 48.

[44] See J. Lebon, *JSM* 23.

share in the activity of divine mercy. Furthermore, Mary accomplished a true work of mediation by the very fact that she became the Mother of God, because by her personal action she rejoined two extremes that had been sundered. Ever thereafter, filled with the same love and desire to serve that had animated her at the incarnation, she could not cease to promote the union of God and man. Her continued mediation is but a prolongation of her divine maternity.

The mediatorial character of Mary's motherhood is traditionally manifested in the ancient theme of the new Eve. By her obedience, her freely yielded *fiat,* she welcomed in herself the incarnation of him who is the source of life, and thus she has given life to the world. Christ is the new Adam, the new first man, in whom man receives a new origin and a new life. The obedience of Christ saves us, as the disobedience of Adam devastated us. Mary is the new Eve, the new first woman, in this resumption of the creative plan, this regeneration of the human race. She is the mother of the newly living through intimate association with him who is their Head.

Woman was created to be the companion of man, his associate in life and particularly in the transmission of life. That is true of the original creation and is true of God's regenerative plan. God becomes man and is the new prototype of the human race. By her motherhood, the woman is associated with him in closest community of life. The man is God, the woman is the Mother of God. To call her the new Eve is to call her his companion. She is associated with him in the divine life of grace and in the propagation of the same divine life of grace.

Her association with Christ is a consequence of her divine maternity. An ordinary mother is not the lifelong associate of her child. In fact, she becomes more and more separated from him as time goes on and he matures. He has his own work and life and finds the complement of his being in another woman. But the divine motherhood is not an ordinary motherhood. The Word existed eternally before Mary was born. He chose her as his Mother, and by becoming incarnate in her contracted with her a bond that has no equivalent in ordinary motherhood and that recalls, while it incomparably transcends, the bond that exists between spouses. Thus Mary's association with Christ stems from the incarnation of the Word in her womb, from her divine maternity.

An exercise of this association is Mary's cooperation in our redemption. Christ's mediation is wrought in three phases: in the incarnation, in the redemption by which the God-man performed the sacrificial act that reunited man with God, and in eternal life whereby the risen Christ communicates to men from heaven, one by one, the graces he merited for them by his passion and death. How could the new Eve, associated with the new Adam in the first and third phases of his mediation, be deprived of a part in the second? This would imply a misunderstanding of the organic linking of these three phases; Mary would have no share in the dispensing of grace if she had no part in its acquisition. And she would have no such function if she were not the consecrated *Socia Christi* by her maternity. To give the incarnate Word to us was not enough for her; in order to have her proper part in the causality of the new life which her Son desires to live in the soul of every man, she had to consent to his death and offer him to God in sacrifice.

What else should we expect? Mary is the perfect mother, entirely mother, with all her energies centered in her only Son and his life's work, for he is her life and apart from him she has none of her own. The perfect mother, she exists wholly for him. She is the only mother in the world who can exist exclusively for her son, for he is the only son in all the universe who is God—her Son, the end of her person and activity. His will is hers, and therefore she cooperates with him in every detail of his life and death. If he suffers she joins him in suffering. If he wills to die, she also will him to die. If he desires to sacrifice himself on the cross for man's salvation, she desires

NBI.

the same and with all her heart offers him to the Father for the redemption of the world.[45]

Thus associated with her Son in the redemptive act of sacrifice, Mary is further associated with him in heaven for distributing the graces of salvation and sanctification that were merited on Calvary. As always, Christ has the main action; but in complete accord with him and dependence on him, the Mother contributes to the birth of the children of God and to their growth in the life of grace.

Christ's total victory over sin entails his total victory over death, the wages of sin, by his glorious resurrection. Mary's maternal contribution to the victory over sin makes intelligible her anticipated glorification in body and soul by her assumption into heaven. The connection between the assumption and the divine maternity is even more direct. The sacred body of the incarnate Word could not be suffered to undergo the corruption of the grave; how could he allow the body from which he issued, with which, in his human nature, he eternally preserves a relation of origin and dependence, to crumble into dust?

Lastly, Mary is the universal Mother. Her whole finality is to be the Mother of God, the God-man Jesus Christ. But Jesus Christ is the Head to which are to be joined the many members who will make up His mystical body, the Church, the two forming a single mystical person, the whole Christ. Therefore, she who has given birth to the Head cannot fail to give birth to the members. Mother of the historical Christ, Mary by her motherhood embraces the whole Christ.

In devotional terms we could say that, at the incarnation, Mary conceived us spiritually, for her maternal action inaugurated the generation of the mystical Christ. On Calvary she bore us spiritually, for there she cooperated maternally to bring about our rebirth in Christ by gaining for us, in subordination to him, the graces of our incorporation into his body. And her

[45] These considerations, succinctly expressed, are the fruit of several discussions with my colleague, Gerald Van Ackeren S.J.

41

mediatory action in heaven is maternal not only by the love that animates it, but also by its proper effect, which is the supernatural birth of men and their growth in divine life. This maternity is the model and the end of all maternity on earth, for nature is for the supernatural, and all men are born to be reborn by being incorporated into the body of Mary's Son.

A mariological synthesis constructed along these lines indicates the hierarchic relation existing between all the truths knowable about the Mother of God. Revelation is the beginning and must be the guiding light throughout. Logic is here in plenty; but it is not the logic of theodicy for the simple reason that theology is not philosophy. It is the logic of revelation.

In consequence of the above considerations, the place mariology ought to occupy in the whole of theology is easily indicated.

3. THE RELATION OF MARIOLOGY TO THE REST OF THEOLOGY

Theology has never neglected the study of the relations existing between the mysteries of revelation and of their bearing on man's last end. Yet the unequivocal doctrine of the First Vatican Council about such procedures has stimulated theological investigation and steered it in the right direction. Reflection on the relations of the mysteries with one another has engendered insights into all phases of revealed truth, and consideration of the connection which each mystery has with man's final destiny has enabled theologians to arrive at a better appreciation of the place of all the mysteries in the economy of salvation.

No part of theology may be erected on its own independent foundation; such isolation would distort perspectives in every part. Scientific labor and didactic method require division of work, but any spirit of divisiveness that results in a closed system is evil and has to be exorcised. The mariological synthesis may not take on even the appearance of autonomy; every chapter must exhibit the vital relations which the treatise has with the whole of theology. Fidelity to the vast, harmonious design of God's wisdom demands the integration of marian theology into the entire Christian mystery.

A tendency in the direction of autonomy appeared in the evolution of mariology during the very centuries that witnessed the decay of all theology, when scholasticism suffered an eclipse. St. Thomas had introduced the Blessed Virgin into his *Summa* in connection with the incarnation of her Son. He raised and solved a number of important questions about Mary, but without giving them the full development they subsequently received. The synthesis composed with masterly skill by Aquinas was a whole, not a congeries of treatises. During the period of transition to such treatises, the followers of St. Thomas were careful to relate them to the various parts of the *Summa,* on which their own works were commentaries. They regarded mariology as a function of christology, and insisted on keeping together the Mother and Son whom God himself had joined. For St. Thomas, the theology of Mary was a sort of chapter in his theology of Christ; for his disciples, the section *De Beata Maria Virgine* became rather an addition appended to the larger division *De Christo.*[46]

Marian theology in the narrower sense is a product of the revival of scholasticism in the sixteenth century. The great theologians of that era were the first to compose distinct treatises about the Blessed Virgin and her part in redemption. Beginning with the seventeenth century a cleavage gradually opened up between mariology and the rest of theology. Mariologists were dominated by the desire to add new jewels to the crown of our Lady, and tended at times to exalt her without reference to the framework of theology as a whole. Scheeben did much to block that movement, although his initial influence

[46] See M. Becqué C.SS.R., *art. cit.* 80f.

was slight. By the end of the nineteenth century the treatise on mariology had acquired its definite position, situated immediately after the treatise on the incarnation and redemption. The decade prior to the Second World War inaugurated a new impetus that has not lost momentum. Contemporary marian endeavor, with its program of a thoroughly scientific marian theology, is surpassing all previous efforts and shows many signs of wholesome progress. Most heartening of all is the firm determination to integrate mariology into the general theological synthesis, to bring out all its relations with every other facet of theological truth. The idea of an independent theology of the Blessed Virgin is happily receding.

Mariology occupies so necessary a place in the divine plan of salvation that without it theology is incomplete and therefore defective. The mystery of Christ is inseparable from the Blessed Virgin through whom the incarnation was accomplished. If we wish to know Jesus, we must know who his Father is; but we must also know who his Mother is. We do not sufficiently understand the work of redemption unless we are aware of the special way Mary was redeemed and the special activity allotted to her in the redemption of the rest of us. We do not perceive the extent of the Savior's love for us unless we appreciate the exquisite kindness that induced him to give his own Mother as our mother. We do not apprehend the deifying power of Christ's grace until we look at her who is full of grace.

Knowledge of Mary leads to knowledge of God himself. And this knowledge is the very purpose of theological study: to know God as fully and deeply as possible by contemplating what he has revealed about himself and about his works in creation, particularly in the creatures he has raised to the supernatural order. The more noble a creature is in this order as a result of God's special love and action, the more such a creature reflects the divine perfections. But among all creatures none has been more favored with God's gifts nor entrusted with a more important mission for the execution of God's designs than Mary.

She is unique by reason of her supernatural endowments and therefore also by reason of her power to make known to us the perfections of the Creator. She is the *Virgo singularis,* never equaled in the past and never to be equaled in the future. She is the only creature who is the mother of God, the only creature conceived immaculate, the only creature who may be called the coredemptress and comediatress along with—but, of course, subordinate to—Christ, and the only creature who is already glorified in body and soul by being assumed into heaven.[47]

Consequently, knowledge about Mary is knowledge about God, because she is, second only to the Savior's sacred humanity, the greatest and most beautiful of his works. She is the ideal woman as Christ is the ideal man.

Any lingering danger that mariology, as cultivated by specialists, may tend to become an independent treatise isolated from the rest of theology can easily be obviated. In our own day it is being offset particularly by the study of mariology in the perspectives of ecclesiology. The two great theological treatises of modern times, mariology and ecclesiology, are being scrutinized in their reciprocal relations, compared in detail and drawn together. Mary and the Church are both mothers of men. The Mother of Christ is the Mother of Christ's mystical body. Christ and Mary and the Church are all for our salvation; as mariology cannot be independent of christology, so neither can it be walled off from ecclesiology.

Another theological discipline that gains valuable insights from mariology is the treatise on the last things. The Blessed Virgin's assumption into heaven bears powerful witness to the truths of eschatology. The coming of the Messiah inaugurated the latter times in the history of the world. Many centuries, perhaps hundreds and thousands of them, may yet unroll; for all we know, we may still be in the early stages of the Christian era. But the kingdom of heaven is near. The last terrestrial phase has been opened by the bodily exaltation of the Mother

---

[47] See J. Lebon, *art. cit.* 25.

of God; with her, the ascent of the human race into heaven has begun.

The importance of mariology in the organism of theology, indicated by these few samplings, is gauged mainly by the place which the Blessed Virgin's person and cooperation with Christ have in the program of salvation. She stands close to the Church but closer to Christ, for the mystery of Mary finds its explanation only in Christ, the incarnate Word, rather than in the Church, Christ's mystical body. Her maternal relation to the Church derives from her maternal relation to Christ, and her collaboration in the genesis and building up of the Church is a consequence of her collaboration with Christ in the redemption of mankind. Therefore, Charles Journet proposes an unacceptable theory when he writes: "Mariology is a part of ecclesiology, that part of ecclesiology which studies the Church at its most excellent point."[48] Mariology is not a part of ecclesiology but a distinct part of theology in its own right. Moreover, even though mariology is connected with ecclesiology, it is far more closely connected with the theology of the incarnate Word.

Theologians have not been entrusted with the responsibility of creating the place mariology occupies in theology. Their task is to scrutinize what God has made known. Since theology is the science of revelation, the position of mariology in theology is the same as the position of Mary in revelation. The place of Mary, and therefore of the theology of Mary, is in the heart of the mystery of God who gives himself to us in Christ and in the continuation of Christ which is the Church; she is in the very depths of christology, which has its prolongation in ecclesiology.[49]

Since the fundamental principle of mariology is the divine maternity, and since the rights of mariology as a distinct part of theology are based on the Blessed Virgin's cooperation in the work of redemption, the treatise on mariology ought to be re-

[48] *L'Église du Verbe Incarné*, Bruges 1951, vol. 2, 293.
[49] See G. Philips, *art. cit.* 8.

lated as closely as possible to the treatise on the incarnation and redemption. To emphasize the relationship is to bring out the force of the truth that God, who could have saved man by the direct causality of his omnipotence, has actually willed to employ mankind itself as the instrument of his saving work. Mankind, plunged into sin by the disastrous decision of its first parents, was to be the instrument of its own restoration. In pursuit of his plan, God drew from Mary the conjoined instrument of our redemption and required her to consent to the incarnation in the name of the human race that issued from Adam.[50] The initiative of our salvation belongs to the Father. But the Father carries out his work through the God-man with his humanity as conjoined instrument and with Mary as subordinate instrument closely linked with the principal instrument.[51] The place thus attributed to Mary in the work of redemption is in full harmony with the teaching of Benedict XV:

Mary suffered so grievously with her suffering and dying Son, and, almost at the point of death herself, so generously renounced her maternal rights over him for the salvation of man and immolated him, so far as lay in her power, to placate divine justice, that she may correctly be said to have redeemed the human race along with Christ.[52]

Mary, Mother of God and of men, inseparably linked with Christ and his redemptive work, is situated at the very summit of the Church, the mystical body of Christ. Theologians are realizing more and more that the theology of Mary will not reach its full development unless its relations with the redemptive incarnation and ecclesiology are clearly apprehended and thoroughly exploited, in causal interactions yet to be worked out. Accordingly, the best place for mariology is between the treatise on the redemption and the theological or dogmatic treatise on the Church.

Theologians of our time are eager to elaborate a scientific

[50] *Summa Theol.* III, q. 30, a. 1.   [51] See E. Druwé, *art. cit.* 30f.
[52] *Inter sodalicia, AAS* 10, 1918, 182.

mariology that will have its true importance and rightful function in theology. They vigorously oppose any deviation toward isolation that would leave marian theology dangling on the fringes of sacred doctrine. Much work remains to be done, but the progress that has been made is an earnest of progress yet to be achieved.

2

The Fundamental Principle of Marian Theology

IF marian theology is to have a sound scientific structure, it must possess a trait that is characteristic of all science. It must marshal all the factors of its material object according to a principle of order. In other words, it must rest on a fundamental principle that will be an immovable base unifying the whole treatise and assuring coherence to all its elements. Furthermore, if marian theology is not a mere appendix to some other branch of theology but is a distinct theological discipline in its own right, it must have its own fundamental principle that will formally distinguish it from other parts of theology and will serve as a source of unity promoting the organization of all the truths knowable about the Mother of God.

Although theologians agree that mariology is scientific theology, they are far from accord when they consider the question of its fundamental principle. The clash of opinions emphasizes a problem that has to be faced. What is the basic principle of mariology? Before this question can be answered, another must be asked. What is the nature of a primary principle in theology?

1. THE NATURE OF A THEOLOGICAL PRINCIPLE

The primary principle of a science is governed by the nature of the science; as sciences vary, their principles must vary. Sacred theology is a science unique in kind; it alone receives its prin-

49

ciples from a higher science that is beyond the reach of the intellect's natural resources. The principles of theology can be known only through divine revelation.

God, the infinite Being, knows himself intuitively and all other beings in himself as participations of himself. Because God has created the universe, he knows the order and intelligibility of all that he has made. The knowledge God has of himself and of all being has been communicated to men, perfectly in the beatific vision, imperfectly in supernatural faith. Yet faith yearns and strives for a knowledge that is less imperfect.

This tendency toward a better understanding of revealed truth operates through an activity of the believer in response to God's initiative. The believer joins his activity to the gift of faith he has received. Thus there arises a new kind of knowledge that starts with faith and engages in an elaboration of the content of faith. The activity is rational and discursive, unfolding according to all the laws, methods and powers of reason. Such intellectual contemplation of the teachings of faith is theology; and, as illuminated and developed in man's reason, it takes the form and obeys the exigencies of all human knowledge. Two such exigencies are particularly imperative in theology: a need of order and a need of unity among the objects of knowledge.

need of :
1. Distinction of Truths
2. Conjunction of these Truths

① God has made all things with order. This order, the product of God's creative knowledge, passes from him to all his works and also to his Word, who communicates some of his knowledge to us. Since reason cannot renounce its need of order, it has to discover order among the objects of the new knowledge which faith inaugurates. The truths given to us for our salvation have to be organized into an orderly body of knowledge, in which what is first in intelligibility is sought as the basis of all the rest, so as to reproduce the order of God's creative knowledge.

② The second exigency, likewise shared by faith and reason, is the need of unity among the objects of knowledge. Reason seeks unity between the knowledge it gains from observation and demonstration and the new truths it receives from faith. The teaching of revelation is developed and illuminated by all the procedures at the disposal of human reason and tends to take a rational form, discursive and scientific, which is theology.

The most important activity of reason in this domain is the organization of the revealed mysteries into a coherent corpus of doctrine; for the revealed mysteries are coherent, both with one another and with all truths that are naturally knowable. Theology draws its very life from the contemplation of such connections and relations.

Some of these mysteries have been revealed directly for their own sake because of the surpassing importance of their content; they are the articles of faith which are also the principles of theology. Others have been revealed for the sake of the main mysteries, which they serve to bring out and illuminate. The truths that constitute the primary object of faith are summed up in the twofold mystery or economy: the necessary mystery of the last end, comprising all that is beheld by the blessed in the beatific vision, and the free mystery of the means by which men are brought to eternal life.[1]

In the work of penetration and intellectual organization of the revealed mysteries, carried on by the study of analogies which natural knowledge furnishes and by the contemplation of the relations which the mysteries have with one another as well as with man's last end, the activity of reason may take different forms, reducible to three: the explanation of revealed truth, the *rationes convenientiae* or perceptions of appropriateness, and deductive theological reasoning.[2] What is most important, how-

[1] See *Summa Theol.* II–II, q. 1, a. 6 ad 1; a. 8; q. 2, aa. 5, 7. *Compendium theologiae* I, cap. 2.

[2] See M. J. Congar, "Théologie," *loc. cit.,* col. 454–456. According to R. Garrigou-Lagrange, "Thomisme," *DTC* 15, col. 849–851, St. Thomas, and with him theologians generally, whatever their theories about the nature of theology, employ eight different procedures, of which only the last and least important is concerned with inferring new conclusions that are not revealed.

51

ever, is not the deduction of new theological conclusions, but rather the explanation of the realities of faith, the gaining of a deeper insight into them, the discerning of their hierarchical relationships, and the understanding of them in their proper function in the whole of revelation. The conclusions themselves are sought not precisely for their own sake, but to aid us in arriving at a more perfect intelligence of the truths of our faith. The entire activity is directed to the goal clearly set forth by the First Vatican Council: that reason, enlightened by faith, may by God's gift acquire a fruitful understanding of revealed mysteries.[3]

If the theologian is to perform his task he must discover a general principle that will dominate the whole of theology or any of its parts, and that will permit its organization. The mind is avid for unity. Revelation is not an accumulation of disparate truths, but God's communication to us of the Word that will save us. Attentive study of each revealed truth will enable us to grasp more clearly the internal unity of the one great mystery. Such investigation requires a basic principle that will regulate the structure of the science. The initial truth sought by the theologian is a principle of intelligibility that will shed light over all the teachings presented by tradition and will empower us to apprehend their basic unity. Theological thought does not proceed exclusively from the one to the many; it also endeavors to gather together many partial visions and reduce them to the original unity of God's knowledge. The movement does not lose itself over the horizon, but with each of its discoveries turns back enriched toward the center.[4]

To serve as primary or fundamental principle of a treatise in theology, a truth must fulfill certain conditions. It must be revealed, for in theology the principles are articles of faith. Since it is revealed, it is absolutely certain, as the principle of any

[3] Const. de fide catholica, chapter 4, Denz. 3016.
[4] See G. Philips, "Perspectives mariologiques: Marie et l'Église," Marianum 15, 1953, 440.

science must be, and therefore can impart its own firmness and consistency to all the elements of the science. Further, it must be theologically rich and fecund, permitting the deduction of theological conclusions and the arrangement of all the factors of the science in logical organization. As the very term denotes, the principle must possess priority that is ontological as well as logical; it must be a supreme, primary reality expressing the basic order of God's knowledge and of his plans for the universe. Finally, the principle must be one. If several principles are put forward, one will have to be the principle of the other, which will then be subordinate and cannot be primary; or else they will be coordinate and independent, with distinct sciences corresponding to the independent principles.

The problem of the primary principle of a theological treatise cannot be settled *a priori*, in accord with the demands of a preconceived system, but must be solved *a posteriori*, after thorough examination of the data of revelation as delivered to us by the magisterium with its interpretations and directives. The task is to investigate what God has ordained; only when we are in possession of the facts can we proceed to work out the harmonies of the divine plan so as to discover what is primary and what is consequent. Who are we to dictate the actions of God by our syllogisms? The theologian must indeed exploit syllogisms—the illative syllogism for drawing conclusions, but mainly the explanatory syllogism as an indispensable instrument for developing understanding. Faith is the principle of this science. Yet even faith is only the proximate principle, for the ultimate principle is the intellect of God, which stamps its imprint on theology.[5]

This problem is basic in the theology of the Blessed Virgin. The primary principle dominates the entire structure of mariology, gives it consistency, confers order on its various parts, and

[5] See *In Boetium de Trinitate*, q. 2, a. 2 ad 7: "*Huius scientiae principium proximum est fides, sed primum est intellectus divinus.*" *Summa Theol.* I, q. 1, a. 3 ad 2: sacred doctrine is "*quaedam impressio divinae scientiae.*"

expedites the unified organization of the whole treatise.[6] With-out it, marian theology cannot be a true science, but only a series of questions or theses succeeding one another without logical coherence.

The primary principle cannot be established independently of revelation. Few treatises are so conditioned by the sources as marian theology. What we know about Mary is not what we may esteem to be most fitting for her, but what God in his wisdom has actually ordained and made known to us. Revela-tion, it is true, does not directly deliver such a principle to us; yet the sources do specify the various offices and functions of the Blessed Virgin, and also indicate the order and subordination among them. God has assigned to her a definite activity in the economy of salvation and has richly endowed her with all the graces and aptitudes needed to discharge it.

The material object of marian theology is made up of the aggregate of graces, offices and privileges with which Mary was invested. The supreme principle that has to illuminate and ex-plain all these elements, thus imparting the unity and consist-ency that will elevate mariology to the plane of science, must express the primary and fundamental mission of Mary in the world, her essence and the very reason for her existence, as well as the precise place she occupies in the program of divine providence.

Yet even when we have found the primary principle, we cannot deduce from it alone all that is knowable about Mary in the shape of certain conclusions which may henceforth dispense with the sources. The tendency of a purely inferential theology is to plumb the depths of revelation in the hope of laying bare a hidden axiom from which all the truths about the Blessed Virgin may be derived by strictly rational methods, as though dogmas such as the immaculate conception or the assumption had to be demonstrated by sheer logic. In that case, a few well-

[6] See G. M. Roschini O.S.M., *La Madonna secondo la Fede e la Teologia,* Rome 1953, vol. 1, 97.

constructed syllogisms would suffice to draw out a string of neatly formulated propositions. If one key concept does not yield the desired result, theologians of this frame of mind come forward with a second—for instance, by supplementing the divine maternity with the idea of coredemption. They then surround these two basic notions with a number of subsidiary norms that will direct the process of exploitation, such as principles of fittingness, transcendence or eminence. Having recast two or three Scripture texts into the form of geometrical theorems, they then go on to deduce an endless series of conclusions. If this method were carried to the extreme, all further investigation of Scripture and tradition and even of the declarations of the magisterium could be bypassed.

No competent mariologist goes that far. Certainly no theologian would be so rash as to think that he could deduce the entire treatise on the incarnate Word from the prologue of St. John's Gospel, or infer all the implications of original sin from a few verses in the Epistle to the Romans. The situation is not different in the theology of the Blessed Virgin.

The mariologist must carefully harvest all the data that revelation proposes about the Blessed Virgin. Under the constant guidance of the magisterium he must search the Scriptures, the Fathers and all tradition. With his intellect attuned to the mind of the Church, he can then contemplate the rich treasures spread out before his eyes. Gradually he will perceive order among his facts.

Exaggerations of the role of deduction in mariology stem from a defective notion of theology. Some authors compare marian theology with theodicy and seek a principle that is the counterpart of the *esse subsistens* from which to derive their whole science by rigorous rational methods. Such a procedure is possible in natural theology because the attributes of God are essential properties that flow necessarily from the principal source, the necessary divine *esse*. But marian theology is quite different in nature from such a metaphysical science which can be developed by reason alone. Metaphysics is concerned with necessary consequences; much of theology, especially in the domain of the economy of salvation, is concerned with free consequences. All the truths of mariology are indeed necessary; not, however, by antecedent, metaphysical necessity, but by the necessity that issues from the free will of God who in his wisdom has disposed matters as he has freely chosen yet could have disposed otherwise.

Mariology is a theological discipline still in formation. Its progress requires that every proposal made for its elaboration should be subjected to wholesome criticism. That is particularly true of its fundamental principle, which is the clue to the mystery of Mary.

2. What Is the Fundamental Principle of Marian Theology?

Concerning this question theologians are far from agreement, and the major differences between them are by no means affairs of mere verbal refinements. Three tendencies are observable in the discussions. Some mariologists propose a single simple principle, some favor a single composite principle, and others, unable to see how the whole of marian theology can be deduced from one principle, frankly acknowledge that there are two. The main reason accounting for the divergence of opinions is the notion authors have about the function of the primary principle in a theological treatise.

Theologians who liken theology to theodicy seek in mariology a supreme principle that will emulate the virtualities of *ipsum esse* or aseity, a principle from which all conclusions can be deduced with strict logic. If the divine maternity does not meet the requirements, they turn to Mary's association with Christ. If neither of these principles is such that all the privileges and functions of Mary are linked to them with metaphysical necessity, they try to combine these ideas in a higher synthesis or, judging that the key ideas are distinct and irreducible, contend that the whole of mariological science rests on two independent principles as on two gigantic pillars.[7]

On the other hand, authors who perceive that all revelation, all faith, and hence all theology are referred to the twofold mystery of God—that is, the necessary mystery of God's trinitarian life and the free mystery of our salvation through the redemptive incarnation—and who likewise note that all the other articles of faith are but applications or explanations of these two essential articles,[8] place marian theology under the second, the free mystery. Therefore, they seek not a connection of metaphysical necessity between the conclusions and the primary principle, but the necessity that is consequent on God's free decrees about Mary's position in the economy of redemption, involving Mary's free cooperation as eternally known and willed by God.

A complete classification of all the opinions need not be reviewed; mariologists are generally content to accept the list compiled by G. M. Roschini.[9] Only the main proposals of recent mariologists will be discussed, including several omitted by Roschini or added since his latest book.

Opinions and Criticisms

1. *The Divine Maternity.* Under various aspects, the Blessed Virgin's divine maternity is regarded by the majority of mariologists as the primary principle of their science. One point of view was ably presented by the Abbé Blondiau in 1921. At the base of the entire edifice of marian theology, veritable cornerstone on which it rests and which assures its cohesion and solidity, is

[7] Thus A. Luis C.SS.R., "Principio fundamental o primario ¿cómo enunciarlo si se da ese único principio?" *EM* 3, 1944, 188f.

[8] See *De veritate*, q. 14, a. 11.

[9] *Mariologia*, 2nd. ed., Rome 1947, vol. 1, 324–347; *Compendium Mariologiae*, Rome 1946, 4–12; *La Madonna secondo la Fede e la Teologia*, vol. 1, 97–115.

this truth, clearly contained in Scripture, affirmed by tradition, and defined at Ephesus: Mary is the Mother of God. The whole of Christianity reposes on this foundation; can we desire for mariology a base more solid than that on which the whole of Christianity logically rests? To this first truth there is attached another, likewise contained in revelation: Mary is the new Eve, the mother of men, associated with the new Adam, Christ, in the order of reparation, as Eve was associated with Adam in the disorder of ruin. The whole theology of the Blessed Virgin flows from these two truths; its assertions are corollaries drawn from them and all its questions are related to what is implicitly comprised in them. Yet the divine maternity is the source of the new Eve relationship, since Mary's spiritual motherhood which is involved in her title of new Eve is dependent on her physical motherhood.[10]

The aspect of the divine maternity concretely considered that is implicit in Blondiau's presentation was insisted on repeatedly by J. M. Bover. He argues that, since Mary's primary reason for existence is her maternity, the germinal idea from which the truths of marian theology issue is the fact that she is the Mother of the Redeemer. However, to serve as the fundamental principle, the divine maternity must be taken not in an abstract sense, but in the concrete and historical sense exhibited in Scripture and tradition. Thus understood, the divine maternity implies another element, namely the principle of association with Christ's redemptive work. This principle of association invests the divine maternity with its historical or concrete significance and makes it the supreme axiom of all mariology.[11]

Bover's insistence on the divine maternity in its concrete and historical sense is taken up by other authors, among them J. A.

[10] L. Blondiau, "Les fondements théologiques de la mariologie," *Mémoires et rapports du Congrès Marial tenu à Bruxelles*, Brussels 1921, vol. 1, 122–125.

[11] J. M. Bover S.J., *Síntesis orgánica de la Mariología en función de la asociación de María a la obra redentora de Jesucristo*, Madrid 1929; "Los principios mariológicos," *EM* 3, 1944, 11–33.

de Aldama, who endeavors to clarify the connection between Mary's motherhood of Christ and her motherhood of men. In the present order the divine maternity essentially implies the spiritual maternity. The supreme principle of mariology is the divine maternity or, if another formula is preferred, Mary's motherhood over the Redeemer. The Blessed Virgin was chosen to be the Mother of the Redeemer. Her maternity as decreed by God must be understood concretely and historically, in relation to the actual Redeemer. Hence her election to this exalted dignity includes: her election to be Mother of God, for the Redeemer is God; her election to maternal union with the Redeemer as such—therefore, the Mother of God must be associated with the Redeemer in a maternal way, for the very work of redemption; her election to spiritual motherhood over men, for redemption is a new communication of divine life brought about by the fact that men, incorporated into Christ as true members, receive from God an adoptive sonship that flows to them from the natural sonship of Christ. Thus Mary's maternal function by which a human nature is given to the Son of God involves our incorporation into Christ. Therefore, Mary, who was made Mother of God for our redemption, is by that very fact Mother of the whole Christ, Head and members.[12]

Other authors have contributed further light to this notion. Elias de la Dolorosa contends that all the secondary principles and conclusions of marian theology can be reduced to the divine maternity, regarded fully and adequately, especially if the *terminus ad quem* is recognized as the main aspect. From this point of view Mary, considered physically and physiologically, is Mother of Jesus-man; considered theologically, she is Mother of Jesus-God; considered morally, she is Mother of Jesus-Redeemer. The moral maternity may be called soteriological because it is wholly directed to the salvation of men and, in its integral concept, embraces both Christ the Redeemer and re-

[12] J. A. de Aldama S.J., "Mariologia," *Sacrae Theologiae Summa* 3rd ed., Madrid 1956, vol. 3, 337.

50 words on a couple of names + what they held.

deemed men who by their solidarity form the mystical body in union with Christ the Head. The point of connection between Mary with Jesus as God and Jesus as Redeemer is the physical maternity. The adequate maternity includes all three modalities.[13]

The necessity of a single primary principle of marian theology is illustrated by M. R. Gagnebet. He recalls that Aquinas, when developing his doctrine on the incarnate Word, employed the single principle of the redemptive incarnation. In this formula the qualification adds not a new principle, but a determination needed to express the concrete form according to which the mystery of the hypostatic union is realized. Throughout the treatise on the incarnation, whether there is question of perfections, of coassumed defects, of consequences of the hypostatic union, or of the mysteries of Christ's life, the principle of explanation is always this integral concept of the redemptive incarnation. In the same way, if the divine maternity is envisaged in its integral concept of motherhood over the incarnate Word-Redeemer, it is seen to be the single first principle of mariology, to which Mary's association in the work of redemption is linked as a consequence. The Mother loves her Son with a love which grace has elevated and adapted to the divine personality of her Son, in order to equip her for her part in the supernatural work of redemption. This love makes her experience in her heart all his joys and sorrows and associates her inseparably with all the actions of his life. Above all, it gives her the power to share in the climactic action toward which every one of his desires and efforts tended. This close union of Mary with Christ makes her the intimate associate of the Redeemer.[14]

A similar parallel between the redemptive incarnation as principle of christology and the coredemptive divine maternity

[13] Elias de la Dolorosa C.P., "La maternidad de María, principio supremo de la Mariología," *EM* 3, 1944, 40f.

[14] M. R. Gagnebet O.P., "Questions mariales," *Angelicum,* 22, 1945, 165f.

as principle of mariology is stressed by M. M. Philipon. In both cases the principle is but one. Throughout his christology, St. Thomas relies in his reasonings on the principles of the hypostatic union and capital grace. But if we look closely, we see that the second flows from the first, after the fashion of a property; the first alone is the fundamental principle. All the christological conclusions, even those derived from Christ's capital grace, are resolved in the last analysis in the light of the hypostatic union that is essentially redemptive, according to the actual plan of Providence; and St. Thomas expressly attaches the second principle to the first in the *Summa*, IIIa, q. 7, a. 13. The situation is the same in mariology. The divine maternity is the basic principle, but other, secondary principles must be appended to the primary principle for the deducing of mariological conclusions.[15]

A formulation of the primary principle proposed by J. Lebon in earlier works is resumed in a later study. Once we admit that, by God's will, the Blessed Virgin is the worthy Mother of the Redeemer as such, the theology of Mary becomes clear, falls into order, and is perfectly unified. All its propositions find a center toward which they converge and from which they radiate to make intelligible the execution, the culmination, and the results of the divine plan.

The formula thus stated is regarded not as a premise from which conclusions are deduced, but as a principle of intelligibility. In its light we are able to understand Mary's unique predestination, her immaculate conception and perfect holiness, her perpetual virginity, and her assumption into heaven. We understand, too, her coredemptive mission that was accomplished in association with and subordination to Jesus. For her maternity conferred on her real rights over the human life of her Son, and these rights she voluntarily renounced to offer him

[15] M. M. Philipon O.P., *op. cit.* 130–136. See also M. J. Dorenkemper C.PP.S., "Subsidiary Principles of Mariology," *MS* 10, 1959, 121–177.

in sacrifice for the salvation of mankind. Finally, we can comprehend that, in consequence of her redeeming merit, she is associated with the Redeemer forever in the distribution of the graces of salvation.[16]

Many other contemporary theologians advocate the divine maternity as the basic principle of mariology.[17] Yet the opinion, especially as proposed by some of its champions, is not without difficulties, and objections have been raised against it.

Appeal is made to authority to dislodge the principle of the divine maternity. The first speculations in the field of marian theology turned around the Eve-Mary parallel. As Adam is the principle of natural life for all men, including Christ, so Christ is the principle of supernatural life for all men, including Adam. The same law of parallelism invites us to consider by what title Eve appeared at the side of Adam; she was not his mother, but his companion and aid. Because of this comparison, we ought to conclude that Mary was primarily predestined as associate; she was to be an aid to Christ, an aid similar to him. This is the reason that accounts for her existence.[18]

Furthermore, the divine maternity seems to provide no norm enabling us to decide which graces and privileges are required by the dignity of God's Mother. Do we merely say that a particular privilege appears to us as suitable for the Mother of God

16 J. Lebon, *art. cit.* 22–24.
17 For example, F. M. Braun O.P., *La Mère des fidèles,* Paris 1953, 99, 115, 181; E. M. Burke C.S.P., "The Beginnings of a Scientific Mariology," *MS* 1, 1950, 121; M. Griffin O.C.D., "The Divine Motherhood, the Basic Principle of Mariology," *MS* 10, 1959, 104–120; H. Rondet S.J., *Introduction à l'étude de la théologie mariale,* Paris 1950, 44. One of the best studies is that of G. de Broglie S.J., "Le 'principe fondamental' de la théologie mariale," *Maria: Études sur la Sainte Vierge,* vol. 6, 297–365. The author argues convincingly that Mary must be regarded as the Mother of God's Son who became incarnate to redeem the sinful race of Adam by a life of expiatory renouncement and by associating mankind, beginning with his own Mother, in his own redemptive renouncements. Thus the divine maternity is essentially oriented to the ends of our economy of salvation, the redemptive finalities to which the life of Christ himself was dedicated.
18 J. F. Bonnefoy O.F.M., "La primauté absolue et universelle de N.S. Jésus-Christ et de la Très-sainte Vierge," *BSFEM* 4, 1939, 90f.

and that another one is not suitable?[19] And even though we regard the divine maternity in the concrete, as historically realized, so that both the divine maternity of Mary and her association with the Redeemer are recognized in her, these two ideas are formally distinct and do not integrate a single principle that could be the foundation of mariology.[20] The divine maternity as such does not include Mary's share in the work of re- demption, for there is no intrinsic connection between it and participation in that work.[21] Therefore, it has to be considered in the concrete, as coredemptive; but then it becomes a composite or complex principle, equivalent to a double principle, and we can no longer speak of a simple primary principle.[22]

Prescinding from this complication, the principle that Mary is the Mother of the Redeemer is not sufficient to contain in germ her entire mission. It indicates her initial association in the work of salvation, in the sense that she brought forth the Redeemer, but does not express the continuation of such association as extending to the objective redemption or to the distribution of all graces.[23] At most, the principle thus formulated suggests that Mary *de facto* cooperated with the Redeemer; but no reason is given. We lack an explanation why the Mother is associated with Christ's work.[24]

The main objection against the divine maternity as the pri- mary principle of mariology seems to be that it is not a source of necessary conclusions. According to Bonnefoy, maternity pertains to the natural order, even for Mary. Therefore, it does not require grace, for grace cannot be demanded or merited by what is natural.[25] L. P. Everett admits that Mary had a right to the state of grace at the moment of the incarnation and a right

[19] E. Druwé S.J., *art. cit.* 22.   [20] *Ibid.* 23.
[21] F. J. Connell C.SS.R., "Toward a Systematic Treatment of Mariology," *MS* 1, 1950, 60.
[22] Roschini, *op. cit.* 112f.   [23] Roschini, *ibid.;* Connell, *loc. cit.*
[24] J. Bittremieux, *Ephemerides Theologicae Lovanienses (ETL)* 12, 1935, 608.
[25] *Art. cit.* p. 93.

never to lose that grace. But he adds that no necessary connection can be found between her other prerogatives and the fact that she was the Mother of God. The immaculate conception, the perpetual virginity, and the office of coredemptress were merely fitting, not necessary.[26] Since all the conclusions of mariology, such as the idea of the new Eve, cannot be deduced from the divine maternity, and since other conclusions are only congruous but not necessary, it cannot be the supreme principle.[27] The doctrine of the divine maternity is not rich enough to comprehend all the perfections and prerogatives of Mary in such a way that they can be derived from it as logical, necessary, definitive conclusions. Therefore, the divine maternity cannot serve as the foundation of mariology.[28]

Critique of Objectors

The attitude of theologians who draw up such objections is quite apparent. They seek an axiom that will contain all of marian theology in germ, a principle from which all the conclusions of the science may be deduced with the metaphysical necessity of a rigorous logical demonstration. Their procedure is like that of the philosopher who undertakes to develop the whole of natural theology from the *ipsum esse* or the aseity of God.

Simple Principle - 2. *The Mission of Coredemption.* Recent proponents of the opinion that the basic principle of marian theology is Mary's coredemptive mission or her function of new Eve build up a strong case. S. Alameda searches into the Fathers for light on the problem.[29] He acknowledges that the Fathers do not speak expressly of a primary principle in the way that the question is phrased by later theologians, but contends that in their discussions of the relations between the various offices of the Blessed Virgin they sufficiently manifest their minds.

[26] L. P. Everett C.SS.R., "The Nexus Between Mary's Co-redemptive Role and Her Other Prerogatives," *MS* 2, 1951, 140–152.

[27] Roschini, *Compendium Mariologiae*, 6.

[28] A. Luis, *art. cit.* 197f.

[29] S. Alameda O.S.B., "El primer principio mariológico según los Padres," *EM* 3, 1944, 163–186.

64

An examination of passages culled from the works of St. Justin, St. Irenaeus, Tertullian, St. Ephraem and a few other ecclesiastical writers up to St. Bernard leads Alameda to the conviction that enough evidence is at hand to show that Mary's mission as coredemptress is the basic idea of marian theology. The Blessed Virgin intervened in our redemption in the way that Eve intervened in our ruin.[30]

The principle thus expressed is not identical with the principle of Mary's general association with Christ. Alameda does not deny the fact of such association, but he is opposed to its errors and inexactitudes. The main reason why he rejects Mary's universal association with all the mysteries and works of Christ as primary principle is that it is not revealed. The view seems to stem from the desire of creating a facile system of mariology: the system of applying to the Blessed Virgin the entire christological soteriology, with certain attenuations. What Christ did, Mary likewise did, although with grace received from him; the graces which Christ had, Mary also had, although in less eminent degree. The system is easy but dangerous; we must remember that Mary is the *ancilla Domini,* far inferior to Christ.[31]

As more correctly stated, the principle derived from the Fathers is the Blessed Virgin's office of coreparation, which in ecclesiastical parlance finds adequate expression in the formula: Mary, the second Eve. This principle is true; the Fathers have employed it since apostolic times to assert that Mary intervened in the work of reparation as Eve intervened in our fall. It is also most firm, since it is formally revealed—as the Fathers insinuate when they comment on the protogospel (Gn 3:15). Further, it is supreme, for it expresses the ruling idea in God's plan, the end to which all the graces, offices and privileges of Mary are ordained. In consequence of this office of second Eve, Mary was made the Savior's Mother. Other consequences follow. Among them is Mary's virginity, for only as a virgin, with a vow of virginity, could she merit to be chosen Mother of the

[30] *Ibid.* 168–177. [31] *Ibid.* 180f.

Savior. Another consequence is her sanctity, enabling her to conquer the serpent, and also her immunity from all sin, original and personal. Mary's title of mother of men, her office of universal mediatress of graces, her assumption, her queenship, and the cult of hyperdulia owing to her are all consequences of her coredemptive mission.

Finally, the principle of the Blessed Virgin's function as coredemptress expresses a single idea, a single fact, that of her intervention in the work of our reparation. At the same time it is so rich that it alone involves all mariological truths and has the added advantage of being a formula consecrated by the Fathers and the whole Church from the beginnings of Christianity.[32] Accordingly, in Alameda's judgment, the coredemptive mission ought to be regarded as the primary principle of marian theology. It guarantees the unity and consistency of mariology as well as, or better than, the principles favored by modern theologians.

L. P. Everett, perhaps the ablest exponent of the view that Mary's office of coredemption is the fundamental principle of mariology,[33] thinks that revelation does not teach a single, simple fundamental principle of marian theology, since the Gospels show the Blessed Virgin fulfilling both the office of God's Mother and that of coredemptress while the Fathers did not treat the question explicitly. However, he adds that, in developing the science of mariology, theologians have a right to put forward a simple, basic principle that will give scientific order and coherence to the discipline.[34]

Mary was chosen to fulfill a twofold office: to bring forth the Savior and to cooperate with her Son in the work of salvation. Of these two offices, which was the more basic? The correct answer will yield the fundamental principle. The divine maternity may truly be called a principle, yet the nexus between it and most of the prerogatives of body and soul possessed by

---

[32] *Ibid.* 183f.   [33] L. P. Everett, *art. cit.* 129–152.
[34] *Ibid.* 151.

Mary is one of fittingness only.[35] An examination of the other alternative results in a perception of absolutely necessary connections. Since God chose Mary to be coredemptress of the human race, he had to confer on her the prerogatives required to fulfill this office. Since her victory over Satan was to be complete, she had to be conceived immaculate and to be preserved from the slightest taint of personal sin. Moreover, because of her association with Christ the Mediator in the work of redemption, she had to be preserved from the consequences of sin; hence she overcame concupiscence and death. Her victory over concupiscence was shown in her virginal maternity, her victory over death by her accelerated resurrection. Finally, by reason of her association with Christ in the acquisition of grace, she merited for herself a strict right to the title of Queen of all men and dispensatrix of all graces.[36]

On the ground of this necessary, causal connection between the coredemption and the other prerogatives, Everett contends that the office of coredemption ought to be accepted as the fundamental principle of marian theology. If any of Mary's singular prerogatives should be removed, she would cease to be the coredemptrix of the human race. Although the divine maternity is the reason why this particular woman, Mary, possessed such great prerogatives, the cause of the prerogatives is not the divine maternity but the coredemption.[37]

In his essay on the structure of mariology, J. Thomas asserts his belief that a study of Mary's predestination leads to the discovery of the true principle that should eventually supersede the principle ordinarily proposed (the divine maternity, understood in the sense that Mary is the Mother of God the Redeemer as such). He regards the principle of the Blessed Virgin's necessary union with Christ the Mediator as more essential than the divine maternity.[38]

---

[35] *Ibid.* 142
[37] *Ibid.* 151.
[36] *Ibid.* 143–149
[38] J. Thomas, *art. cit.* 113.

Mary's mediatorial association with Christ, her *consortium mediativum,* is the principle that unifies the treatise. She is the comediatress with Christ because she is the Mother of the Mediator as such. She is associated with Christ in all that he is and does because she was thus willed by God. As the man Christ Jesus is the Mediator between God and men, she is the mediatress with the Mediator. This principle governs the whole internal structure of mariology, causing its unity and determining its development.[39]

critique

Despite the patristic evidence adduced by Alameda and the argumentation worked out by Everett, the theory that the basic principle of marian theology is found in the doctrine that Mary is the new Eve, associated with the new Adam in redeeming the world, has not commanded much support among theologians. J. Bittremieux dismisses it on the ground that it is excluded by tradition, which considers the divine maternity as the foundation of mariology.[40] In the judgment of A. Luis, no argument of weight can be urged in its favor. Although the idea of the new Eve is the earliest form under which Mary's intervention in salvation appears in tradition and may have been the first of her prerogatives that presented itself chronologically to the Fathers, that does not mean that ontologically it had to precede the idea of the divine maternity.[41] According to G. M. Roschini, the Fathers did emphasize the idea of Mary as second Eve. But we go beyond their thought and their words if we say that in their minds the divine maternity was a consequence of the office of second Eve or a means to realize that office. The Fathers do not say this and they cannot say it. Alameda makes the Fathers assert much more than they actually do assert.[42] Although the Fathers are aware of a relationship between Eve and Mary, the new Eve in patristic tradition is the Church rather than Mary.[43]

[39] *Ibid.* 124.   [40] See *ETL* 12, 1935, 608.
[41] *Art. cit.* 200f.   [42] *Op. cit.* 249.
[43] C. Moeller, *Lumen Vitae* (*LV*) 8, 1953, 249.

Moreover, as Luis observes, in treating of the supreme principle of mariology we may not prescind from the divine maternity, Mary's most sublime prerogative; and the divine maternity cannot be deduced from the principle of association. Reasons of fittingness may be urged in favor of uniting both privileges in the same person, but such reasons are not enough to found a scientific system.[44] The same difficulty occurs to F. J. Connell, who asks: "How does this doctrine include the divine maternity?" Even though some connection could be shown, the subordination of the divine motherhood is highly incongruous.[45] Roschini agrees that it is wrong to degrade the divine maternity to a secondary place. Besides, the divine maternity cannot be deduced from the principle of *consortium,* for God could have conferred on Mary the quality of new Eve without elevating her to the dignity of being his Mother.[46] If the association is understood concretely, in the sense that it presupposes the divine maternity on the ground that Mary is Christ's *socia* because she is the Mother of God, then the divine maternity itself and not the idea of new Eve is prior and ought to be recognized as the fundamental principle.[47] By what right does anyone make the divine maternity depend on the office of second Eve? The contrary is true: the office of second Eve depends on the divine maternity.[48]

3. *Twofold Principle: Mother and Associate.* Dissatisfied with the principles thus described and in despair of finding a single principle from which the whole of marian theology may be deduced, some theologians contend that two primary principles must be acknowledged. Others, who are generally of the same mind, deny the existence of two such principles, but propose theories that actually assert two distinct principles.

With complete candor, J. Bittremieux prefers to speak of two

Two Primary ?

---

[44] A. Luis, *art. cit.* 200.   [45] *Art. cit.* 60.
[46] Roschini, *art. cit.* 113.
[47] Roschini, *Compendium Mariologiae,* 7.
[48] Roschini, *La Madonna secondo la Fede e la Teologia, loc. cit.*

principles: the Blessed Virgin is the Mother of God and she is the associate of her Son the Redeemer. A theoretical reason favors this preference: divine maternity and association in the office of the Redeemer are distinct. They are connected; association presupposes the divine maternity as its foundation, and the maternity is ordered by God to the association. Yet to be mother is one thing and to be associate is another. A practical reason supports the same view: mariology can thus be constructed on the model of christology. Theologians generally divide this treatise into two parts, of which one treats of the incarnate Word, the person of Christ, and the hypostatic union with all its consequences, and the second treats of the office of Christ the Redeemer. Accordingly, we have a parallel: as Christ is God and Redeemer, so Mary is Mother of God and associate of the Redeemer.[49]

This duality cannot be denied. Mary's maternity and her association in Christ's work do not coalesce into a single concept. Yet the duality is coherent. It is fitting that the new Eve should stand at the side of the new Adam and that men should have a mother and coredemptress at the side of Christ the Redeemer.[50] Although these two offices are realized in the same person, they are not necessarily connected, for the association cannot be reduced to the divine maternity. Therefore, they are two formally distinct principles.

In his work on the mariology of St. Alphonsus Liguori, C. Dillenschneider presents these two principles: Mary is the worthy Mother of God, and she is the worthy associate of Christ the Mediator.[51] Yet these two primary principles are not simply parallel; there is a close bond between them. Our Lady's divine maternity and her mediation, or her divine maternity and her maternity of grace, are inseparable and imply each other. The

[49] J. Bittremieux, "De principio supremo mariologiae," *ETL* 8, 1931, 250f.
[50] J. Bittremieux, *ETL* 12, 1935, 609.
[51] *La Mariologie de St. Alphonse de Liguori,* Fribourg 1934, 56.

first is ordered to the second and the second finds its ontological foundation in the first. However, they are not reducible to a single concept; the active role of mediatress or of new Eve cannot be strictly inferred from the title "Mother of God." The two ideas ought to remain formally distinct and may not be mingled in theological reasoning.[52]

During a discussion of this question at a later date, Dillenschneider remarked that he preferred speaking of a single concrete reality (the Blessed Virgin Mary) with two different formal principles. The original unity has to be guarded, but for reasoning the two principles are required.[53]

After observing that any science is more solid and harmonious in proportion as the truths integrating it are more perfectly contained in its generating principle, A. Luis asserts that mariology, to be a genuine theological treatise, must combine the traits of true science. In addition to ordering its material object systematically, it must be founded on a principle from which its theses are derived with impeccable logic and to which all its truths converge. As in theodicy all authors admit *actus purus* or aseity as a basic principle, so in mariology it is necessary to assign a note, quality or perfection that is the fundamental principle from which all the other excellences and prerogatives of the Mother of God are deduced, a principle that accounts for their unity.[54]

But none of the activities of the Blessed Virgin as Mother of God and men may be omitted from the formulation of the supreme principle. Mary's mission is twofold: to invest the

---

[52] *Ibid.* 58–61. The same theory is shared by J. Keuppens, *Mariologiae Compendium,* Antwerp 1938, 12, and by G. Alastruey, *Mariologia,* Valladolid 1934, 3.

[53] See *BSFEM* 2, 1936, 41. This renowned mariologist subsequently modified his views in favor of the proposal that the basic principle of an organic mariology is Mary's divine, messianic maternity in its personal, soteriological and ecumenical dimensions. See his book, *Le principe premier d'une théologie mariale organique,* Paris 1956, esp. 172. This work is a notable addition to the literature on the subject.

[54] A. Luis, *art. cit.* 188.

Word with human nature and to cooperate with him in restoring the human race.[55] The Mother of God is the spiritual mother of men because she supplies them with the life of grace, aids them in developing it, and preserves them in it. This spiritual maternity is so important for a grasp of Mary's saving mission that it may well replace the principle of association to designate her activity as coredemptress of mankind.[56]

Thus the principle must include the divine maternity and the spiritual maternity in the full sense of its soteriological functions. Is this principle single or double? Luis feels impelled toward a single principle because of his conviction that mariology is *one* science, and to be *one* it cannot be better governed than by a single principle. Yet he is unable to see how the entire coredemptive mission of Mary can be derived from the concept of divine maternity.

He agrees that Mary, by giving birth to Christ, Head of the mystical body, concurred in the initial phase of our regeneration and so is mother of men in an inceptive way. But he does not see how that first cooperation in the redemptive work includes her association in the whole of redemption.[57] Until further clarification of the union between the two maternities is forthcoming, in such a way that the maternity of grace is shown to be formally included in the divine maternity, he reluctantly gives his adherence to the theory of a double basic principle.

Reflection on the problem has led Roschini to relinquish his former position in favor of a new theory. However, the earlier point of view had exerted considerable influence and hence is included in our survey. According to the opinion he subsequently abandoned, neither the divine maternity nor association with the Redeemer can constitute the supreme principle of mariology; therefore, the mind has to turn elsewhere.[58] Although the idea of the divine motherhood is quite distinct from the idea of

[55] *Ibid.* 189.   [56] *Ibid.* 212.
[57] *Ibid.* 216f.
[58] Roschini, *Mariologia,* 1st ed., Milan 1941, vol. 1, 433; *Compendium Mariologiae* 7.

72

association, the two can be combined into a single supreme principle which is not simple but complex. In other words, the two distinct ideas are closely linked and thus enable us to speak of one principle; for coordination and connection imply unity, which is like a middle term between duality and simplicity. The primary (but complex) principle of mariology should be thus formulated: "Mary is the Mother of God and associate of the Mediator." From these two truths, aptly combined in this fashion yet equivalent to two irreducible principles, all the conclusions of mariology can be inferred.[59] This "conciliatory opinion" is substantially identical with Bittremieux's teaching, as Roschini himself avows.[60]

Support for this view is given by A. Mouraux,[61] who turns to the texts of the New Testament that describe the place and role of Mary in the economy of salvation. These passages disclose the principle of mariology and are summed up by Pius XII in *Munificentissimus Deus:* "Sacred Scripture proposes to us, as before our eyes, the gracious Mother of God in closest union with her divine Son and always sharing his lot."[62] The Pontiff's words indicate the very principle of marian theology, which contains two ideas that are connected though distinct: the maternity of Mary regarding the Redeemer as such and the close association between Jesus and Mary.[63]

The formulation of this double principle is said by E. Druwé to represent true progress in the scientific elaboration of mariology. The authors who hold it bring out the fecundity of each of these principles, but also insist on the intimate connection of Mary's two missions. However, they have to concede that the two ideas remain formally distinct and that no process of strict reasoning permits passage from one to the other. Yet who does not sense that in the divine mind the idea realized in Mary must imply a higher unity in which both of these aspects are synthe-

[59] *Ibid.* 11f.
[61] *Art. cit.* 31–76.
[63] Mouraux, *art. cit.* 62.
[60] In *Mariologia.*
[62] *AAS* 42, 1950, 768.

sized and fused?[64] The desired higher synthesis has been disclosed by Scheeben, who may well have discovered the true principle of mariology.[65]

Working in his own personal and original way, Scheeben had unearthed a vein of patristic tradition that led him to the concept of bridal maternity (*braütliche Gottesmutterschaft*), meaning that Mary was at once the mother and the spouse of Christ, as Eve had been given to Adam as his wife and aid. The divine maternity itself is the main, basic and central privilege to which all the privileges are joined as subordinate, derived attributes.[66] But the factor that distinguishes Mary's motherhood from all others and constitutes her personal character[67] is a special, supernatural union with the person of her divine Son which cannot be better designated than as a divine matrimony in the strictest sense of the word. "Mary, as united with the Logos, is taken up by him in complete possession; the Logos, on his part, as infused and implanted in her, gives himself to her and takes her to himself as partner and helper in the closest, fullest and most lasting community of life."[68]

Scheeben makes this personal, materno-sponsal character of the Blessed Virgin the keystone of his entire mariology. Mary is the Mother of Christ because she gave birth to him; she is the bride of Christ because she is joined to him in a union like that of husband and wife. The motherhood itself is bridal because of Mary's freely given consent to be God's Mother. All the truths of mariology are derived either from Mary's motherhood or

[64] E. Druwé S.J., *art. cit.* 23.   [65] *Ibid.* 29.

[66] M. J. Scheeben, *Hundbuch der katholischen Dogmatik,* Freiburg im Breisgau 1882, vol. 3, 489.

[67] On Scheeben's views concerning Mary's "personal character," see H. Mühlen, "Der 'Personalcharakter' Mariens nach J. M. Scheeben: Zur Frage nach dem Grundprinzip der Mariologie," *Wissenschaft und Weisheit* 17, 1954, 191–213. In dependence on Scheeben, the author inquires whether mariology ought to be erected on the principle of the distinction between nature and person, which is essential to the dogmas of the Trinity and the incarnation. He inclines toward an affirmative answer.

[68] Scheeben, *op. cit.* 490f.

from her consortship with Christ, yet neither concept can be logically deduced from the other. Thus Scheeben bent all his efforts to the discovery of a higher synthesis that would include both the motherhood and the consortship. Ultimately, he found this higher synthesis in the formula: Mary's "bridal motherhood."[69]

The ideas put forward by Scheeben have been further reworked by C. Feckes,[70] who shows that according to tradition the fundamental principle of marian theology must include the divine maternity; yet the divine maternity alone is not enough. Even the so-called adequate maternity is not a sufficient basis for Mary's role as associate. If the title "new Eve" is taken as principle, the way to the maternity would be unsafe. The solution consists in combining both concepts into the bridal motherhood of God, in which "the two apparently disparate ideas are joined in Mary because they are connected in the one divine idea."[71] The divine maternity requires Mary's assent; since the assent is free, the concepts of Mother of God and of associate appear united, and Mary is at once mother and spouse of God. The bridal motherhood is a single idea; Mary is Mother because her first service as associate was her maternal contribution, and she is bride because her maternal service had a bridal character through her *fiat*.[72]

Although E. Druwé regards the proposal of a double principle as a sign of progress in marian theology, he prefers Scheeben's formula, which involves more than a mere juxtaposition of two distinct concepts that are united only *de facto* in the actual realization of the redemptive economy. The "bridal motherhood" is a single concept in which the formal aspects of spouse

---

[69] Perhaps the best exposition of Scheeben's doctrine on the primary principle is found in C. Feckes, "Scheeben, théologien de la mariologie moderne," in H. du Manoir, ed., *op. cit.* 564–568.

[70] "Das Fundamentalprinzip der Mariologie," *Scientia Sacra,* Köln-Düsseldorf 1935, 252–276.

[71] *Ibid.* 268.   [72] *Ibid.* 269.

and mother are intrinsically united so as to integrate a reality that is perfectly one.[73]

Criticism of the double principle has been far more widespread than acceptance of it. Few mariologists would agree with the encomium pronounced by J. Coppens on the occasion of a review of the theological career of Bittremieux: "There is question here of the keystone of the whole system. . . . If it is well cut and placed, the entire edifice holds solidly together. . . . Bittremieux has followed an impeccable logic so as to assure to each of the parts the needed firmness."[74]

In fact, the theory of two principles, consisting in the divine maternity combined with the principle of association or with that of coredemption or with that of spiritual maternity, is judged inadmissible. Since there are two principles, the unity of mariology is shattered. The device of joining the principles into a complex formula fails to save the situation; the artificial formula does not change the reality.[75]

The basic reason advanced in favor of this dualism is rejected by Elias de la Dolorosa. Authors who affirm two fundamental principles in mariology are misled by the comparison they make between mariology and theodicy. They seek a principle from which all the conclusions of the science can be deduced with metaphysical necessity. They analyze the concept of maternity and are unable to find the coredemption included in it; the ideas of maternity and coredemption are ontologically distinct and independent. Therefore the coredemption does not flow from the divine maternity; hence the latter is not by itself the supreme principle of mariology and requires the principle of coredemption as its companion principle. The false reasoning consists in the misguided notion that the two sciences are identical in structure, whereas they are wholly diverse. We must focus the powerful light of Scripture and tradition on Mary's

[73] E. Druwé, art. cit. 26.   [74] J. Coppens, ETL 23, 1947, 348.
[75] S. Alameda, "El primer principio mariológico según los Padres," EM 3, 1944, 181.

maternity. If the divine maternity, thus illuminated by the light of revelation, is found to include the coredemption, we easily perceive that it is the supreme principle of mariology. The source of the connection is not the nature of the relation between the abstract concepts of maternity and coredemption, but the will of God who intends his Mother to be his associate in the work of salvation. Accordingly, those who assert that the divine maternity and Mary's association in redemption are irreducible principles have been seduced by their erroneous notion of the nature of theology.[76]

Like every branch of theology, mariology must have one simple principle; otherwise it would not be a single treatise. Roschini's composite principle does not elude the difficulty. For if one of its members is not reducible to the other, then we have two principles; if it is thus reducible, then there is only one simple principle.[77]

Although in his earlier writings Roschini had no quarrel with the twofold principle, he objected to the doctrine taught by Terrien in *La Mère de Dieu et la Mère des hommes* and later resumed by Luis that the supreme principle is composed of Mary's divine maternity and her spiritual maternity. He argued that, on the contrary, the concept of association is wider than that of spiritual maternity and is to be preferred, since the basic principle ought to be most universal. The concept of association is not limited to Mary's association in the supernatural regeneration of men (spiritual maternity), but includes her association in the reconciliation of men (objective redemption) and in the distribution of graces (subjective redemption).[78]

Roschini finds little to commend in Scheebens' theory of bridal maternity. The idea seems to him too novel; it is unknown to the Fathers and was apparently personal with Scheeben. Actually, it means nothing else than coredemptive

---

[76] E. de la Dolorosa, *art. cit.* 38–44.
[77] M. R. Gagnebet, "Questions mariales," *Angelicum* 22, 1945, 165.
[78] Roschini, *Compendium Mariologiae* 11.

maternity. Therefore, it should be called coredemptive maternity, which is a more precise theological term.[79] But even then, Mary's association in the work of the Redeemer is not sufficiently expressed. The initial association is indeed expressed—in the sense that Mary truly gave birth to the Redeemer—but the continuation of such association is not brought out. Therefore, we must come back to the complex principle: "Mary is Mother and associate of God the Redeemer."[80]

But in that case the theory is exposed to all the ruinous attacks launched against the views of Bittremieux. Scheeben's notion does not go beyond a mere verbal junction[81] and so does not represent any substantial advance toward a solution of the problem.[82] To understand Mary's intimate and loving association with the work of her Son, we need not have recourse to the confused concept of bridal maternity that is so dear to Scheeben's disciples, for such cooperation is a manifest consequence of her maternal relationship with Jesus Christ, the Redeemer.[83]

The assertion that Mary is not only Mother but also spouse of Christ has no foundation in revelation. Nowhere in Scripture do we read that Mary is spouse of the Word; she is exclusively his Mother. This union between Mother and Son surpasses the union of husband and wife. In other words, Mary is truly associated with Christ in his redemptive work—not however as his spouse, but as his Mother. Her motherhood eminently includes all that the biblical image of spouse suggests.[84] Nor do the Fathers lend support to Scheeben's view. They do not, as it is sometimes averred, teach that Mary is related to Christ as Eve is related to Adam. They established a certain relation between Eve and Mary, and then resumed the relation between Adam and Christ that is brought out by St. Paul. For the Fathers, the

[79] *Ibid.* 9f.   [80] *Ibid.* 8.

[81] C. Moeller, *LV* 8, 1953, 248.   [82] Luis, *EM* 3, 1944, 206.

[83] Gagnebet, *art. cit.* 166.

[84] F. M. Braun O.P., "Marie et l'Église, d'après l'Écriture," *BSFEM* 10, 1952, 15f.

new Eve as spouse of the new Adam is not Mary, but the Church.[85]

Thus the Mother of God is not identified with the spouse of God either by Scripture or by the Fathers. The combination "bridal motherhood" is the invention of Scheeben, who mingles the flowery and figurative language of the Fathers with the formal and abstract vocabulary of the scholastics and tries to include the disparate qualities of mother and spouse in a single, unthinkable concept.[86]

4. *Mother of the Whole Christ or Universal Mother.* A frame of mind common to mariologists who eventually come to two principles is the persuasion that all the prerogatives and offices of Mary cannot be strictly deduced either from the formal concept of divine maternity or from her position as second Eve. García Garcés shares this attitude. However, he prefers a formula that, in appearance at least, is simple, even though it may contain two virtualities which are actually reduced to two principles. Moreover, he desires to supplant the idea of Mary's association with Christ by her spiritual maternity, which enjoys greater favor in ecclesiastical usage and is more easily grasped.[87] Combining the divine maternity and the spiritual maternity in a single principle is not difficult; to express Mary's motherhood over Christ and over us, we have an apt formula: "The Blessed Virgin is the Mother of the whole Christ." This principle discloses God's will of associating Mary's physical motherhood regarding Christ, Head of the mystical body, with her spiritual motherhood over men, Christ's mystical members. It also emphasizes Mary's special characteristic: she is always and completely mother. With the aid of this principle, we can deduce all conclusions pertaining to the nature, properties and exercise of her spiritual maternity.[88]

[85] M. J. Congar O.P., "Marie et l'Église dans la pensée patristique," *Revue des Sciences Philosophiques et Théologiques* (*RSPT*) 38, 1954, 3–38.

[86] G. Philips, *Marianum* 15, 1953, 443.

[87] N. García Garcés C.M.F., *Mater Coredemptrix,* Turin-Rome 1940, 121f.

[88] *Ibid.* 123f.

In his earlier works, Roschini had slight esteem for this opinion. He held that the concept of *consortium* was wider than that of spiritual maternity, since it included, besides Mary's cooperation in the spiritual regeneration of men, her association with Christ in the reconciliation of mankind with God and in the distribution of graces.[89] Moreover, two ideas or two really distinct principles—divine maternity and universal mediation—are discerned in this proposition, with the added inconvenience that the two diverse ideas are joined in a vague and obscure formula which has merely an illusive appearance of a single principle.[90]

Nevertheless, the views of García Garcés influenced Roschini's subsequent thinking and led him to take a similar position. Roschini confesses that he had formerly agreed substantially with Bittremieux, for he thought that two supreme principles had to be admitted—the divine maternity and association with the Mediator—because the divine maternity is quite distinct from the idea of association in the work of mediation, so that one could not be reduced to the other.[91] By the time the second edition of his *Mariologia* appeared, in 1947, he had abandoned this position and was in quest of a formulation of the primary principle that would express Mary's august mission in a simpler and more universal way. After long reflection he felt he had at length found the desired principle: the universal maternity of Mary: Mary is the Mother of Christ and of his mystical body, of the Creator and of creatures; briefly, Mary is universal Mother. This principle is formally one and virtually complex, since the universal motherhood comprises all beings, the Creator as well as his creatures.[92]

The concept of universal motherhood dissolves all the seeming antinomies found in the theory of two principles. This universal maternity is a most simple concept: the concept of maternity. Hence it is a single, simple principle and accounts for

[89] *Compendium Mariologiae* 11.   [90] *Ibid.* 10.
[91] Roschini, *La Madonna secondo la Fede et la Teologia* 1, 114.
[92] *Ibid.*

all of Mary's prerogatives, which God conferred on her either in preparation for or as a result of her divine maternity with relation to Christ and her spiritual maternity with relation to men. Even Mary's mediation is a consequence, not a source of the universal maternity. Mary is mediatress because she is a Mother, not Mother because she is mediatress. Thus the idea of universal mediation, which is diverse from the idea of Mother of the Creator, is not diverse from the general idea of universal Mother, that is, Mother of the Creator and of creatures. Hence the idea of mediatress of creatures coincides with the idea of mother of creatures. Consequently, the supreme and simple principle of all mariology is found in the idea of universal Mother.[93]

Patrons of such theories try to join the divine maternity and the spiritual maternity in a single principle, and they think they succeed because the formula "Mother of the whole Christ" or similar variants possess a specious unity. Yet, as Alameda observes, formulas of this kind involve the acquisition of two ends, the exercise of two offices, the discharging of two missions: the giving of physical life to the Savior and of spiritual life to men. Since the ends and missions are different, not all can aspire to the honor of being first. The illusive unity of the formula is the result of a desire to reduce the principles of marian theology to one and thus to safeguard its integrity.[94] But all the objections lodged against the double principle retain their validity.

Furthermore, the substitution of Mary's spiritual maternity for the coredemption is a step backward. The spiritual maternity implies the coredemption; Mary is our spiritual mother because she bore us spiritually by coredeeming us. Roschini's conversion to his new opinion was unfortunate. He now holds that Mary's universal mediation and queenship flow from the universal maternity. But the truth is that the universal queenship and the spiritual maternity are consequences of the universal mediation.[95]

Roschini's aim has been the discovery of a formula that would

[93] *Ibid.* 115.   [94] Alameda, *EM* 3, 1944, 181f.
[95] L. P. Everett, *MS* 2, 1951, 135f.

join the two essential ideas, mother and associate, into one basic principle. At first he found his solution in the complex proposition, "Mary is the Mother of God and associate of the Mediator." This was a mere makeshift. The two ideas are correct, but lack functional unity. Later he adopted the simple formula "Mary is the universal Mother," that is, Mother of God and mother of men. The new solution has the aspect of greater unity but, like the old one, is wanting in strict logical coherence.[96]

The most penetrating criticism is that of A. Luis. He is ready to admit that the formula "Mary is Mother of the whole Christ" has a fair appearance. But it labors under the heavy disadvantage in that the term "mother" has a tremendously different value as applied to the Head and to the members of the whole Christ. The term has two senses, which vary as it is applied to the diverse parts making up the whole Christ. Mary is Mother of Christ according to nature and mother of men according to grace. The principle revolves around a twofold maternity and so is reducible to two distinct principles.[97] This theory does not bring us a single step closer to a satisfactory solution of the problem.

5. *Mary, Prototype of the Church.* Most of the difficulties inherent in the question of the fundamental principle of marian theology vacillate between two poles: Mary is Mother of Christ; Mary is associate of Christ. Some authors attempt, without notable success, to surmount the dichotomy by reducing the first term to the second or the second to the first. Others resign themselves to the embarrassing duality. Otto Semmelroth proposes a new solution. The two principles are merely two aspects of a third that is more basic. The true fundamental principle is Mary regarded as the archetype or prototype of the Church.

The divine maternity, even when qualified as bridal, can be traced back to a more fundamental mariological principle. We can find this principle if we compare the mysteries involving

[96] A. Müller, "Um die Grundlagen der Mariologie," *Divus Thomas* 29, 1951, 387, 390.

[97] Luis, *EM* 3, 1944, 211.

Mary in an endeavor to perceive how one of them results from another until we come to one that cannot be reduced any further. This principle is Mary, as prototype of the Church. Even the divine maternity has its basis in this idea. Mary was called by God to be his Mother in order that she might be the archetype of the Church.[98]

If we go on to ask which of all the marian mysteries most closely links the Blessed Virgin with the economy of salvation, we again come to Mary as prototype of the Church. The basic principle of marian theology must be that mystery which, while conferring unity on the science, is also the point at which it is inserted into the whole of theology. Mariology is theologically significant only because of Mary's vital relationship with the work of redemption. The center of the economy of salvation is not the physical, historical Christ, but the whole Christ, that is, Christ with his Church, which as his bride appropriates his work by receiving from him its fruits and distributing them to the various members. Therefore, the basic mystery of mariology is the one which brings Mary into closest proximity with the Church, and that is the mystery of Mary as prototype of the Church. This mystery places Mary in the very center of the economy of salvation, the Church in its essential function as intermediary of redemption. As prototype of the Church, Mary is the Church in germ; hence she possesses the fullness of the grace of the Church, and this grace she imparts to the Church as it develops in space and in time.[99]

The main interest in this point of view is the new conception it offers of Mary's association with the mystery of redemption. The principle of Mary as prototype of the Church enables us to attribute to her a coredemptive function not like that of Christ, but like that of the Church. The role of mankind, represented and typified in the Blessed Virgin, is not an active, causal, pro-

[98] O. Semmelroth S.J., *Urbild der Kirche*, Würzburg 1950, 37f. English translation, *Mary, Archetype of the Church*, New York 1964, 49.
[99] *Ibid.* 48.

ductive cooperation in the work of redemption, but exclusively a free receptiveness, under the influence of grace, of saving union with God.[100] The acceptance of redemption was made by the Church, in the person of Mary, at the time Jesus was accomplishing his work on Calvary. Thus Mary had a real office in the order of objective redemption; but this was entirely an office of receiving, with a causality that was purely receptive.[101]

Commentators tend to take a dim view of Semmelroth's thesis. The idea of Mary as prototype of the Church is an illuminating aspect of mariology, but can hardly be its foundation. If it were, it would have to be derived directly from Scripture and the patristic writings of the earliest centuries. On this capital point, the author's interpretations of the passages he adduces are far from being decisive.[102] The view that Mary is a type of the Church is undoubtedly found in some witnesses of tradition, but the contention that this notion is the basis of marian theology cannot derive support from them.

A notable weakness of this solution is that it reduces the divine maternity, which is more fundamental, to the Church, which is a consequence of Mary's motherhood.[103] The theory errs in subordinating the divine maternity, which is revealed in Scripture, to the Church, which presupposes the dogma that Mary is Mother of Christ.[104] The difficulty is compounded by the fact that in the Christian consciousness the parallelism between Mary and the Church is much less clearly perceived than the divine maternity. How, then, can it serve as principle?[105]

At the beginning of his study, Semmelroth shows that marian

---

[100] *Ibid.* 89.

[101] Further consideration of these views about Mary's part in our redemption is reserved for our chapter on Mary and the Church. An interesting question arises: is Semmelroth's primary principle the source of his coredemptive theory, or did the latter inspire his quest for a primary principle? In any case, they are likely to stand or fall together.

[102] J. Bésineau S.J., *Sciences Ecclésiastiques* 6, 1954, 283; see Congar, *RSPT* 34, 1951, 627.

[103] R. Laurentin, "Marie et l'Église," *VS* 86, 1952, 299.

[104] C. Moeller, *LV* 8, 1953, 248.

[105] G. Philips, *Marianum* 15, 1953, 453.

theology has suffered grievously from being based on a double
principle such as "Mother of God and new Eve," "Mother of
God and spouse of the Word," and the like. But the new principle he advocates does not dissipate this ambiguity. Mary's relation to the Church supposes a term that is common to both of
them, and what is this if not the divine maternity? Thus his
principle expresses a double enunciation: "Mother of God and
type of the Church."[106] The theory is a sort of appendix to
Scheeben's thought.[107] And Semmelroth admits that Scheeben's
"bridal maternity" expresses more or less the mystery he himself
has in mind when he speaks of Mary as prototype of the
Church.[108] Hence the objections brought against Scheeben's
thesis can be effectively turned against Semmelroth's essay.

With regard to the consequence drawn from the principle of
prototype, that Mary's role in redemption is one of mere receptivity, we may well ask whether Semmelroth's presentation of
the concept of coredemption does not destroy the concept itself.
This distorted idea of Mary's coredemptive function hardly does
justice to the declarations of the popes, especially of Pius X and
Benedict XV.[109]

6. *Fullness of Grace.* Like Semmelroth, Alois Müller derives
inspiration from Scheeben. The theory he advances is the fruit
of his book *Ecclesia-Maria: Die Einheit Marias und der Kirche*
(Freiburg in der Schweiz 1951), a patristic inquiry into the
nature of Mary and the Church. Müller himself summarizes the
main points brought out in his book:

1. Mary's decisive act with regard to salvation was her motherhood of Christ; here the Fathers are unanimous. Mary's contribution was her faith and obedience to God. By faith she conceived the Word of God.

2. From the beginning the Church, too, was designated
"Mother of God." The two scriptural truths, that Eve is ful-

---

[106] Bésineau, *loc. cit.*   [107] Moeller, *loc. cit.*
[108] *Op. cit.* 21f.
[109] J. Brinktrine, *Theologie und Glaube* 44, 1954, 473.

filled in the Church and that she is likewise fulfilled in Mary, prepared the way for recognizing first the Church, and then Mary, not only as Mother of God, but also as bride of God. The Church is the virgin that conceived of the Holy Spirit and thus became Mother of God.

3. Christ is conceived in the hearts of his followers by the fact that they hearken to the Word with faith, and he is born in them through baptism and the grace of sanctification. This birth of Christ in the hearts of the faithful and in the Church is the accomplishment of the work of redemption, a divinization and sanctification of mankind in Christ, a union with God as Christ's human nature was united with the Logos.

4. Therefore, the chief mystery of Mary and the essential mystery of the Church coincide: it is the bridal union with God through grace which leads to divine maternity. This mystery was accomplished in Mary and in Christians under the same conditions: by opening the soul for the Word of God by faith, and the union is based on the real union of Christ with his mystical body. Hence the mystery of the divine motherhood in the Church is not a special mystery, but is simply the general mystery of grace, of man's salvation.[110]

The final conclusion of the patristic investigation is that "Mary is the perfect [realization of the] Church—the essential mystery of the Church is the mystery of Mary."[111] And the mystery of Mary is the mystery of man's salvation, of the union with God granted by God and received by the creature.

This doctrine, which in Müller's interpretation is taught by the Fathers, gives rise to a problem. At the bottom of the problem two truths are found. The first truth is the identity of Christ with his mystical body. The second truth is that men or the Church form members of Christ, become mothers of Christ, by the act of faith, that is, by conceiving the word of God. Mary also conceived Christ by faith in the word of God. Consequently,

[110] A. Müller, *loc. cit.* 389.   [111] *Ecclesia-Maria,* 232.

Mary's divine maternity and reception of grace in the Church are one and the same thing. Hence the mystery of the Church and the mystery of Mary are one and the same mystery, that is, the mystery of human salvation, the mystery of the union between God and the creature, a union in which the creature has the function of spouse and mother. Thus Mary is the absolute, universal and perfect realization of the Church, that is, of God's salvific plan.[112]

At this point a question arises: is a new fundamental principle of mariology required by this teaching of the Fathers? Up to now, the divine maternity has been put forward as the basic principle. But according to Müller, this principle is simply and purely grace which, however, has always been regarded as subordinate to the divine maternity and as coming to Mary in consequence of that dignity. How are sanctification through grace and the divine maternity related?[113]

In undertaking a reply to this question, Müller insists that Mary's divine, bridal motherhood is identical with the bridal motherhood of the Church; the former is the perfect realization of the latter. Hence we can take as the fundamental principle of mariology that Mary is (the archetype of the Church or) the perfect Church. Here the Church is regarded in its most general and primary aspect of bridal reception of grace in Christ. And so there emerges the fundamental principle of mariology which was first heard from the angel's lips: Mary is the one who is full of grace. Here we stand at the foundation and beginning of the whole theology of salvation. All we know of grace and the Church has its perfect form in Mary, and all we know of Mary has a counterpart in the Church and in the life of grace.[114]

Now the question can be answered. If Mary and the Church are equal in divine motherhood and if this motherhood rests on

---

[112] A. Müller, "L'unité de l'Église et de la Sainte Vierge chez les Pères des IVe et Ve siècles," *BSFEM* 9, 1951, 36.
[113] "Um die Grundlagen der Mariologie," 386.
[114] *Ibid.* 390.

reception of grace, we are forced to the conclusion that Mary's physical motherhood of Christ is the immediate consequence, a kind of formal effect, of her perfect sanctification through grace. Müller is quite aware that this contention will be rejected by most theologians, who generally represent Mary's fullness of grace as the first necessary consequence of her predestination to the divine maternity, as Christ's created grace is the consequence of the hypostatic union.[115]

Nevertheless, Müller thinks that his position is correct, for there is only one plan of salvation: to unite human nature to God in the Son and to divinize mankind by participation in Christ. This participation is brought about by the free decision of man, who surrenders himself to God as bride to her husband through faith and by the sacrament of baptism. By this receptive act, which is like that of a wife, man conceives and gives birth to a member of Christ, and so is rightly called a mother of Christ. But Mary conceived and gave birth to the physical body of Christ by the same act. Therefore, her act is compared by the Fathers to the act of faith made by every Christian, and the birth of the natural body of Christ is compared to the birth of the mystical Christ. Since sanctifying grace, in conjunction with the baptismal character, makes the Christian a mother of Christ, it also causes the divine maternity in Mary. Immediately a new question emerges: is Mary's divine maternity, caused by grace, different only in degree and not in kind from the maternal dignity of every Christian? Would any Christian, on condition that he had as much grace as Mary, also become literally mother of God?[116]

With the admission that a definitive solution of this difficulty is not at present available, Müller advances several proposals which he thinks are in the right direction. He lays down the principle that all habitual grace is a maternal and sponsal participation in the incarnation. For by receiving grace the Christian becomes mother of Christ, in a partial, limited sense, with reference

---

[115] *Ibid.* 393. [116] *Ibid.* 395.

to the mystical body of Christ. Therefore, perfect grace is the most perfect possible materno-sponsal participation in the incarnation, namely physical maternity of the physical body of Christ.[117]

This principle is then applied to the case of Mary. The grace which the Blessed Virgin received is the perfect grace of the Church carried to its culmination; it is the universe of grace which God has wished to give to mankind. This grace has made Mary the Mother of God, for it caused her to give supreme feminine, materno-sponsal collaboration to the work of redeeming mankind. Every grace is given by God and produces its proper effect when it is accepted by man. Therefore, every man who receives grace gives, partially, a maternal, feminine collaboration to the redemption. Mary has done so universally.

Mary's unique, incomparable privilege consists in the fact that she alone has received the universal grace of the Church; all other persons receive it only in part. This difference between the perfect and the imperfect does not change the species, but it is more than a difference of degree. For difference of degree exists between different grades of the imperfect, whereas the perfect stands above such gradations. Accordingly, the entire Church has received the grace to be the mother of the whole Christ, Head and body, but this supreme grace has not been realized except in one individual, Mary, who alone, therefore, is literally Mother of God.[118]

Müller holds that his hypothesis is supported by the most ancient tradition: God has only one plan of salvation and has established only one order of grace. This grace is essentially ordained to the divine maternity, which is realized where grace is perfect, in Mary. Therefore, "mother of God" means simply "full of grace." The concept "fully endowed with grace" is at the very

---

[117] In connection with this inference, H. Lennerz, "Maria-Ecclesia," *Gregorianum* 35, 1954, 92, is tempted to ask: "Is the same to be said of the perfect grace in the soul of Christ? If so, a marvelous conclusion follows"—Christ would be his own mother!

[118] *Art. cit., BSFEM* 36f.; see *art. cit., Divus Thomas* 396f.

basis of Mary's existence; the divine maternity is its interior fruit, its formal effect.[119] Thus the fundamental principle of marian theology is the Blessed Virgin's fullness of grace.

The praise awarded by scholars to Müller's patristic exposition in his book *Ecclesia-Maria* has been withheld from the two articles in which he ventures into the realms of theological speculation. Of the critiques that have appeared, one of the fairest is the appraisal made by H. Lennerz.

Basic to Müller's theory is the identity he perceives between habitual grace and the divine maternity. The assertion of such identity begets a great difficulty. Habitual grace is a created gift that is infused in justification, whereby man becomes a sharer in the divine nature and is made an adopted child of God. And this same grace is said to be a participation in the incarnation, by which the divine Word is conceived according to human nature. Therefore, the generation by which man "becomes God" is a participation in the generation by which God becomes man. This idea is hard to grasp. True, in both the incarnation of God and the justification of man, there is union between God and man. But these two unions are essentially diverse. In fact, they are opposed to each other: in the incarnation man does not become God, but God becomes man; in justification the opposite occurs: man "becomes God."[120]

The reason habitual grace is said to be a participation in the incarnation is that, when the Christian receives grace, he becomes, in some limited sense, the mother of Christ with reference to the mystical body. This concept is not without merit, and similar things are found in the Fathers. But it has nothing to do with a participation in the incarnation. Members of Christ's mystical body are generated in the Church, but the incarnate Word of God is not generated in the Church. Certainly, the Church is the mystical body of Christ, but the Church is not Christ and Christ is not the Church. The Church, mystical body

---

[119] *Art. cit., Divus Thomas* 398f.
[120] H. Lennerz, "Maria-Ecclesia," *Gregorianum* 35, 1954, 92.

of Christ, is a visible society founded by Christ; but Christ is not a visible society founded by Christ; thus the Church is not the incarnate Word. The Church is the mother of Christians but is not the mother of Christ. Therefore, the maternity of the Church regarding the members of Christ's mystical body is utterly diverse from the Blessed Virgin's maternity regarding Christ—and Müller's thesis collapses.

Do the Fathers really teach what Müller asserts they do? The very first "truth" he thinks he finds in the Fathers arouses doubt. Christ is the divine Word incarnate, Son of the Virgin Mary. The mystical body is the Church, a visible society instituted by Christ. Identity between them means that the divine, incarnate Word is the Church, a visible society. But the Fathers did not teach this. Hence the "identity" cannot be understood in a strict sense, but only in some wider sense which leaves intact the difference between Christ and the Church.

The second "truth" is: just as men form members of Christ and consequently become mothers of Christ by an act of faith, so Mary conceived Christ by faith in God's word. Müller concludes from this premise that Mary's divine maternity and reception of grace in the Church are one and the same thing. If to "form members of Christ, to become mothers of Christ" is understood of the grace of regeneration, it is not true that this is accomplished by the act of faith. Although an act of faith is required of adults as a disposition for justification, man is not justified or regenerated by the act of faith. The Blessed Virgin believed what the angel said, but she did not conceive Christ by an act of faith. In the generation of Christ, God was made man; in the regeneration of a Christian, man is made an adopted son of God. Far from being identical, the generation of Christ and the regeneration of the Christian are diametrically opposed.[121]

Finally, the Church guards the firm conviction that the Blessed Virgin was adorned with her matchless privileges of grace precisely because she was to be the Mother of God. To

[121] *Ibid.* 92f.

91

perceive this truth, we have only to read the beginning of the bull *Ineffabilis Deus* or the prayers of the liturgy; no theologian of note teaches otherwise. Müller's inversion, that Mary's divine maternity was the effect of her fullness of grace, is completely inadmissible.[122]

7. *Mary as the New Paradise.* In a survey of mariological literature written some years ago, M. J. Congar recalls that Thomist tradition has clung to the formal notion of divine maternity as the primary principle of mariology. However, he believes that the developments of piety have led us to pass beyond this point of view which, confined within its proper limits, does not account for Mary's recognized role in the economy of salvation. Efforts are made to explain Mary's coredemptive office by applying the theme of the new Eve and that of prototype of the Church. But the difficulty is that the Fathers recognized not the Blessed Virgin, but the Church as the new Eve who is spouse of the new Adam. Rather, according to the Fathers, Mary is the new paradise.[123]

This hint was taken up and developed by Charles Moeller in an article that is somewhat lacking in theological precision. The author was engaged in tracing two lines of thought—Mother of God and spouse of the Word—that stem from positive data. Could these two be referred to a third that would contain them? Or must we place one in front and attempt to lead the other to it? This third cannot be Scheeben's "bridal maternity" or Semmelroth's *Urbild* or the "new Eve." These aspects of Mary are interesting speculative elements of marian theology, but the entire science cannot be erected on any of them. A fourth idea includes the three preceding ones but does not exhibit their disadvantages; it is the idea of Mary as the new paradise suggested by Congar.[124]

Moeller thinks that this idea unifies mariology. By the im-

122 *Ibid.* 93.
123 Congar, *art. cit., RSPT* 624f. and note 79.
124 C. Moeller, *LV* 248f.

maculate conception, Mary is the new paradise of God, the new creation. By the assumption, Mary represents the eschatological paradise, anticipated in her. By the divine and virginal maternity, she appears as the paradise in which God is wholeheartedly received, the enclosed garden in which the betrothal of God and mankind is accomplished in the incarnate Christ. Paradise itself is a creature, but a creature that is transparent to the divinity dwelling within it. Mary, the new paradise, remains in the order of creation; as a perfect creature, the paradise of God, she verifies the perfect notion of creation, cooperating with the grace of God in the work of God.[125]

The idea of the new paradise integrates mariology into theology: into christology, for Christ is the new Adam of this paradise regained; into ecclesiology, for the Church is also a paradise, the new Eve of the new Garden of Eden, the Jerusalem adorned as bride for her husband; into "pneumatology," for, as the Spirit of God moved over the waters of the abyss at the first creation, he later operated mysteriously in the virginal maternity for the sanctification of Mary and the Church; into eschatology, for the horizon of the history of salvation, from Genesis to the Apocalypse, is dominated by the kingdom that will be realized in the paradise of God.[126]

Such is the idea which Moeller prefers because it keeps Mary's motherhood and betrothal in the same line, without subordinating one to the other; it is also patristic.

Reaction to this suggestion has been negligible. Philips acknowledges that it avoids amalgamating the qualities of mother and spouse in a single unthinkable concept, such as Scheeben's "bridal motherhood." And it is patristic. However, Moeller's idea is not an idea at all, but only an image.[127] As such, it canenunciations of the fundamental principle or principles of marian theology.

8. *Perfect Redemption of Mary.* One of the more recent

[125] *Ibid.* 249f.   [126] *Ibid.* 250.
[127] G. Philips, *Marianum* 15, 1953, 443.

theories, proposed by Karl Rahner, presupposes that Mary did not actively cooperate in the objective redemption wrought on Calvary. Mary's cooperation is limited to her consent that made the redemption possible by permitting it to be accomplished in her and through her, for the salvation of all. The concept and term "coredemptrix" ought to be avoided, for it evokes the idea that Mary cooperated in the redemption on the level and in the function reserved for the one Mediator.[128]

At the time of the incarnation, Mary wholly accepted, in soul (by faith) and in body, the Word of God who was made flesh for the redemption of mankind. By doing so, she also accepted God's mercy for herself, in the order of her own subjective redemption. Thereby she took her stand entirely on the side of the redeemed. By her faith she surrendered herself unreservedly, in soul and body, to the gift of the incarnate Grace of the Father. Accordingly, she is the perfect model of redemption, the perfect type and representative of the Church.

Clear affirmations of Scripture (mainly Gn 3:15, the *fiat* and fullness of grace reported in Luke, and Mary's position at the foot of the cross as described in John) convey a knowledge of the Blessed Virgin's person and place in the history of salvation. This makes possible the formulation of the fundamental principle of marian theology: Mary is she who by grace has been perfectly redeemed, the one who realizes and represents most perfectly what the grace of God achieves in mankind and the Church.[129]

The various theories proposed about the basic principle from which are derived all the properties and functions of the Blessed Virgin come more or less to the same thing: Mary, by her divine maternity, occupies a unique and decisive position in the history

128 K. Rahner S.J., "Le principe fondamental de la théologie mariale," *Recherches de Science Religieuse* 42, 1954, 494f. In footnote 23 the author states that he associates himself with the criticisms made by Goossens, Lennerz, Köster and Semmelroth against the theological teaching, widespread today, about Mary's coredemptive function.

129 *Ibid.* 503, 505.

of salvation. The formula here advocated: "Mary is the one who has been redeemed in the most perfect way," is not opposed to the other theories. For redemption is a reception of salvation, bestowed by God in the flesh of Christ, a reception that cooperates in this salvation; consequently, the most perfect redemption is reception of the incarnate Word in a perfect cooperation of both soul and body and is, moreover, cooperation in the salvation of all.[130] Because of such considerations, Rahner holds that his proposal implies all the elements stressed in other enunciations of the fundamental principle or principles of marian theology.

Rahner believes that his formula has several advantages. For one thing, it results more directly from Scripture. More clearly than others, it traces the line connecting Mary's perfections with the fundamental principle. Thus the immaculate conception is the effect of preservative redemption; exemption from all sin is its perfect grace; Mary's holiness is the most eminent found among creatures; and the assumption is a consequence of her place in the history of salvation. We cannot deduce absolutely everything from it, for we must know from other sources what is possible in the case of a redemption that is brought about in the most perfect manner.[131]

A confirmation of the solidity of this principle is at hand: some truths cannot be known except in the hypothesis of this basic principle. Certain mariological truths which are the object of the teaching and the faith of the Church were not always, from the beginning, expressly and clearly attested in the direct sources of the faith. Among them are the immaculate conception, the permanent freedom from all sin, and the perpetual virginity. Some principle is needed in these cases, since the truth that is deduced or deducible has not always been explicitly taught. This does not mean that the fundamental principle must always have been present in the reflective consciousness of the faith of the

[130] *Ibid.* 508ff. [131] *Ibid.* 510f.

Church, for it may have existed in a general and obscure way, without explicit formulation. Regarding, for example, the immaculate conception, as implicitly contained in patristic affirmations about Mary's absolute freedom from sin: we cannot include freedom from original sin in these affirmations unless we suppose that a redemption realized in the most perfect manner (hence a preservative redemption) was present in the minds of the Fathers. So also, as regards Mary's eminent holiness and exemption from all personal sin, the Church possessed in this fundamental idea the point of departure for further clarification.[132]

Rahner thinks that, after the reflections and indications he has mentioned, it is not necessary to show that the great central truths of marian theology—the divine motherhood and Mary's unique place in the history of salvation—are contained in his principle.[133] However, the importance of the principle is not so momentous with regard to these truths of faith, because they are immediately knowable in the sources of revelation and hence are more independent of the principle.[134]

Whatever may be the best formula (which is variable according to the numerous points of view possible), behind all the affirmations of the teaching of the Church about the Blessed Virgin is found a fundamental, global, nonreflective but clear conviction: redemption, definitively taking hold of the world in the person of Mary, body and soul, has been realized in her in the most perfect manner.[135]

The inversion of revealed truths, criticized in Alois Müller's theory, seems to be the main defect of Rahner's proposal. That

---

[132] *Ibid.* 512–515. Rahner has some difficulty deriving Mary's perpetual virginity from his fundamental principle, and requires four or five pages to make his point; the end result is not very convincing.

[133] With regard to the divine maternity, one of the pertinent "indications" seems to be that perfect reception of redemption in body implies reception of Christ, through whom alone salvation comes, into one's body by a literal maternal conception. In that case, a male could not be redeemed "in the most perfect way."

[134] *Op. cit.* 513.   [135] *Ibid.* 521f.

Mary was perfectly redeemed is certain and we all gladly believe that she was. The question is whether her perfect redemption can be taken as the ultimate, basic principle of mariology.

In this connection, we might consider Rahner's final summing up: behind all the particular affirmations of the teaching of the Church about Mary is the conviction that redemption, taking hold of the world in the person of Mary, body and soul, has been realized in her in the most perfect manner. But is this conviction really behind all the particular affirmations? It is certainly not the conviction of the Church, for the Church has a conviction that behind Mary's perfect redemption is the basic reason underlying it: because she is the Mother of God, she was perfectly redeemed; for the same reason she occupies so marked a place in salvation history. Thus, concerning Rahner's whole thesis, the question always persists: *why* was the Blessed Virgin redeemed so perfectly? And the answer is no less persistent: because she was to be, and actually was, the Mother of God. This concept is behind the perfect redemption and therefore is the reason and the principle of all the rest.

A good example is Rahner's point about the immaculate conception, which is forcefully made. It is quite true that we cannot regard freedom from original sin as implied in patristic affirmations about Mary's absolute freedom from sin, unless we suppose that a redemption realized in the most perfect way, and consequently a preservative redemption, was obscurely present in the minds of the Fathers. But what is the source of their conviction concerning Mary's perfect redemption if not their appreciation of the supreme dignity of the divine maternity? The same holds for their teaching about Mary's eminent holiness and permanent freedom from personal sin.

Furthermore, going far beyond Rahner, we can show that Mary could be, and was, coredemptress by the very fact that she was God's Mother. Rahner does not admit this. He is not even willing to allow the concept or the term "coredemptrix." The basis for Rahner's attitude, and seemingly the support of his

97

entire thesis, is the view that the Blessed Virgin's part in the redemption, aside from her consent which made salvation possible, is purely receptive.

Eventually the question is whether Mary is the Mother of God because she is perfectly redeemed or whether she is perfectly redeemed because she is the Mother of God. Which of the two is the reason accounting for, underlying the other? In other words, which is the fundamental principle of marian theology: the perfect redemption or the divine maternity? Consultation of the official teaching authority of the Church leaves no doubt concerning this choice of alternatives.

The Mind of the Magisterium

Strange neglect of directives furnished by the teaching authority of the Church has attended discussions of the primary principle of mariology.[136] The more important the question, the graver is the theologian's duty of consulting the teaching of the magisterium. In the theology of the Blessed Virgin, the problem of the primary principle is supremely important, since the primary principle dominates the structure of the science, imparts consistency to it, confers order on all its parts, and makes possible the unified organization of the treatise.

In his bull that defines the immaculate conception, Pius IX tells us that God had eternally foreseen the fall of the human race which would result from Adam's disobedience and had decided to bring the first work of his love to a successful completion through the incarnation of the Word. Therefore, from the beginning and before all time, God selected for his Son a Mother of whom he would be born, and on her he lavished a profusion of divine gifts such as no other creature would ever receive. In addition to everything else, she was forever to be

---

[136] The necessity of heeding the guidance of the magisterium is clearly set forth by Pius XII, *Humani generis, AAS* 42, 1950, 567; also 563, 569, 576. On encyclicals as instruments of the Supreme Pontiff's exercise of his ordinary magisterium, see *ibid.* 568.

free from all sin; wholly beautiful and perfect, she was endowed with a fullness of innocence and holiness unexcelled under God and incomprehensible except to God. "It was altogether fitting that this Mother should always be radiant with the splendor of most perfect holiness and that, completely unsullied even by the stain of original sin, she should win a triumphant victory over the ancient serpent. For on her the Father had bestowed the gift of his only Son."[137] Here the reason assigned for Mary's perpetual sinlessness, incomparable fullness of grace and holiness, immaculate conception, and triumph over the devil is her divine maternity. The notion that her fullness of grace or perfect redemption is the source of her divine motherhood is an inversion of the order of divine providence.

Faithful to the same line of thought, Leo XIII wrote in one of his rosary encyclicals: "The Virgin who had no part in original sin, having been chosen to be the Mother of God, because of that very fact was given a share in the work of saving the human race, and so she possesses such grace and power with her Son that no human or angelic nature has ever received or can receive greater."[138] Here again, the reason why God has endowed the Blessed Virgin with such incomparable gifts, including her association in the work of redemption, is her divine maternity.

The derivation of Mary's spiritual motherhood from her divine motherhood is brought out by Pius X in words of great beauty:

Is not Mary the Mother of Christ? Therefore, she is our mother also. . . . As the God-man, Christ acquired a material body as all men do; but as the Savior of our race he acquired a kind of spiritual and mystical body, which is the society of those who believe in Christ. . . . In one and the same womb of his most chaste Mother, Christ took to himself human flesh and at the same time added to it a spiritual body made up of all those who were to believe in him. Therefore, Mary, while carrying the Savior in her womb, may be said to have carried

---

[137] *Ineffabilis Deus, Collectio Lacensis,* vol. 6, col. 836.
[138] Leo XIII, *Supremi apostolatus, ASS* 16, 1883–1884, 114.

likewise all those whose life was contained in the Savior's life. All of us, consequently, who are united to Christ and are, as the Apostle says, "members of his body, of his flesh, and of his bones" (Eph 5:30), have come forth from Mary's womb, like a body attached to its head. That is why, in a spiritual and mystical sense, we are called Mary's children, and she is the Mother of us all.[139]

Accordingly, formulas such as "Mary is the Mother of the whole Christ" or "Mary is the universal Mother" cannot be accepted as the primary principle of mariology. Of the two elements comprised in these formulas, the divine maternity and the spiritual maternity, the second is dependent on the first; therefore, the first is the principle of the second. Moreover, as the Pope goes on to state, Mary distributes the treasures of Christ's merits by title of her divine motherhood, which invests her with a kind of right.[140] Finally, the special reason why the Blessed Virgin was preserved from original sin is the fact that she was to be the Mother of God.[141]

In an encyclical to commemorate the fifteen-hundredth anniversary of the Council of Ephesus, Pius XI affirms: "From the dogma of the divine maternity emanate, as from a deep and hidden spring, Mary's unparalleled grace and her eminent rank, the highest under God." The Pope proceeds to quote two great authors, with complete approval:

As Aquinas so aptly writes: "The Blessed Virgin, because she is the Mother of God, possesses a certain infinite dignity resulting from the infinite good which is God" (*Summa*, Ia, q. 25, a. 6 ad 4). The same truth is stated and explained in greater detail by Cornelius a Lapide: "The Blessed Virgin is the Mother of God; therefore, she far excels all the angels, even the seraphim and cherubim. She is the Mother of God; that is why she is all pure and all holy; that is why, under God, greater purity than hers cannot be conceived" (*In Matthaeum* I, 6).[142]

In this passage the Pope teaches that the divine maternity is the most basic source of Mary's greatness. Her position at the sum-

---

[139] St. Pius X, *Ad diem illum, ASS* 36, 1903–1904, 452f.
[140] *Ibid.* 455: "*materno veluti iure.*"   [141] *Ibid.* 458.
[142] Pius XI, *Lux veritatis, AAS* 23, 1931, 513.

mit of creation, her exaltation above all the angels, her fullness of grace, and her supreme purity and holiness are all consequences of the fact that she is the Mother of God.

Before coming to the definition of the Blessed Virgin's assumption into heaven, Pius XII summarizes the historical development of the doctrine. Discussion of the evidence gathered from the patristic period is followed by an examination of scholastic theologians. Speaking in his own name later in the encyclical, Pius continued:

All these proofs and considerations of the holy Fathers and theologians are ultimately based on the sacred writings, which set the loving Mother of God before our eyes as most closely associated with her divine Son and ever sharing his lot. Consequently, it seems impossible to think that she who conceived and gave birth to Christ, nursed him with her milk, held him in her arms and clasped him to her breast, should, at the close of her earthly life, be separated from him in body, even though not in soul. . . . Since he had the power to grant this great honor to his Mother, to preserve her from the corruption of the grave, we must believe that he actually did so.[143]

In this excerpt the Holy Father teaches that Mary's holiness and loving union with her Son, her association with him throughout his career, and her glorious assumption into heaven, are all consequences of her divine maternity.

Proclamation of the Marian Year (1954) was the occasion for an encyclical which conveys, in unmistakable terms, the doctrine that the divine maternity is the basic reason underlying the extraordinary greatness of the Blessed Virgin.

Among all the holy men and women who have ever lived, there is only one about whom we can say that the question of sin does not even arise. It is likewise clear that this unique privilege, never granted to anyone else, was given to Mary by God because she was raised to the dignity of Mother of God. . . . A higher office than this does not seem possible; since it requires the greatest dignity and sanctity after Christ, it demands the fullest perfection of divine grace and a soul free from

[143] *Munificentissimus Deus, AAS* 42, 1950, 767f.

every sin. Indeed, all the privileges and graces with which her soul and her life were endowed in so extraordinary a manner and measure, seem to flow from this sublime vocation of Mother of God, as from a pure and hidden source.[144]

The divine maternity is the basic reason for many of Mary's greatest graces and functions, which are specified here and elsewhere in papal documents. This is altogether certain. Moreover, Pius XII believes that her maternity is the source of all her privileges and graces, although he does not state this teaching as certain. Hence he contents himself with saying that it "seems" to be the universal source.

That the divine maternity is the source of Mary's queenship is asserted by the Pope with all the firmness that may be desired in the document in which he decrees the feast of Mary as Queen.

The basic principle on which Mary's royal dignity rests is beyond doubt her divine maternity. . . . She is Queen because she brought forth a Son who, at the very moment he was conceived, was King and Lord of all creation even as man, by reason of the hypostatic union of his human nature with the Word.[145]

This truth is unassailable. However, the Pope adds:

The most Blessed Virgin is to be called Queen not only on account of her divine maternity, but also because by the will of God she had an exceedingly important part in the work of our eternal salvation. . . .[146] By God's will, Mary was associated with Jesus Christ, the principle of salvation, in procuring spiritual salvation, in a way similar to the way Eve was associated with Adam, the principle of death. . . . Hence we may draw the sure conclusion that just as Christ, the new Adam, must be called King not only because he is the Son of God, but also because he is our Redeemer, so, by a kind of analogy, the Blessed Virgin is

144 Pius XII, *Fulgens corona, AAS* 45, 1953, 580.

145 Pius XII, *Ad Caeli Reginam, AAS* 46, 1954, 633.

146 This teaching lends powerful support to the opinion that Mary cooperated immediately in objective redemption. The "important part in the work of our eternal salvation" that is here attributed to the Blessed Virgin cannot refer either to her divine maternity, from which it is distinguished, or to her activity in dispensing graces from heaven, for the latter is an exercise of her queenship, not a principle of it.

Queen not only because she is the Mother of God, but also because, as the new Eve, she was associated with the new Adam.[147]

Yet the divine maternity is the ultimate principle of Mary's unique rank and therefore of the lifelong association with Christ and his work that is summed up and has its crowning culmination in her queenship.

Perhaps the most decisive passage of all is found in the allocution by Pius XII to the World Union of Feminine Catholic Organizations in 1957:

> The dignity of Mother of God has called down on Mary exceptional graces and extraordinary privileges, her preservation from original sin and from every personal fault, the splendor of her virtues and gifts of the Holy Spirit, her intimate participation in all the mysteries of Christ's life, his sufferings, death and resurrection, the continuation of his work in the Church and his sovereignty over all creatures. All this was given to her because she was the Mother of God and therefore had a unique function to perform in the redemption of the world.[148]

From this brief examination of a few pontifical documents, therefore, it is clear that of all the proposals that have been made about the fundamental principle of marian theology, only one is consonant with papal teaching: Mary's divine maternity.

Theological Vindication

Many theologians, especially among those who advocate a double principle, would admit that the divine maternity is the basic principle of marian theology were it not for their fear that the divine maternity does not offer a secure way to Mary's association with Christ in the work of redemption. These theologians maintain that the notion of divine maternity does not necessarily contain the notion of Mary's cooperation in redemption. Analysis of the first does not yield the second; therefore, the second can-

---

[147] *Op. cit.* 633ff.

[148] *AAS* 48, 1957, 912. For other pertinent texts see W. F. Hogan, "The Fundamental Principle of Mariology according to the Magisterium," *MS* 10, 1959, 47–68.

not be deduced from the first. Consequently, if our mariology is to safeguard the Blessed Virgin's coredemptive activity, some other principle is needed.

To solve this difficulty we need but distinguish, with St. Thomas, between the necessary mystery of God's trinitarian life and the free mystery of our salvation through the redemptive incarnation.[149] All the other articles of faith, and with them all theology, are reduced to these two supreme articles. The main task of marian theology is to discover the place and the function of the Blessed Virgin in the divine plan; consequently, mariology belongs to the free mystery of salvation that is achieved through the redemptive incarnation.

In the stratosphere of abstract ideas, cooperation in the redemption cannot be deduced with metaphysical necessity from the notion of divine maternity. Prescinding from the free design of God's infinite wisdom, we cannot know that the Mother of God is associated with Christ in the enterprise of salvation. Yet there is a connection, and it is necessary, because God has eternally planned to associate his Mother with himself in redeeming us, and he wills the execution of his plan. Such is the clear teaching of Pius XII: "By God's will [ex Dei placito—God's free will—sociata fuit] Mary was associated with Jesus Christ. . . . as the new Eve, she was associated with the new Adam."[150]

This parallel between Eve and Mary is the most ancient form found in tradition to describe the Blessed Virgin's cooperation in redemption.[151] It is also the most basic theme in marian theology after the principle of the divine maternity. The parallel implies a contrast: as Eve was associated with Adam in the disorder of ruin, so Mary, the new Eve, is associated with Christ, the new Adam, in the order of reparation. It also involves a comparison: as Eve, on the natural plane, is mother of all the living, so Mary, on the supernatural plane, is likewise mother of all the living.

[149] See De veritate, q. 14, a. 11.   [150] Ad Caeli Reginam 634.
[151] See W. J. Burghardt S.J., "Mary in Western Patristic Thought," Mariology, ed. J. B. Carol, Milwaukee 1955, vol. 1, 110–117.

Yet the relationship is not the same in each case. Eve is the mother of all who have natural life because she is the wife of Adam, whereas Mary is the mother of all who have supernatural life because she is the Mother of Christ. Mary is a maternal, not a bridal associate of her Son.

Sacred Scripture never refers to Mary as the spouse of the Word. She is exclusively his Mother. But she is fully his Mother not only because she brought him into the world, but because she sustained him in his vocation up to the supreme sacrifice. That is the lesson Scripture scholars are perceiving more and more clearly from her presence at the foot of the cross.[152] Any element of pertinent truth connoted by the figure of spouse is eminently included in Mary's motherhood, but in a way that incomparably transcends the image. Rightly did St. Justin and St. Irenaeus find in the recital of the annunciation a reason for contrasting Mary's obedience with Eve's disobedience; yet they fell far short of St. John in penetrating the mystery. For the Evangelist, Mary did not merely obey the angel's proposals by consenting to be the Savior's Mother; she went much further and acquiesced in his immolation and thus shared in his victory over mankind's ancient enemy. As Mother of the Savior, inseparably united to her Son, she verifies the promise of Genesis: "I will put enmities between you and the woman, and your seed and her seed; she shall crush your head" (Gn 3:15). She is the new Eve because she is the Mother of the new Adam.

By the very fact that Mary is the Savior's Mother, she cooperated in our redemption, at least in its initial stage. There is no metaphysically necessary reason why her intervention should not have terminated at this stage, if the Father had so willed. Christ could have carried on and achieved his redemptive work without any associate at all. Yet such a cessation would hardly be consonant with the exercise of divine Providence as it is ordinarily manifested. We should rather expect that the association begun should have a further cooperation as its complement.

[152] See F. M. Braun, "Marie et l'Église, d'après l'Écriture," *BSFEM* 15.

This expectation is readily justified. Mary's maternity elevates her to the hypostatic order, in the sense that the hypostatic union between Christ's assumed human nature and the Person of the Word was accomplished through her and in her; her Son is a divine Person. In the actual economy of salvation the hypostatic order is for the redemption of the human race. Consequently, anyone who belongs to this order has a redemptive function. Therefore, the divine maternity, which introduces Mary into the hypostatic order, is also the cause of her redemptive mission. "The Virgin who had no part in original sin, having been chosen to be the Mother of God, because of that very fact was given a share in the work of saving the human race."[153]

Nevertheless, a doubt remains. To cooperate actively in objective redemption, Mary had to have some significant part in the very sacrifice of the cross, the climax of Christ's redemptive life. To have such an office, she had to know about it, consent to it, and effectively discharge it. All this has to be shown, and in such a way as to make clear that her coredemptive activity is an exercise of her divine maternity.

To what extent did this woman, who had been chosen by God to be the Mother and associate of the Redeemer, understand the part she was to play in the history of salvation? She was a Jewish girl, a daughter of Israel, the race that lived on the "promises" (Rom 9:4), and she shared the hopes and longings of her people. The first promise of the redemption had been made to the original parents of mankind (Gn 3:15) and was progressively clarified in the course of the long centuries. Abraham received from God the promise that all nations would be blessed in the people of which he was to be the father. David was given the assurance that one of his descendants would be the Savior who would wield divine power and possess sacerdotal dignity. Yet, as the prophet Isaiah foretold, this Savior would be a man of sorrows and would be born of a virgin.

The chosen people of the Old Testament were called by God

153 Leo XIII, *Supremi apostolatus, ASS* 16, 1883–1884, 114.

for a definite purpose; each new revelation inaugurated a new period in the history of redemption and marked an advance over the preceding epoch. The vocation of an individual was never a private affair but always betokened a communal call: Abraham, Moses, David and the prophets were summoned forth by God for the salvation of mankind. Among the individuals thus chosen was Mary, whose election was the crowning point in the general election of the people of God. The annunciation was the fulfillment of all the earlier annunciations.

The Jewish maiden, well acquainted with the traditions of her race, was aware of all this when the angel Gabriel, carrying out the prophecy of Isaiah, brought her the message from God: "You will conceive in your womb and will bring forth a son." Prior to any response on her part, he told her that the time had come for establishing the everlasting messianic kingdom, the new empire of salvation. Her cousin Elizabeth, filled with the Holy Spirit, knew that Mary was the Mother of the divine Savior and bore witness to the Virgin's association with Jesus: "You are blessed among women, and blessed is the fruit of your womb." Even the shepherds were informed, shortly after Christ's birth, that Mary was the Mother of the Redeemer: "This day is born to you a Savior, who is Christ the Lord." In the temple Simeon told Mary: "This child is set for the fall and for the resurrection of many," and announced that she would share in her Son's future conflict: "Your own soul will be pierced by a sword."

How could Mary's knowledge fail to measure up to her vocation? All her life she cherished the memory of every word that was spoken about her son or by him, and she would ponder on all these utterances in her heart. How could God neglect to enlighten her more and more fully, as time went on, about all the implications of her calling? "We may not doubt that the Blessed Virgin received most excellently the gift of wisdom."[154] Illuminated by this gift of wisdom which, like all the infused virtues

[154] *Summa Theol.* III, q. 27, a. 5 ad 3.

107

and gifts of the Holy Spirit, is proportionate to her fullness of grace, she penetrated ever more deeply into the abyss of the mystery of Jesus. "Those who were nearest to Christ, whether coming before him, like John the Baptist, or coming after him, like the apostles, had a fuller knowledge of the mysteries of faith."[155] But who ever stood so close to Christ as his own Mother? Pius X perceived this very clearly:

> She was the only one who enjoyed the intimate association of family life with Jesus for thirty years, as is right for mother and son. Who understood better than his Mother the stupendous mysteries of Christ's birth, of his boyhood, and especially of his incarnation, the very beginning and foundation of our faith? She kept and pondered in her heart all that happened at Bethlehem and in the temple of the Lord in Jerusalem. Beyond that, she shared in the thoughts and the hidden plans of Christ; indeed, we must say that she lived the very life of her Son. . . . From the home at Nazareth to the hill of Calvary, Mary was the constant associate of Jesus; she understood the secrets of his heart better than anyone ever did.[156]

The question whether Mary grasped all the implications of her consent to the incarnation is basically unimportant. Full consent to God is abandonment of one's life to consequences that cannot be completely foreseen, because the person who surrenders himself to God without condition or reserve loses himself in God's immensity. Some obscurity is inevitable in such a consent but does not lessen its value, for the surrender is made to God who is incomprehensible. Mary knew enough; she knew that she was saying yes to him whom the angel called the Son of God, come to accomplish our redemption.[157]

Mary's free consent to the incarnation is explicit: "Behold the handmaid of the Lord; be it done to me according to your word." The consent itself stems from her faith for which she

[155] *Ibid.* II–II, q. 1, a. 7 ad 4.

[156] *Ad diem illum, ASS* 36, 1903–1904, 452, 454.

[157] See K. Rahner, *art. cit.* 492. The first part of this article expresses some beautiful truths which will be further applied in this study. Unfortunately, Rahner does not draw out the full consequences of the premises he so convincingly establishes.

is declared blessed: "You who have believed are blessed among women," and is the effect of grace, which makes it an event in the history of salvation, supposing both a call from God and her own personal response. Thereupon the Virgin, through the action of the Holy Spirit, became the Mother of the Savior of the world.

The initiative is God's. He alone decides who is to have a commission and power in the economy of salvation. His was the will to save the fallen race through the God-man. For him God chose a human mother, and out of all the women of the earth, from Eve to the last girl that would ever be born, he selected Mary, who thereby received from God a charge affecting the eternal lot of all mankind. In response to God's call, Mary gave her consent to be the Mother of the Redeemer; she understood clearly from the angel's message that her Son was the promised Messiah.

Because of her consent Mary suddenly found herself at the decisive point in salvation history; through her the central act of God in the world was accomplished. All previous history led in a straight line to this act, and here also the future of mankind was decided, although redemption still had to receive its definitive consummation in the death and resurrection of the incarnate Word.

Can we go further and say that Mary, who consented to be the Redeemer's Mother, continued her consent to God's redemptive plan to the very end as she stood under the cross of her Son? The answer must unquestionably be affirmative, if we can show that such was God's will.

Christ is the Redeemer not only by his own will, but also because the Father sent him for the purpose of redeeming us on the cross by the sacrifice of his life. Likewise, the presence of Christ's Mother under the cross was willed by God; in God's plan Mary was to have a part in the passion of her Son. Otherwise God would certainly have spared her this excruciating pain.

109

Accordingly, Mary was the associate of the Redeemer at his very act of redemption, because God had predestined her to be the *Mater dolorosa* and because she fully cooperated with God's program. She was drawn into the redemptive suffering of her Son precisely because she was his Mother. She, the Immaculate, the one who is full of grace and blessed among all women, did not have to suffer anything for her own redemption, and therefore she was engaged exclusively in the work of her Son for the redemption of all mankind. The whole of her life, from the moment of the annunciation to the hour of the cross, with all the periods of suffering in between, has to be understood in this way if it is to have any meaning at all.[158]

The inevitable consequence of the incarnation was the death of Christ; the effect of Mary's acquiescence is both the incarnation and the cross. Together they are the indivisible object of her *fiat*, which is a consent efficacious for salvation, a cooperation in the order of objective redemption.[159]

This cooperation was given. Mary's maternity conferred on her real rights over the human life of her Son. God required the sacrifice of this life for the redemption of man. The sacrifice entailed Christ's voluntary renunciation of his personal rights and Mary's renunciation of her maternal rights over a life that, in different ways, belonged to both. Mary made that renunciation. Instead of willing to save her Son from death, she offered him, as he offered himself, because she knew that it was the Father's will that the Son should redeem the world by the cross. Accordingly, the Son is the Redeemer, the Mother is the co-redemptress.

That Mary's cooperation extended to the sacrifice on Calvary is clearly taught by some of the more recent popes. In addition to giving birth to the victim for man's salvation, "she was commissioned to watch over the same victim, to nourish him, and

[158] See J. Auer, "Salve Maria, Regina Mundi," *Geist und Leben* 27, 1954, 343.
[159] See K. Rahner, *art. cit.* 492ff.

110

even, when the appointed time came, to place him on the altar."[160] Her lifelong association with her Son's career included the last hours.

The scope of Mary's maternal cooperation is clearly set forth by Pius XII: it reaches as far as the sacrifice of Christ and embraces all the descendants of Adam. "Free from all sin, personal as well as original, and always most closely united with her Son, as another Eve she offered him on Golgotha, along with the holocaust of her maternal rights and motherly love, to the eternal Father for all the children of Adam."[161] Thus Mary's coredemptive activity is a function of her motherhood.

Since Mary is the Mother of Christ, she is also the mother of his mystical body. "She who corporally was the Mother of our Head, by the added title of suffering and glory became spiritually the Mother of all his members."[162] It could not be otherwise. "The unbroken tradition of the Fathers from the earliest times teaches that the divine Redeemer and the society which is his body form a single mystical person, that is, as Augustine says, the whole Christ."[163] As Mother of the Head, she was able to be mother of the members. When she conceived the Head, she conceived also the members. In due time she gave birth to the Head, who did not as yet actually have his members. On Calvary, cooperating as coredemptress, offering her Son in sacrifice, she gave birth to the members in principle, and they become members in actuality as they are successively joined to the Head by being incorporated into him at their baptism. Truly she is the new Eve, mother of all the living, for she is the Mother of him who is our life.

Thus from the basic truth that Mary is the Mother of God, everything else follows. By reason of her divine maternity she is the new Eve, the associate of the Redeemer, the coredemptress

[160] Pius X, *Ad diem illum* 453.
[161] *Mystici corporis Christi, AAS* 35, 1943, 247.
[162] *Ibid.*
[163] *Ibid.* 226. See *Summa Theol.* III, q. 48, a. 2 ad 1: "*Caput et membra sunt quasi una persona mystica.*"

and mediatress of all grace, Mother of the mystical body, universal mother, the archetype of the Church, the new paradise, the one full of grace, the one who is perfectly redeemed, the Queen of heaven and earth. None of these consequences, revealed or deduced, can be the primary principle of mariology; they all proceed, by the ordering of God's wisdom, from the Blessed Virgin's predestination to be the Redeemer's Mother, inextricably united with her Son in the one eternal decree. The divine maternity is the basis of Mary's relationship to Christ; hence it is the basis of her relationship to the work of Christ, to the whole Christ, to all theology and Christianity. Therefore, it is the fundamental principle of marian theology.

3

Mary and the Church

THE inquiry into the relations between Mary and the Church *NB !*
has become one of the dominant concerns of modern day
theology. It is drawing more closely together the two treatises
notably developed in modern times: ecclesiology and mariology.
Both Mary and the Church are mothers of men; they should
be united. If we wish to penetrate more deeply into the mystery
of Mary, we must contemplate it in its connections with other
basic mysteries, especially the Trinity, Christ and the Church.
The parallel between Mary and the Church is not a secondary
theme that is situated merely on the periphery of Catholic
teaching; it is necessary for comprehending the redemptive incarnation. Although the comparison was a minor object of
patristic and scholastic thought, it is part of the reserves of
Christian tradition, and we of today are beholding its entrance
into theology.

Before a comparative study of Mary and the Church can be
undertaken, we must define the terms of comparison, that is to
say, Mary and the Church. In speaking of the Blessed Virgin,
the risk of equivocation is slight, but the notion of the Church
is complex and admits of diverse senses.

Ordinarily, when we speak of the Church, we invest it with
a personality of its own. Though it is a society composed of
individuals, we think of it as an organism that lives its own

113

life. As such, it can be understood in two ways: the name "Church" may designate① the totality made up of Christ the Head and all the members that are joined to the Head, or it ②may designate only the body that is united to Christ the Head.[1] The second sense emphasizes the distinction between the person of the Savior and the persons who have been saved by him and respond to his love. Clearly, Mary is comparable to the Church understood in the second sense.

Scripture presents the Church, as distinct from Christ, under various images and figures. St. Peter calls the Church "a holy nation, a purchased people" and "the people of God" (1 Pt 2:9f). Hence the Church is the new people of God, the new Israel, in continuity with the ancient Israel but surpassing it. This new people of God is the posterity of Abraham, not according to the flesh, but according to the spirit; the true descendants of the father of believers are the followers of Christ, who is the seed of Abraham (Gal 3:16, 29). Mary is comparable to the Church regarded as the new people of God, for she is the ideal personification of the Church and the perfect realization of what God wishes to accomplish with the coming of his Son.

The Christian community is the people of God in union with Christ the Head, whose life circulates in it. From the idea of the people of God united to Christ, we pass naturally to the concept of the Church as the body of Christ. Under this figure, the Blessed Virgin is the first and most important member of the body, the one closest to the Head, surpassing the rest in excellence and eminence, because her position as Mother and associate of the Savior is superior to that of all the other members.

A third symbol, the image of conjugal union between Christ and his Church, eliminates the danger of misunderstanding our connection with Christ. The title "spouse of Christ" reminds us that, notwithstanding our insertion into Christ the Head, we

[1] Thus St. Thomas, *In IV Sent.*, dist. 49, q. 4, a. 3 ad 4.

retain our separate personalities and our individual consciences. The Church, bride of Christ, preserves an attitude of submission, receptivity and love toward him. Under this figure, which emphasizes the distinction between Christ and the Church, the Blessed Virgin is again the first member, in whom the union of the redeemed with the Redeemer reaches a perfection unattainable by anyone else.

Accordingly, in comparing Mary with the Church, we are considering the Church as the mystical body of Christ and the spouse of Christ, an extension of the image under which the prophets designated the chosen people in anticipation of the Church. These figures are complemented by another one, likewise ancient, that depicts the Church as the mother of the faithful.

In pondering the relationship between Mary and the Church, we are not thinking of the Church in a wide sense, as including those who have been saved before the advent of Christ in virtue of their faith in the coming Redeemer. We mean rather the community of the baptized that was founded by Christ, the Church on earth and in its culmination in heaven. To carry out the comparison, we must set the Blessed Virgin apart from the rest of the Church. The Church is here understood not as a whole composed of Mary and all other Christians, but only as that part of the Church which is made up of the latter. The comparison is between two parts of the same whole, the Blessed Virgin on one side and all the rest of the members on the other.

1. The Foundation of the Analogy

Development of the parallel between Mary and the Church, a theme capable of contributing clarification to mariology, is in the domain of speculative theology. The structure must rest on a solid foundation, which has its deepest base in the designs of God for man's salvation.

115

Mary and the Church in the Divine Plan

The key to the mystery is offered by St. Thomas: "It belongs to the essence of goodness to communicate itself to others. . . . Hence it pertains to the Supreme Good to communicate himself to creatures *summo modo,* in the highest possible manner."[2] The world created by God adds nothing whatever to him and profits him not at all. We can assign no reason for God's creative activity other than the inclination of the Supreme Good to communicate himself. Creation is the beginning of his self-communication. Participation in God's goodness and reflection and representation of the divine perfections are the aim of all creatures. Since no individual thing can be a sufficient image of the infinite Good, a universe of beings, a hierarchy with the spirit world at its summit, was called into existence.[3]

God can give himself in a more perfect way than by producing feeble vestiges of himself. He can make himself known and loved by admitting intellectual beings into a supernatural participation of his own nature and his own acts of knowledge and love. In this case, besides mere resemblance, there is union between Creator and creature. Such union leaves the created person at an infinite distance from the Creator. But God has the power to give himself wholly, to associate a created nature substantially in his own existence, to be one with such a nature by communicating himself *summo modo.* This is what God has done by becoming incarnate. He has communicated himself *summo modo* to a created nature issuing from the Virgin Mary. But his intention in thus communicating himself envisioned the universe. Through the one created nature assumed by the divine Word in hypostatic union, all other beings are offered a participation in divinity. In particular, all men are summoned to receive from Jesus Christ a share in the divine nature.

The Church, in the eternal plan, is the prolongation of Christ;

[2] *Summa Theol.* III, q. 1, a. 1.   [3] *Ibid.* I, q. 47, a. 1.

116

it is his body, in which every member has a definite place, an individual way of resembling the God-man, a spiritual vocation and a supernatural activity. Complete self-communication would be lacking if the power of action were not conferred. Christ makes his members his cooperators by granting them the redemptive energy of charity and the ability to merit, pray and act for mankind's salvation. Human nature is social, and the grace of Christ that is given to human nature is social. The community of the redeemed is socially organized into a body that is the complement of Christ and his fullness. The multitude of persons composing it form a unity, which the Son of God has taken to himself and espoused.

In the divine plan Mary has a place and function analogous, though vastly superior, to those of the Church. The Second Person of the Trinity became incarnate not in a nature created for this purpose, but in the womb of the Blessed Virgin. Her union with the Word is not hypostatic, as is the union between the assumed human nature and the Son of God; it is a union of person with person, the intimate relationship of motherhood. God utilized the woman in the incarnation not because he needed an instrument, but because he wished to exploit to the utmost, *summo modo,* the possibilities of union with the incarnate Word which the maternal powers of woman presented to him.[4]

Christ admits all his members to a share in his activity. To his Mother he gave a greater and a higher power of acting than to any other member. As she participated in the hypostatic union at the very instant of the incarnation, so also did she cooperate with her Son at the very moment of redemption.

Thus the theology of the Blessed Virgin is closely connected with the theology of the Church. The underlying principle is the same in both cases: God's intention to communicate himself

[4] M. J. Nicolas O.P., "Marie et l'Eglise dans le plan divin," *BSFEM* 11, 1953, 165.

supernaturally to the world, in a self-communication that enables mankind to collaborate with him for its own salvation.

The Relation of Mary and the Church to Christ

In Scripture, tradition and the liturgy, the Church is often personified in feminine imagery. This femininity characterizes the relationship which St. Paul, following the lead of the Old Testament, discerned between Christ and mankind. Femininity is receptivity of being; it is an attribute that well describes the creature in its sincerest attitude toward the Creator. The receptivity that is common to every creature is especially typified by woman in relation to man, who is, according to the apostle, the head of the woman as Christ is the head of man (Eph 5:23). Quite naturally, then, the creature who is loved by God appears under the symbol of woman. Any particular creature is too imperfect to be the beloved spouse of God. Only the universe of creatures, by the concert of their many complementary perfections, can suitably be called an image of God; only mankind in its entirety can be regarded as the adequate spouse of Christ.

The fullness of grace, which overflows to the Church, abounds in the soul of Christ, Head of the Church and supreme principle in the order of grace, of whose plenitude all receive. Therefore, the Church is completely dependent on the incarnate Word.

Mary's relationship to Christ essentially transcends that of the Church. She is not an ordinary member who simply participates, even in a uniquely privileged way, in the common relationship which all the other members have with Christ. She is united to the incarnate Word in a way that is exclusive to her and that surpasses the relations which the rest of the Church has with Christ by grace. Her personality and her life are dominated by her divine maternity; every grace that is given to her is gauged by her state as Mother of God and is not imparted to her through the agency of the Church. Her relations with Christ are defined by her divine motherhood which, in the order of the divine decrees, is prior to the establishment of the economy of grace and the founding of the Church.

Yet Mary is related to the Church through the relations which both she and the Church have with Christ. The kinship between Christ and Mary is comparable with the kinship between the Church and Christ's members. Mary is the Mother of Christ; and the Church, through grace, generates Christ in the souls of the baptized; as Mary cared for and nourished the infant Christ, so the Church cares for, nourishes and cherishes Christ in souls. Mary is the new Eve, and the Church also is the new Eve; each is mother of all the supernaturally living. Furthermore, because of the mystical oneness of the Church with Christ, Mary's relationship with the physical Christ is extended to his members; the mother of the Head is also the mother of the body. The underlying cause of the likeness is the fact that the Church, along with its head, is the mystical Christ, according to the Savior's own words: "I am Jesus whom you persecute" (Acts 9:5). Consequently, the Mother's relationship to her Son necessarily flows over to the Church. Christ stands in the middle between them, uniting both. Thus all comparison between the two terms arises from the relationship of each term to Christ: Mary is the Mother of Christ, the Church is the body of Christ, the mystic Christ himself.

Mary Considered apart from the Church

Although Mary is a member of the Church, she may be considered apart from it. First of all, she is prior to the Church. Because of her, Christ was never without his Church; in her, who belongs to the era of Christ's grace and of explicit faith in him, the Church was a concrete person before it was a mystical person or an organized institution.

Her predestination, too, differs from that of all other persons. Like all of us, she was redeemed. The grace that was given to her came from the foreseen merits of him who was to be her Son. But she was redeemed quite otherwise than the rest of men; she was preserved from contracting the sin of nature. She was redeemed apart and therefore placed apart. Her fullness of grace, which grew in her all her life, was not dependent on the Church, but has its explanation in her divine maternity, its rule and measure. Thus she constitutes an order apart, so that she alone can enter into comparison with the rest of the Church. This fact makes possible an analogy between her, a particular person, and the collectivity which is the Church.

The Blessed Virgin's association with the Church in the divine plan draws them together, yet at the same time shows how unique Mary's situation is in the universe. The bond linking her to Christ is unattainable by other Christians. However, although all supernatural graces have in her their most eminent perfection, the hierarchical and sacramental powers that essentially constitute the Church were never conferred on her. Hence the Church adds something to Mary. The divine maternity is greater than all the functions and offices exercised by the Church, but is radically different from them. Among the countless members of the Church, therefore, the Blessed Virgin can be considered apart from all the others and then be compared with them.

Ultimately, the foundation of the parallelism between Mary and the Church is the incarnation, which is God's effort to communicate himself to all mankind. Except for the hypostatic union, this communication reaches its highest point in the Blessed Virgin, Mother of God. Her divine maternity, with all the consequences that flow from it, sets her apart, so that she alone is comparable and superior to all the rest of the Church. Yet the Church, too, has the closest relationship with the incarnate Word; through him, Mary and the Church are related. What the Church is collectively, Mary is first individually.[5]

[5] *Ibid.* 169.

2. THE ANALOGY PRESENTED

In the problem of Mary and the Church, the comparison is between Mary and all the rest of the Church. Understood in this way, Mary and the Church can be brought together for study and analogies between them can be perceived. From early times, in fact, Mary, mother and virgin, has been likened to the Church, mother and virgin. Such resemblances, however, involve a number of essential differences. Thus Mary is the Mother of the divine Word, whom she generated according to his human nature; the Church is mother not of the divine Word, but of Christians, whom it regenerates not according to human nature, but for participation in the divine nature. Mary is literally a virgin; the Church can be called a virgin in that it has never adulterated the faith, but has always remained true to Christ's teaching. The Church is mother of the faithful, and Mary is also mother of the faithful.

Doctrines such as these are the ancient and common patrimony of the Christian people. But they do not exhaust the possibilities of our knowledge about Mary and the Church. Further investigation can be undertaken and is being vigorously carried on, with the hope of imparting greater intelligibility to both mariology and ecclesiology.

In tracing the parallel between Mary and the Church, a simple and at the same time systematic method may be followed. It consists in pondering one by one the main attributes, perfections, activities and mysteries of the Blessed Virgin, and then inquiring whether their analogies are discernible in the Church.

The Maternity of Mary and the Church

In the supernatural order, the Mother of Christ is also the mother of the Church and therefore our mother. The Church, too, is our mother. What are the meaning and value of this twofold maternity? This is the initial problem confronting us.

121

The present inquiry proposes to put in order and synthesize the data acquired from Scripture and tradition, with the aim of bringing out several conclusions. In particular, does any conclusion derived from this twofold maternity possess any power to promote clarification of the relations between Mary and the Church?

1. *The Divine Motherhood.* Mary is the true Mother of the divine Word. She brought him forth into the world and sustained him in his vocation up to the sacrifice of his life for the redemption of mankind. The divine maternity is absolutely unique; only the incarnation could make it possible. The assertion that Mary is the Mother of God involves no metaphor; she is God's Mother in the same sense as other women are mothers of their children, by actual physical generation. No application of the term "Mother of Christ" can be made except in reference to her. Hence her maternity offers to mariology an unshakable and sharply delineated substructure. As we observed above, the theology of the Blessed Virgin could not but suffer if it lost sight of this unique point of departure, or if attempts were made to construct it on other, less stable foundations. Intelligibility in the study of marian theology comes ultimately from the maternity, and we must start here if we wish to illuminate all other aspects of her position in the plan of salvation and to clarify her function in the career of her Son and in the Church.

2. *Mary, Mother of the Church.* Tradition exhibits the relationship between Mary and the Church in various ways. According to St. Augustine, "Mary is a part of the Church, a holy member, an excellent member, the most eminent member, but still a member of the whole body."[6] St. Ambrose asserts that she is "a type of the Church."[7] St. Bernard saw the Blessed Virgin as intermediary between Christ and the Church: "Mary

[6] *Sermo 25 de verbis evangelii Matth., PL* 46, 938.
[7] *In Lucam* 2, 7, *PL* 15, 1555.

is placed between Christ and the Church."[8] Titles of this kind express some aspects of Mary's relationship to the Church. Which is the most basic, central, illuminating? As we mentioned above, a few contemporary authors, such as Semmelroth and A. Müller, select the view that Mary is the prototype of the Church. But this idea is not primary and is not wholly valid, since Mary is not the prototype of the ecclesiastical hierarchy which is essential to the Church. None of the formulas proposed completely explains why Mary is the foundation or model of the Church. The truth that is most securely anchored in the sources of revelation and most clearly defines the relations between Mary and the Church is the simple fact stated by Leo XIII that the Blessed Virgin is the mother of the Church.[9]

Mary had been prepared for the divine maternity by her immaculate conception and all the graces flowing from it. When the angel announced God's proposal, Mary offered to God her free acquiescence and in return received the Son of God into her womb. In consequence of her consent to be the Mother of the Messiah, she entered into a relationship with all the subjects of the messianic King. Mary became the Mother of Christ; beyond that, her maternity extended to the entire Christian populace, to the whole Church founded by Jesus Christ.

That the Blessed Virgin is mother of the Head and body, hence of the Church, is completely certain from tradition. The only question is how and in what way Mary is mother of the Church: is she our mother only morally or juridically, or in some deeper, more ontologically real sense?

The moral and juridical maternity is clear; Mary embraces all the faithful with motherly love and helps them from heaven with her prayers. But tradition asserts more. She is our mother because she generates us, causing in us a real origin of supernatural life. When did she give birth to us? Three main alterna-

[8] *In dom. infra oct. Assumpt.* 5, PL 183, 432.
[9] *Adiutricem populi*, ASS 28, 1895–1896, 130: "*verissime quidem mater Ecclesiae.*"

123

tives occur: the incarnation, association in the redemption, and heavenly intercession. The last is an aspect of her moral maternity, and the incarnation is only a remote origin of our supernatural life. Hence Mary's spiritual maternity depends mostly on her coredemptive activity. The more closely she was associated in the work of redemption, cause of our regeneration and birth of the Church, the more truly she is our mother.

The incarnation establishes a direct continuity between Mary and the Church, for the faithful are the body of Christ, who is generated and formed in them. By consenting to become the Mother of Jesus, Mary had also to take under her maternal charge his mystical body. The birth of the Redeemer from a daughter of our race inaugurated solidarity between him and all mankind. From the moment of the incarnation, Christ contained in mysterious fashion all the members of the mystical body he came to redeem. Mary gave him the power to make our nature his own; in her and from her virginal flesh Christ took to himself the humanity that makes him our kinsman.

Therefore, the womb of Mary is the womb of the Church. Such is the authoritative doctrine of Pius X:

> In one and the same womb of his most chaste Mother, Christ took to himself human flesh and at the same time added to it a spiritual body made up of all those who were to believe in him. Therefore, Mary, while carrying the Savior in her womb, may be said to have carried likewise all those whose life was contained in the Savior's life. All of us, consequently, who are united to Christ . . . have come forth from Mary's womb, like a body attached to its head.[10]

Mary's spiritual maternity is rooted in the mystery of the incarnation. When Mary consented to the incarnation, she represented all mankind and spoke in the name of the whole human race.[11] When she conceived Christ, she spiritually conceived all the faithful. Because she is Mother of Christ the head, she is

[10] *Ad diem illum* 452f.
[11] See *Summa Theol.* III, q. 30, a. 1: "*Per annuntiationem expectabatur consensus Virginis loco totius humanae naturae.*"

124

mother of the whole body. This is not a mere moral maternity, but is a supernatural reality, for Christ's members form one mystical person with the individual Christ, Son of Mary,[12] a situation which has no counterpart in the relationship between a natural society and its founder. Accordingly, the incarnation establishes a vital union between us and Christ, and consequently between Mary and the Church.

The maternity which thus has its inception in the incarnation is the ontological reason why Mary's cooperation with the Redeemer on Calvary could be elevated by God to a true generation of members of the mystical body. Although she was already the mother of the faithful because she was Mother of Christ, she did not become our mother in the fullest sense except from the moment when she was present on Calvary. At that solemn hour, Jesus made her the mother of John, type of all the disciples whom Christ and his Father love. At a stroke, her maternity acquired a new dimension. United to her Son in the sacrifice, she received from him her maternal mission with regard to the Christian community. This is the proper understanding of the words "Woman, behold your son," for the beloved disciple represented all those who, like him, lovingly adhere to the Savior.[13] From that time on, Mary is fully the mother of the whole Church. Analogically speaking, the Blessed Virgin spiritually conceived the mystical body of Christ along with the Head at the conception of Jesus and, as associate of the Redeemer, gave birth to it under the cross when the Church itself was born.

Thus, on the basis of her divine maternity, Mary is the spiritual mother of the Church; her spiritual maternity is the

---

[12] *Mystici corporis Christi* 226: "The divine Redeemer and the society which is his body form a single mystical person, that is, in Augustine's words, the whole Christ."

[13] F. M. Braun O.P., *La Mère des Fidèles*, 113, 181. See Leo XIII, *Adiutricem populi*, 28, 1895–1896, 130: "In John, as the Church has always perceived, Christ designated the person of the human race, especially of those who would cleave to him by faith."

prolongation of her maternity over Christ. The two maternities are analogous, for her spiritual maternity refers not to the God-man, but to his members, and is not according to the flesh but is exercised on a higher, more spiritual level.

To perceive the relations between Mary and the Church in their proper perspective, we must always come back to the basic idea that she is the mother of the Church.[14] Maternal foundation of the Church, she is, so to speak, the very womb of the mystical body.

3. *The Church, Mother of Christians.* The Blessed Virgin is our mother, for her maternity with respect to Christ is continued in her relations toward the Church. Yet the Church, too, is our mother, for from her we receive our supernatural life and education. This maternity, exercised by the Church, is founded on the divine maternity of Mary. The expression "Mother of Christ" has no meaning apart from the incarnation of the Son of God in Mary. But the incarnation is prolonged in the Church, for grace is a participation in the divine life that is fully possessed by Christ in his humanity. Therefore, to be born to the life of grace is to be born to the life of Christ.

Consequently, as we noted previously, every Christian who receives sanctifying grace gives birth to Christ in himself; he becomes the "mother of Christ" in a limited sense, that is, with reference to the mystical body of Christ. Jesus himself said: "Whosoever shall do the will of God, he is my brother and sister and mother" (Mk 3:35; see Mt 12:50). No paternal title is here mentioned; the reason is that the soul which gives birth to Christ in itself acts in complete dependence on the initiative of the eternal Father and so contributes a cooperation that bears some resemblance to the feminine role of mother.

Furthermore, if birth to the life of grace is a new birth of Christ, everyone who collaborates in the birth of Christ in others is also a "mother of Christ." St. Paul told the Galatians

14 F. M. Braun, "Marie et l'Église, d'après l'Écriture," *BSFEM* 10, 1952, 7.

that he was suffering the pains of childbirth until Christ would be formed in them (Gal 4:19). The same idea is applied by St. Augustine to all who bring about the birth of Christ in others.[15] With much greater reason the maternal function attributed to anyone who collaborates in the work of salvation is attributed to the Church, the very organism of salvation. In a sense more profound than for any individual, the Church is Christ's mother. "The mother of Christ is the whole Church, because by God's grace it gives birth to his members, that is, his faithful."[16]

Christ's own words: "Whosoever shall do the will of God, he is my brother and sister and mother," guard us against an erroneous understanding of this maternity. The three titles "brother," "sister" and "mother" cannot, of course, be taken in their actual sense. Literal motherhood is excluded; the three terms are metaphors expressing the close union between Jesus and those who carry out his Father's will. Such persons have sanctifying grace and consequently share in Christ's sonship; they become united to him by a tie that resembles the union between brothers and sisters. And since their birth to the life of grace is not brought about without their own free cooperation, each of them acquires a kind of maternal relationship to him.

Thus the title "brother" or "sister of Christ" must be understood in an analogical sense: as brothers and sisters are related in a particular way because of their reception of life from the same parents, so Christ and we have the same life of grace, and we are all children of the same Father. As for the term "mother of Christ," it is verified literally in Mary; when applied to us, it is only a metaphor indicating a certain functional likeness between our collaboration with God and maternal collaboration;

---

[15] De sancta virginitate 5, PL 40, 399: "Mater eius est omnis anima pia faciens voluntatem Patris eius fecundissima caritate in iis quos parturit, donec in eis ipse formetur."

[16] Ibid.; see Serm. 192, 2, PL 38, 1012: "Caput vestrum peperit Maria, vos ecclesia."

127

it is not a true exercise of the functions of motherhood. And the Church itself, in its entirety, is the mother of Jesus in the sense that in it and through it God continues to give his Son to the world by forming for him a body, the mystical body of Christ.[17]

Therefore, Mary's motherhood with regard to Christ incomparably transcends the metaphorical maternity that is ascribed to each of the faithful and to the Church. Müller's theory that the two maternities occupy the same ontological level and that Mary is literally the mother of Christ only because she, unlike us, possesses grace in plenitude is inadmissible. According to this opinion, grace of itself requires divine maternity, conformably with the text from Mark quoted above; hence Mary's maternity would be an effect of her fullness of grace. If this line of reasoning were correct, we would also have to conclude that Mary is literally the sister of Christ, which is nonsense. The argument from analogy requires a delicate touch in theology, especially when the question concerns metaphor rather than proper analogy. In the present case, the maternity of the Church does not clarify the incarnation or Mary's maternity; in fact, it is not even intelligible except in dependence on the maternity exercised by the Blessed Virgin. We can be regarded as Christ's brothers and sisters only in the sense that we are admitted by grace into the divine life that is fully possessed by him in the sacred humanity he derived from Mary; and we do our part to bring about his birth in ourselves and others, thus imitating Mary's maternity in a remote fashion and on an essentially lower level, only in the sense that we freely collaborate in the reception of his grace. But Mary's grace was not the cause of her maternity; it was the cause of the faith and love which produced in her the disposition that enabled the power of the Holy Spirit to act on her for the conception of Christ. Hence her maternity, far from being a privileged instance of the maternity

[17] On this point see J. Lécuyer, C.S.SP., "Marie et l'Église comme Mère et Épouse du Christ," *BSFEM* 10, 1952, 33f.

common to all believers, is forever first and unique and belongs to a totally different order.[18]

When we compare Mary's spiritual maternity with that of the Church, we easily see that the former is the nobler and is the source of the latter. Mary's maternity acts and is actuated in the maternity of the Church. But these two mothers do not have two separate families or give birth to different children; they exist in the same Christian family; they have the same sons and daughters whom they cherish with a common love. The same kind of spiritual maternity is realized in Mary and the Church; yet the first is the foundation of the second.[19] One never operates without the other. Mary's maternity brings forth the whole body of Christ, the Church, which is also the mother of Christ's members; for Mary, by Christ's will, gave birth to the Church so that it too might be the mother of Christians.[20]

The maternity of the Church, which receives its power of generating from the Blessed Virgin in subordination to Christ,[21] visibly and strikingly manifests Mary's maternity. Both maternities coalesce into a single, continual communication of life to the faithful, so that they are two aspects or functions of one spiritual maternity rather than two adequately distinct maternities. As Christ is socially prolonged in his mystical body, so Mary's maternity is prolonged in the Church.

The Church is our mother mainly as minister of the sacraments, without which no supernatural life is given. Mary is our mother because she cooperated in Christ's redeeming sacrifice to gain for us the grace without which the sacraments

---

[18] See Lécuyer, *art. cit.* 34. Müller's speculative development goes far beyond the patristic evidence he gathered in his book *Ecclesia-Maria* and owes more to Scheeben than to the Fathers. Among the many criticisms and correctives of his notions about the maternity of Mary and the Church, see H. Lennerz, "Maria-Ecclesia," *Gregorianum* 35, 1954, 91–94, and Y. M. J. Congar, "Marie et l'Église dans la pensée patristique," *RSPT* 38, 1954, 31–35.

[19] Congar, *art. cit.* 37.

[20] I. Vodopivec, "Beata Virgo Maria typus et mater ecclesiae," *Alma Socia Christi* 11, 1953, 290f.

[21] See below, on the coredemptive activity of Mary and the Church.

cannot cause life in us. Mary's spiritual maternity more directly influences the internal, spiritual nature of the Church, but thereby also reaches the social, hierarchical structure of the body. For, as St. Augustine points out, the Blessed Virgin co-operated by charity, not by authority, that Christ's members might be born.[22] Authority belongs to Christ, who committed it to the apostles and their successors. But the hierarchy continually receives supernatural power from the source of the cross, whose saving grace Christ confers on the Church through his Mother.

The Spouse of Christ

Occasionally in past centuries and more frequently in recent times, the title "spouse of Christ" has been applied both to Mary and to the Church.

The notion of God's espousals with his people is very ancient, and Christian usage of the idea owes much to the Old Testament, in which it is a favorite theme. God's alliance with Israel is likened to the matrimonial bond that unites man and woman and that requires an unswerving fidelity from both parties. If the chosen race is unfaithful to God and slips into idolatry, it commits adultery.[23] Thus the vocation of the people of Israel has a feminine trait. God chose the race of Abraham, formed it into a nation, and took it to himself as his spouse.

But the chosen race of the old covenant prefigures the chosen race of the New Testament. God wishes to take all mankind into his love. The true spouse is not Israel according to the flesh, but the spiritual posterity of Abraham: the Church.

This transition involves an important change, resulting from

[22] De sancta virginitate 6, PL 40, 399: "[Maria est] plane mater membrorum eius, quod nos sumus, quia cooperata est caritate ut fideles in ecclesia nascerentur."

[23] The main texts are given by C. Dillenschneider, Le Mystère de la Corédemption mariale, Paris 1951, 111–114.

the unique event that ushered in the new era. God became man in Christ; the Word was made flesh. Since human nature and divine nature are united in him, we may speak of the espousals of humanity and divinity on the day of the incarnation. And since the Church is his body, we are led to the further metaphor that the Church is his bride. This union is the great mystery or sacrament: "They shall be two in one flesh" (Eph 5:31); St. Paul adds expressly that he is referring to Christ and the Church.

Transfer of this metaphor from the Church, regarded collectively as a moral person, to each individual belonging to the society is quite justified. Titles that are proper to the Church, such as "spouse" or "temple of God," can be attributed to every member of the body. For Christ loves each member of his body and calls each of them to be his bride.

If every member of the Church can be called the spouse of Christ because of the love to which each soul is invited to respond, can the same title be applied to Mary? Of all the members of the Church, she is the one most richly endowed with divine grace, the one most closely united in love to Christ, the one who has most perfectly responded to God's advances.

The tradition of the Church, however, is unfavorable to this suggestion. Nowhere in Scripture do we read that Mary is the bride of the Lamb or the spouse of the Word.[24] The Fathers, too, are silent on the subject. Although they established between Eve and Mary a relation analogous to that which St. Paul discerns between Adam and Christ, they know nothing of the bridal relationship exploited by some contemporary mariologists, who imply that Mary is to Christ what Eve is to Adam. For the Fathers, the new Eve associated with the new Adam *as his spouse* is not Mary, but the Church.[25] They never join the two

[24] Braun, "Marie et l'Église, d'après l'Écriture," *BSFEM* 10, 1952, 15.
[25] Congar, "Marie et l'Église dans la pensée patristique," *RSPT* 38, 1954, 3; the author gives a number of examples typical of patristic teaching.

expressions "Mother of God" and "spouse of the Word"; the spouse is not the Blessed Virgin, but human nature assumed in Mary's womb.

The idea that the Blessed Virgin is the spouse of Christ hardly occurs prior to the middle ages. St. Ephraem has a hymn in which he calls Mary "thy mother, thy sister, thy spouse, thy handmaiden"; but the condition of the text is not good and the meaning is not clear. In the eighth century, an obscure passage of a sermon by Pseudo-Augustine refers to Mary as "bride of Christ." Apparently Rupert of Deutz, that "untidy thinker," is the chief innovator in this matter, and passed his fancy on to French divines of the seventeenth century and to Scheeben two centuries later.[26]

An earlier and more trustworthy tradition represents the incarnation as the nuptials between the Son of God and the human nature he assumed. Although the Fathers did not speak of a bridal relationship between Christ and Mary, they observed that the virginal womb of the Mother is the *thalamus* or bridal chamber in which the mystery of the nuptial union between divinity and humanity was accomplished. This theme was quite universal in patristic times.[27] Hence the Blessed Virgin is personally implicated in this mystic marriage, for the Word sought her free consent to the union and, as soon as it was given, formed a body for himself from her flesh. Her place in the mystery has been signalized by St. Thomas in a celebrated passage that has influenced all subsequent thinking on the subject. One of the reasons he assigns for the message brought to Mary by the angel is "that there might be made known a sort of spiritual marriage between the Son of God and human nature. At the annunciation, therefore, the consent of the

[26] See the review of the sparse evidence by J. H. Crehan S.J., "Maria Paredros," *TS* 16, 1955, 414–423.

[27] St. Augustine has many passages on the subject, e.g. *Enarr. in psalmos*, 90, *PL* 37, 1163: "*Verbum sponsus, caro sponsa, et thalamus uterus virginis.*"

Virgin was awaited in place of that of the whole human race."[28]
Thus the incarnation is like a marriage between divinity and
humanity. But the humanity that is thereby joined to the Word
embraces, in addition to the individual nature hypostatically
united to him, the whole of human nature that is mystically
included in the body of Christ, that is, the Church.

Mary, however, did not contract the matrimonial union in
her own behalf. She acted as a representative or proxy. "The
true bride of Christ, the Church, was not yet of age at the date
of the annunciation and therefore someone had to act for her.
God's prevision had provided such a proxy."[29] Mary herself
is not the spouse; she represents the spouse—that is, the Church
—whose consent is expressed by her *fiat*. "The eternal Son of
God, when he wished to take man's nature to himself and so
contract a mystical marriage with the whole human race, did
not do so before obtaining the perfectly free consent of the
one chosen to be his Mother, who thus acted in the person of
the human race itself."[30]

The metaphor of spouse, however, rich in content though
it may be, discloses only a partial aspect of Mary's vocation.
Penetration of its meaning leads inevitably to her divine maternity. With reference to the Blessed Virgin, the term "spouse"
is always equivocal and cannot correctly describe the union of
Jesus with his Mother.

The relationship between this Son and this Mother is much
stronger and more comprehensive than the relationship between
spouses, although it contains all the perfection found in the
union of a man and a woman who are linked in the same
destiny. Mary is Christ's Mother associated with him in his redemptive mission and verifies eminently, but transcendently,

[28] *Summa Theol.* III, q. 30, a. 1. Leo XIII quotes this passage several
times in his encyclicals on the rosary, and Pius XII uses it in the epilogue
of *Mystici corporis Christi.*

[29] Crehan, "Maria Paredros," *TS* 16, 1955, 421.

[30] Leo XIII, *Octobri mense, ASS* 24, 1891–1892, 195. Immediately after
these words, the Pope quotes the passage from St. Thomas mentioned above.

all that the biblical imagery of spouse conveys.[31] Hence Mary is not aptly called the spouse of the incarnate Word; she is his Mother and she is likewise the mother of his mystical body which is the Church, the spouse of Christ. Maternal union and bridal union are here expressed; the first exists between Christ and Mary, the second between Christ and the Church. The two categories should not be intermingled.

Whatever is significant in the metaphor of spouse in connection with Mary is not an attribute added to her maternity, but a perfection of her maternity. The Blessed Virgin is the *Socia Christi* and the Church is the *Sponsa Christi.* Although the two ideas ought to be kept distinct, they are very close and, through Christ, draw Mary and the Church closer to each other.

The New Eve

Some modern mariologists endeavor to plumb a relationship between the Blessed Virgin and her Son according to the formula: what Eve is to Adam, Mary is to Christ. This is a relationship of bride to bridegroom and would make Mary the spouse of Christ. Neither Scripture nor the Fathers allude to such a parallel. Yet both Scripture and the Fathers recognize between Eve and Mary a relationship analogous to that which St. Paul establishes between Adam and Christ: as Christ is the new Adam, Mary is the new Eve. On the other hand, the Church is also celebrated as the new Eve.

Adam is the type of the One who was to come (Rom 5:14), and the latter is identified in the same context as well as in 1 Cor 15. He is Jesus Christ, the new Adam. Although the apostle does not speak of a new Eve, he places at the side of the new Adam a female figure: the Church that submits and unites herself to Christ in love; this is his spouse and our mother (Eph 5:22–23). Here the idea of the new Eve is at least foreshadowed, if not implicitly indicated. Does the Bible also suggest that Mary

[31] Braun, "Marie et l'Église, d'après l'Écriture," *BSFEM* 10, 1952, 16.

is the new Eve? The prophecy of Simeon associates the Savior and his Mother together in a way that recalls the woman and her seed in Gn 3:15. Several passages in the Gospel according to St. John point to the same parallel.[32] In the opinion of many exegetes, the words uttered by Christ on the cross: "Woman, behold your son," contain an allusion to the woman of Genesis.

Scholarly examination of Ap 12 has indicated that the woman in that exalted passage is Mary.[33] Many proofs are brought forward, e.g. that the woman in question is the Mother of the Messiah. One of the arguments is particularly pertinent here; it consists in a comparison between Ap 12 and Gn 3:15. In both texts the encounter of the woman with the adversary is emphasized, and in both the woman is mentioned first. The adversary-dragon is identified with the adversary-serpent of Genesis. Both passages identify the dragon's opponent as the offspring of the woman. In Genesis the offspring gains the final victory over the serpent; the same is true in the Apocalypse, but with a clarification: the victory of the collective offspring is won by reason of the individual, the Lamb. The same closed unit of woman and offspring is discerned in both texts. "So many and such close points of contact between Ap 12 and Gn 3:15 point to the same actors in the scene. Since the woman in Gn 3:15 is Mary, the mother of the Messiah, so also here in Ap 12."[34] And because the woman in Genesis is she who is known as the new Eve, the woman in the Apocalypse is likewise the new Eve.

Furthermore, although the woman of the Apocalypse designates a definite person, the Blessed Virgin, this person embodies in herself a collectivity. "Just as the male Child represents at the same time the historical Christ and the mystical Christ . . . so the woman signifies, first, the personal Mother of Jesus, and

[32] See A. M. Dubarle O.P., "Les fondements bibliques du titre marial de nouvelle Eve," *RSR* 39, 1951, 49–64.

[33] For example, B. J. LeFrois S.V.D., *The Woman Clothed with the Sun*, Rome 1954, especially the evidence presented in 38–47.

[34] *Ibid.* 222.

then the people of God, as realized in the Church."[35] Under the figure of the woman in the Apocalypse, St. John portrays Mary as the Church; the individual personifies a collectivity, and the collectivity is embodied in a concrete person. The great task of the Virgin-Mother is perpetuated in the gigantic task imposed on the Church, the regeneration of all mankind in Christ.[36] Consequently, as Mary is the new Eve, so also is the Church the new Eve.

Under this aspect of the new Eve, Mary and the Church are identified with each other. The two unite in their opposition to the ancient serpent. Yet Mary and the Church are not the new Eve in the same way. Mary is the new Eve because Christ, her issue, crushes the head of the serpent, and hence because she is the Mother of Christ. The maternal function with which she is charged makes her, after victory over Satan has been won, the "mother of all the living," as Eve is (Gn 3:20); these are "the rest of her seed, who keep the commandments of God and have the testimony of Jesus Christ" (Ap 12:17). The Church, on the contrary, is called the new Eve because it is the spouse of Christ (Eph 5:31f), prefigured by the spouse of the first Adam.[37]

The theme of the new Eve is developed by the Fathers in their reflections on the idea of recapitulation (*recirculatio, recircumlatio*) that is so prominent in St. Irenaeus.[38] God's plan had been clear from the very outset: a man and a woman, Adam and Eve, were to transmit to all mankind a life of union with God. Restoration of the plan so tragically compromised soon after its inception was to be made by another man and another woman. The man is Jesus Christ, the new Adam. A woman had to have her place in the restoration, for the feminine sex was

[35] Braun, *La Mère des Fidèles*, 143.   [36] LeFrois, *op. cit.* 262.

[37] See C. Sträter S.J., "Marie, Mère de l'Église," *EM* 4, 1954, 442.

[38] For a summary of patristic teaching on the second Eve, see N. F. Moholy O.F.M., "Saint Irenaeus: The Father of Mariology," *Studia Mariana*, Burlington, Wis. 1952, vol. 7, 151–172; W. J. Burghardt S.J., "Mary in Western Patristic Thought," *Mariology*, 1, 110–117.

meant to cooperate in the redemption. The Fathers recognized this woman. The new Eve is Mary and the Church.

Evil and death had been introduced into the world by the woman in consequence of her gross disobedience. It would seem necessary that a woman should reintroduce life by obedience and faith. This teaching is found in most of the Fathers, with the exception of those who only apply this idea to the Church. However, Mary is the new Eve not because she is the spouse of the new Adam, but because she is the Mother of Christ and, in him, of regenerated mankind. Thus St. Irenaeus, like his predecessor St. Justin, and his imitator Tertullian, compares Eve, virgin and spouse of Adam, to Mary, virgin and spouse of Joseph. The former was disobedient to God and so was the cause of death; the latter was obedient to God and so became the cause of salvation. But she caused the regeneration of humanity by generating her Son.[39] Accordingly, the principle of *recirculatio* from Eve to Mary is based on the Blessed Virgin's divine maternity.

Not only the Church, therefore, but also Mary is celebrated in tradition as the new Eve, mother of all who live the new life brought by Christ.

Later ages made a further application. If Mary is mother of all the living, she is associated with her Son in his work of redemption. The consent which she freely gave at the annunciation to be the Mother of Christ and which was necessary for carrying out the recapitulation was enlivened anew at the crucifixion. By cooperating in the redeeming sacrifice, she is the new Eve in a heightened sense, source of our life, mother of the body as she is mother of the Head.

Thus the comparison between Eve and Mary leads to the idea of Mary as the mother of the Church. If the Blessed Virgin is mother of the Head, she is mother of the Church which is Christ's body. It leads further to the concept of Mary's coredemptive function, for if she is truly mother, she had a part in the true birth of the Church that occurred on the cross. And in the

[39] St. Irenaeus, *Adversus haereses* 3, 22, 4; 4, 33, 4, in *PG* 7, 959, 1074f.

conviction of many theologians, the most important aspect of Mary's spiritual maternity was Calvary.

The parallel between Eve and Mary, which was studied early in Christian thought, has proved attractive to contemporary theology. As Eve contributed to our ruin, so Mary and the Church cooperate for our redemption; the affinity between the mystery of Mary and the mystery of the Church is very close. Some authors go so far as to make the idea of Mary as new Eve and type of the Church the basic principle of mariology. The proposal is quite untenable, because the title "new Eve" is dependent on and included in the divine maternity. Mary is the new Eve because she is the mother of the Redeemer.

The Virginity of Mary and the Church

From ancient times Mary, mother and virgin, has been likened to the Church, mother and virgin. This comparison, however, involves a number of differences. Mary is the Mother of Jesus Christ; the Church is the mother of Christians who are "other Christs." Mary is literally a virgin; the Church is a virgin in the sense that it has never adulterated the faith but has always been true to Christ's doctrine. Maternity and virginity are literal for Mary, but analogous and metaphorical for the Church.

In Judeo-Christian writings, a virgin is a person or a community that is given to God and remains faithful to him. Sexual connotations are nonexistent or unimportant. In the Old Testament, the matrimonial union with God, a common theme, consecrates and guarantees virginity and at the same time makes it maternally fruitful, so long as Israel does not abandon its divine Bridegroom for false gods. Virginity in this connection means fidelity; heresy and apostasy are a kind of adultery that destroys virginity.[40] Faith and nuptial fidelity are linked together; infidelity is disruptive of both. Union with God shelters virginity

[40] G. Philips, "Perspectives mariologiques: Marie et l'Église," *Marianum* 15, 1953, 455.

and hallows it by enriching it with a fecundity that is free from all corruption. Its fruit is an imperishable life of which the Holy Spirit is the transcendent cause.

Therefore, the Church, spouse of Christ, is a virgin. "Christ is the Bridegroom, the Church is his bride: spouse in her love, a virgin in her integrity," as long as she does not commit adultery against truth; for "adulterers are all they who seek to adulterate the truth of faith and wisdom."[41] As applied to the Church the notion of virginity is always linked to the purity of faith. The very maternity of the Church is virginal because, pure in faith and undefiled by heresy, she brings forth the children of God by the action of the Holy Spirit, without the intervention of any unchaste agent.

When the biblical idea of virginity refers to persons, it implies, of course, bodily integrity, especially as a sign of spiritual fidelity, total consecration to God, and permanent union with him. Mary, Mother of God and Virgin of virgins, is the ideal of virginity in every respect. Her divine maternity is entirely according to God, by reason of her incorruptible reception of the Word in the complete yielding of faith. She conceived and bore her Son with unimpaired virginity, through the action of the Holy Spirit and to the exclusion of all power of this world. Her spiritual maternity, too, is wholly virginal. Christ is the Bridegroom of the Church, drawing it from the spiritual womb of Mary by the activity of his Spirit, and no alien causality has anything to do with the existence or life of the Church. Like Christ, the members of his body are born of Mary as children of God solely by the power of the Holy Spirit.[42]

The virginity of the Church helps us to understand the virginity of Mary. The Church is not only one flesh but one spirit, with Christ: "He who is joined to the Lord is one spirit" (1 Cor 6:17). Though real, the union is spiritual and mystical. The

[41] St. Ambrose, *Expositio Evangelii sec. Lucam* 8, 9, in *Corpus Scriptorum Ecclesiasticorum Latinorum* (CSEL) 32.4, 395.
[42] See Sträter, "Marie, Mère de l'Église," *EM* 4, 1954, 443.

virginity of the Blessed Virgin is also real, but spiritual and mystical. Her virginity is not only the absence of carnal relations with any man, it is also the absolutely spiritual and mystical union of her soul with God that preceded the actual incarnation.

By the perfection of its virginity, therefore, the Church draws ever nearer to the virginal Mother of God.

The Holiness of Mary and the Church

As the virginity of the Church aids us in arriving at a deeper appreciation of Mary's virginity, so also does Mary's holiness assist us in understanding the holiness of the Church. The holiness of Mary is essentially the same as the holiness of the Church; it is a sanctity that comes from the same God, leads back to the same God, and is the formal effect of the same grace. The main difference lies in the respective receptivity of Mary and the Church.[43] Human liberty is a power of reception, but also of refusal. No refusal or even reluctance ever marred Mary's attitude of acceptance toward God's advances; the Church, however, is a collectivity made up of men and women who have never completely held their souls open to God's boundless generosity.

Like us, Mary was redeemed. All the graces given to her are owing to the foreseen merits of her Son's charity and his sacrifice on the cross. But unlike us, she never contracted the sin of nature from which the rest of men have to be liberated. The fullness of grace with which she was endowed surpasses the totality of the grace ever given or to be given to all mankind and the angels. Her grace recapitulates the whole order of grace, which achieves its highest perfection in her, for it was conferred on her by reason of her divine maternity.

[43] R. Laurentin, "Sainteté de Marie et de l'Église," *BSFEM* 11, 1953, 11. The first ten pages of this article present an excellent discussion of the notion of sanctity.

All men are called to holiness in a collective vocation, that is, in the society known as the Church. This society is holier than the sum of the individuals composing it, for the individuals are united to the God-man, the divine Head who divinizes the Church. Christ's Spirit, the Holy Spirit, dwells in the Church which thus possesses within itself a divine principle of holiness.

The Church is holy because it has received from God means *NB!* of holiness in great profusion—faith and the sacraments which are vitalized by Christ its Head and by the Holy Spirit who animates it as its soul. These means of grace infallibly produce holiness in the members of the body. The Church, to be sure, is not without sinners, but it is without sins. The defects and faults which result from the weakness of its members do not stain the Church, for the Church is *ex maculatis immaculata.*[44] "The mystic spouse of Christ has never been contaminated in the course of the centuries, nor can it ever be contaminated."[45] The fragility and infirmity of the members can never be attributed to the Church itself.[46] However, its members are subject to many defects and sins that interfere with and hamper the diffusion of its holiness.

Comparison between the holiness of Mary and the holiness of the Church discloses the differences that separate the two and brings out the superiority of Mary's sanctity over that of the Church. The Blessed Virgin's fullness of grace is measured by the deeper capacity for grace which God opened in her and by her higher destiny. Mary was called to be literally the Mother of the Savior; the Church is called to be his metaphorical spouse. Hence Mary was summoned to share in the mysteries of Christ's life; the Church begins its career with Christ's death. Mary was given the office of cooperating in the mysteries of the incarnation and redemption; the Church is limited to the task of dispensing the graces of these mysteries. Corresponding to the

[44] St. Ambrose, *Expositio Evangelii sec. Lucam,* 1, 17, *CSEL* 32.4, 21.
[45] Pius XI, *Mortalium animos, AAS* 20, 1928, 14.
[46] Pius XII, *Mystici corporis* 225.

Blessed Virgin's incomparable vocation is a holiness that vastly surpasses the holiness of the Church.

The Coredemptive Mission of Mary and the Church

The renewal of biblical and patristic studies, combined with a more adequate comprehension of ecclesiology, has led theologians in recent years to seek a more precise understanding of the role providentially assigned to Mary and the Church in the economy of salvation. Mary's maternal relation to the person of Christ occupied the attention of theologians for many centuries; today their efforts are concentrated on her relation to her Son's work.

Investigation of the contributions made by Mary and the Church to man's redemption is not new. The study has a history, and in that history three phases are discernible.[47] The first period begins with St. Irenaeus and runs on for a thousand years. It produced no more than vague gleams of insight, seeds for future growth. Yet these rough outlines of doctrine concerning Mary's share in the redemption were sketched against the background of the Church. Mary's faith at the time of the incarnation was contrasted with Eve's infidelity at the time of the fall and was set in parallel with the faith of the Church.[48]

From the twelfth to the end of the nineteenth century, the Blessed Virgin's cooperation in the sacrifice of the cross was recognized more and more distinctly. However, as views about the coredemption took firm shape, the connection between Mary and the Church was gradually obscured. The seventeenth century, so important for the development of ideas on the coredemption, is also the century in which the ties linking Mary and the Church became so tenuous as almost to fall apart.

[47] Laurentin, "Rôle de Marie et de l'Église dans l'oeuvre salvifique du Christ," *BSFEM* 10, 1952, 44f.

[48] For some pertinent texts, see H. Holstein S.J., "Marie et l'Église chez Pères anté-nicéens," *BSFEM* 9, 1951, 13–19.

Scheeben inaugurates the third period, which has come to a climax in our own time. Of the two forms of the modern enterprise, one is a reaction that has gone to excess. In opposition to an exaggerated assimilation of Mary to Christ, it advocates an exaggerated assimilation of Mary to the Church, depressing her cooperation in salvation to the level of the cooperation furnished by the Church. Mary's contribution has been reduced to pure receptivity; the Mother of the Savior is said not to have collaborated productively in the redeeming work of her Son.

1. *Theories of Receptive Coredemption.* The impetus to the contemporary effort along this line was supplied by H. M. Köster.[49] Controversy on the coredemptive problem had revolved around two positions—the thesis that Mary cooperated productively in objective redemption, and the antithesis that such cooperation undermines the transcendence of Christ, sole efficient cause of redemption. Köster puts forward a synthesis: Mary did cooperate actively in objective redemption, but not by way of efficient-productive causality. Her cooperation was limited to receptivity; in the name of all mankind she accepted redemption.

In reaction against an excessive likening of the Blessed Virgin to Christ, Köster argues that salvation is accomplished in an alliance or covenant which supposes two subjects or poles, God and man. God gives salvation, man receives it. Christ, the unique Mediator, offers the grace of redemption; the human race must accept it. Such reception is the function of the Church and also of Mary, both acting as the responsible representative of mankind. Since Christ is not a human person, he cannot receive and confirm the treaty of redemption in the name of men. Christ is the mediator between God and men, but only in his divinity,

---

[49] Köster's most important publications on this subject are *Die Magd des Herrn,* Limburg an der Lahn 1947, and *Unus Mediator,* Limburg 1950. The first proposes the new theory, the second undertakes to defend it against criticisms. In a second edition of *Die Magd des Herrn* (1954), the author elaborates his thesis and again endeavors to answer his many adversaries.

according to Köster. Although he is the absolute summit of humanity, he lacks a human personality and has no need of salvation; therefore, he cannot express mankind's solidarity, co-operation and acceptance of God's gift. Someone is still required to represent the human race in this attitude; some summit in the order of human persons having need of salvation has to ratify the alliance in which salvation objectively consists. The desired summit is found in Mary, who thus is assigned a "free place" in the economy of redemption that does not encroach on the place reserved for Christ. As a human person, Mary fills a lacuna which Christ's divine personality had to leave open. Mary is the only one who can give the response exacted of collective mankind. Hence Christ alone is the active principle of salvation; his Mother's office, like that of the Church, is purely receptive. The consent to salvation which each individual must pronounce in the order of subjective redemption, Mary pronounces for us all in the order of objective redemption. As Christ is wholly turned toward the Father, Mary is wholly turned toward the Son, so that to be incorporated into Mary is to be taken up into her momentum toward Christ.

This theory finds for Mary a place different from that of Christ and assigns to her a role in objective redemption without attributing to her a causality that belongs exclusively to Christ, the *unus mediator*. All objections against Mary's mediation melt away. Since her cooperation is completely receptive and implies no productive causality in the sacrifice of Calvary, she no longer infringes on Christ's transcendence; yet she retains an unequaled position in the history of man's restoration and has a more manifest intervention in the distribution of graces.

Defects and weaknesses inherent in Köster's proposals called for immediate criticism and led to definite rejection. The very title of his book, *Unus mediator,* demands repudiation. Christ is in all truth the *unus mediator,* but this mediator is "*homo Christus Jesus*" (1 Tim 2:5). A mediator is one who stands between extremes to unite them, but Christ in his divinity does not stand between God and man. He is mediator as he is priest, in his *human* nature. Köster erects his edifice on a foundation that is perilously shaky; he interprets the Greek *diatheke* as a bilateral contract in the strictest sense. While the word does have this meaning, especially in the Old Testament, it means primarily a testament in the new law. Man's cooperation is needed not to contract a bilateral treaty with God, but to apply the fruits of redemption to himself.

Köster develops a theory of mediation between the Son and mankind. But the alliance is really between God—that is, the Father—and mankind in the incarnate Son, "through the redemption that is in Christ Jesus, whom God has proposed to be a propitiation through faith in his blood" (Rom 3:24f). Christ is on the side of man; although he is not a human person, he has a true human nature, a human will and a human love. Instead of saving Christ's transcendence, which needs no saving, the author compromises the truth of the Savior's incarnation by slighting his human nature and thus devaluates the sufficiency of his mediation. A "free place" is found for the Blessed Virgin by removing the sacred humanity from its rightful position; to make space for Mary, the theory tends to separate Christ from the rest of men.

Furthermore, according to all tradition, "the man Christ Jesus" is the first to receive the grace which he in turn communicates to the members of his mystical body. "Of his fullness we have all received," for he alone is our head. But in Köster's theory, Mary is our summit and our head; she, not Christ, stands on our side to transmit to us the grace she has received. Incorporated into her, we enter into her movement toward Christ. To be consistent, then, we should have to speak of the mystical body of Mary, not of Christ's mystical body.[50] But "the idea of a personal summit of fallen mankind other than Christ is dia-

[50] See Congar, *RSPT* 34, 1951, 628f.

145

metrically opposed to [the Fathers'] teaching on redemption."[51]

Mariologists have in general concurred in the verdict with which Dillenschneider sums up his refutation of Köster. The theory simultaneously asserts too much and too little. It assigns too much to Mary, because it makes Mary, to the detriment of Christ, the personal summit of mankind in need of redemption; her representative role is needed to make up for Christ's insufficiency in this regard. It also gives Mary too little, because it reduces her salvific cooperation to a mere "acceptance," made in the name of us all, of the redemptive effects caused by Christ alone.[52] Mary's whole contribution is the "reception" of salvation for herself and for mankind. The current of tradition has carried the doctrine of Mary's coredemption far beyond this stage, which leaves her standing on the level of subjective redemption.

Hardly any theologian has accepted the full theory proposed by Köster. However, several have followed the main lines of his thought concerning Mary's part in our redemption. Semmelroth, in particular, owes much to Köster, although he recoils from the traces of Monophysitism discernible in his predecessor's works. Semmelroth insists that Christ is the summit of mankind and the representative of collective humanity.[53] Apart from such corrections, however, Semmelroth's theory is scarcely an improvement over Köster's. Thus he writes:

If Christ is to offer his representative sacrifice for mankind, and if this sacrifice of the God-man is to be truly the sacrifice of mankind, he must in a certain sense be established by mankind as its representative. Mankind must take its place behind him and make his sacrifice its own. The God-man's solidarity with mankind must be perceived not only by God the Father, who accepts his sacrifice, but also by the men for whom he offers himself in sacrifice.[54]

[51] Dillenschneider, *Le Mystère de la Corédemption Mariale,* Paris 1951, 129.

[52] *Ibid.* 61. See also J. B. Carol O.F.M., "Our Lady's Coredemption," *Mariology,* vol. 2, 381.

[53] O. Semmelroth S.J., *op. cit.* 61ff.   [54] *Ibid.* 84.

Here occurs Mary's opportunity to cooperate in our restoration. Christ alone, as representative of mankind, offers the sacrifice. But Mary is there at his side, representing the acceptance of men who are to be redeemed and pronouncing the *fiat* by which they are to appropriate to themselves the alliance with God that is wrought in Christ. The Blessed Virgin is able to discharge this function because she is the *Urbild,* the archetype of the Church. To her is attributed a "coredemption" not of the same kind as that of Christ, but the same as that of the Church, the community of redeemed men, who cooperate in their redemption by "freely accepting" it. Each person must voluntarily receive redemption for himself; but reception of redemption by the whole Church, a "living totality," was made, at the time Jesus was accomplishing his work, in the person of Mary. Thus she has a place in the order of objective redemption. But her contribution is not productive of the redemption; hers is a "receptive" coredemption. According to Semmelroth's own summation of his thesis, "Mary is the type of the mediating Church in the sense that, by appropriating for herself the work of Christ, she receives its fruits for herself and at the same time for the whole Church."[55] She stands on the side of mankind to receive salvation, not on the side of Christ to give salvation.

This theory makes little account of the tradition of many centuries and pays slight heed to the statements of modern popes about Mary's coredemptive activity. It also overlooks the fact that Christ is on the side of man as well as on the side of God, for he is mediator between God and man. He is on the side of man even considered as redeemable, for he has taken upon himself our sins. His divine personality does not prevent him from being the supreme expression of man and his need of redemption. Furthermore, mankind's acceptance of salvation, which is undeniably necessary, is not an integrating factor in the concept of redemption, but a condition of its efficacy for man and it

[55] *Ibid.* 60.

147

presupposes redemption as already accomplished. Most important of all, man's response to the Redeemer's sacrifice of himself implies much more than mere reception of salvation; it must be a will to contribute to the reparation of sin and reunion with God. Mary's *fiat* at the foot of the cross is far more than a simple reception of salvation wrought exclusively by Christ; it is a wholehearted will to cooperate in redemption by a love like his, a love of complete conformity to the Father's will, and an oblation. Mary on Calvary truly represents the Church, but precisely by this active cooperation.

The theory of Mary's receptive coredemption, advocated by Köster and further developed by Semmelroth, reaches a high point in the writings of Alois Müller. In a conclusion to his study of the Fathers on the unity between Mary and the Church, Müller distills what seems to him to be the essence of patristic theology about Mary and the Church: "Mary is the perfect [realization of the] Church. The essential mystery of the Church is the mystery of Mary."[56] The mystery is one of feminine, receptive collaboration in redemption. "The mystery of Eve is the mystery of Mary and the Church; the mystery of the Church is the mystery of Mary; and the mystery of Mary is the mystery of man's salvation, of the union with God that is given by God and received by the creature."[57] Mary stands on the side of mankind; as the Mother of the Savior she is the most eminent member of the Church, the person most perfectly redeemed. She is rightly called our coredemptress not in the sense that she, along with Christ, gives us salvation, but in the sense that she has "received" salvation from Christ in our name and for us.[58] The Blessed Virgin is placed at the head of receiving mankind because she is the summit of redeemed humanity; as such, she is the first and universal mediatress of salvation, the associate of

[56] A. Müller, *Ecclesia-Maria: Die Einheit Marias und der Kirche*, Freiburg in der Schweiz 1951, 232. A second edition of this book was published in 1955.
[57] *Ibid.* 229.   [58] *Ibid.* 218.

the Savior; but only in the way and in the measure in which the entire Church has this same function.[59]

Müller's explanation places Mary on the side of men; it insists that her attitude in the presence of her Son is receptive like that of the Church, and that she distributes the graces of redemption as the Church does. That is quite true, but we may not neglect other data that are well founded in revelation merely because they do not fit into a narrow framework. We are not justified in concluding that, because Mary is on the side of men, she cannot be the active associate of Christ. No such choice is imposed; we must retain both truths. We do not have to detach the Blessed Virgin from her Son in order to keep her close to us. She stands near Christ without letting us go; she is precisely the link that fetters us to him. Her association with the Redeemer does not cut her off from us sinners.[60]

Undoubtedly, Christ alone is the origin and source of redemption and of all grace. No theologian is tempted to duplicate the one Mediator. But this unique Mediator has willed to associate his Mother with himself in effecting our redemption. All she has, she has received from him. Her attitude is receptive, certainly, but her cooperation is also productive. From Christ she has received a supernatural activity that cannot be reduced to a mere reception of the fruits of redemption for subsequent distribution to the Church. This office has, of course, been given to her, but it flows from another that is more fundamental. Standing at the foot of the cross and having, like her Son, learned through painful experience what obedience is, she associated herself in the sacrifice and offered the Victim who belonged to her. Yet it is true that she contributed to the sacrifice no element that did not have its source in this very immolation, and all her

[59] A. Müller, "L'unité de l'Église et de la Sainte Vierge chez les Pères des IVe et Ve siècles," *BSFEM* 9, 1951, 37. J. Bur, "La médiation de Marie. Essai de synthèse spéculative," *Maria: Études sur la Sainte Vierge,* 471–512, is of the same mind; see especially p. 496f.

[60] G. Philips, "Perspectives mariologiques: Marie et l'Église," *Marianum* 15, 1953, 462–467.

merits and her cooperation itself came to her from her Son. Thus she collaborated with the Savior in a way that is both receptive and productive.

Accordingly, Müller's insistence about the place of Mary exclusively on the side of men is an incomplete expression of the truth; she also stands at the side of Christ. Extremist theories are easy to grasp, but the oversimplification involved in them exposes them to error. Depiction of the Savior as a purely active principle, and of Mary or the Church as purely receptive, issues in an illusory clarity. Mary and the Church are, in their own order, active causes; and Christ is also receptive. He is Mediator in his humanity, and as man he is the active principle of salvation.

2. *Doctrine of Productive Coredemption.* Theologians of the minimizing persuasion, with Köster, Semmelroth and Müller at the lead, share a common ambition. They seek to clarify the part played by Mary and the Church in our redemption; particularly, they desire to check a movement that has at times excessively assimilated the Blessed Virgin to Christ and that has failed to relate her salvific role to the Church. In reaction against such deviations, they tend to detach Mary from Christ and to assimilate her excessively to the Church. This reaction has, in turn, stirred up a counter-reaction; most contemporary mariologists and ecclesiologists endeavor to eliminate all distortion, so as to leave intact Mary's active cooperation in the redemptive task of Christ. Many contributions toward a solution have been offered. They bring into clearer light the truth that Mary, as representative and even as personification of the Church, collaborated with Christ in the three great steps of the mystery of redemption: the incarnation, the cross and the resurrection. Both Mary and the Church have a mission in the economy of salvation; that of Mary was exercised on an essentially higher level and is consequently far superior to that of the Church.

During the first phase of her salvific activity (from the incarnation to Pentecost), which is the foundation of all her subsequent offices on behalf of the human race, Mary preceded the Church, taking her place at the side of Christ to cooperate with him in the accomplishment of our redemption. The Son of God became man and in his person inaugurated the reunion of God with man; when the appointed hour arrived, the God-man saved the world by the sacrifice of his life. Mary collaborated actively in both mysteries.[61]

In response to God's proposal, conveyed by the angel, Mary replied: "Behold the handmaid of the Lord." Her consent was given in the name of the whole human race: "*loco totius humanae naturae,*" says St. Thomas,[62] and his many commentators have approved the formula as definitive. And the Angelic Doctor's insight has been consecrated by the teaching authority of the Church. "The eternal Son of God, when he wished to take man's nature to himself and so contract a mystical marriage with the whole human race, did not do so before obtaining the perfectly free consent of the one chosen to be his Mother, who thus acted in the person of the human race itself."[63] In the name of the entire human race, she gave her consent for a spiritual marriage between the Son of God and human nature."[64] Thus, in the mystery of the incarnation, Christ the Redeemer, Bridegroom of the Church, and the Church personified in Mary give themselves to each other out of obedience to the Father who decreed this salvific union.

According to all Catholic tradition, from the time of St. Justin, St. Irenaeus and Tertullian, the object of Mary's faith and consent was God's whole plan for salvation. Therefore, since Mary made her acts of faith and consent in the name of the entire Church, the Church, spouse of Christ, as personified in

[61] Cf. Laurentin, "Rôle de Marie et de l'Église dans l'oeuvre salvifique du Christ," *BSFEM* 10, 1952, 50–59.

[62] *Summa Theol.* III, q. 30, a. 1.

[63] *Octobri mense, ASS* 24, 1891–1892, 195.

[64] *Mystici Corporis* 247. Mary's representative function has been studied extensively in a symposium published by the German Mariological Society and edited by C. Feckes under the title *Die heilsgeschichtliche Stellvertretung der Menschheit durch Maria,* Paderborn 1954.

her, uttered its consent to its own salvation and through her cooperated in its own redemption.

Much more than mere receptivity is found in Mary's response to God. She was active spiritually, for she elicited an act of perfect faith. She was active in giving her consent, both interiorly and exteriorly, as evidenced by her words: "Behold the handmaid of the Lord," which expressed her active and definitive adherence to God's plan. Of necessity she was active physically —by conceiving her divine Son and continuing, for nine months, to form the Savior's body that would be immolated on the cross and the blood that would be shed for our redemption.

At the time of the incarnation, Mary represented the Church and in the name of mankind pronounced the words that express our desire for redemption. But we may not say that from then on Christ simply represents God and that the Blessed Virgin represents the human race. For Christ perfectly represents mankind; though a divine Person, he is the perfect man. His redemptive actions and sufferings are human; in the crucified Christ all humanity, embraced by him who is our Head, offers to God a human reparation for human sin, although he who offers the sacrifice is God.

What, then, remains for Mary? Has her presence on Calvary any redemptive meaning? The incarnate Word fully represents humanity; but by God's will, Mary represents aspects of humanity which Christ did not assume. She represents the mere creature, whereas Christ is the Creator; she is a human person, whereas Christ is a divine person; she represents the redeemed, for Christ is not redeemed.[65] On Calvary, therefore, by the will of God, Mary represents the cooperation of the redeemed in their own redemption, the union and fellowship of the faithful with their Savior.

Her very maternity over us acquires a new perfection by reason of her suffering. Her first childbearing, which made her the Mother of God, was without pain; her second childbearing,

[65] See Laurentin, *art. cit.* 54.

152

by which she became fully the mother of us sinners, was painful in the extreme. Wounded in her divine maternity by the death of her only Son, she offered her grievous sufferings, along with her Son, for the salvation of mankind. While the Son offered himself for the redemption of us all, who are responsible for his death, his Mother made her oblation for the same purpose and, by cooperating in our birth to supernatural life, became the mother of the Church that issued from the Savior's side.

Mary's contribution to the work of redemption far surpasses that of the Church. Not only did she precede the Church during the mortal life of Christ, but she was integrated into the very foundation of salvation, the very passion that procured our reconciliation with God. She cooperated in the birth of the Church not merely by giving human nature to the Savior, but by suffering with him. She who was one with him at the incarnation was one with him at the moment of redemption. The activity of the Church is exercised only in the application of the merits and atonement of Calvary. Mary was associated with our redemption as its beginning and achievement, whereas the Church is associated with it according to its successive realization in time and place. By her universal merit she shared, in subordinate fashion, in the Savior's quality of universal cause of grace. At the redemption, as at the incarnation, the activity of the Mother of God unfolded in an order (the hypostatic order) and on a level (the level of objective redemption) essentially higher than that of the Church. In itself, the Church does not enter this order and cannot rise to this level; but it does so in the person of Mary, who preceded it and represented it as she stood with Christ.

A second phase of Mary's salvific mission in the Church extended from Pentecost to the assumption. During this period, Mary lived in the Church and cooperated in the application of the redemption by her prayers and merits. She had preceded the Church, but was now in the Church, a woman effaced in the multitude, without official voice in its councils. Like other members of the Church, she was submissive to the authority of the apostolic hierarchy, as she had always been submissive to God. However, although she possessed no office and occupied no position of authority, she was still the first and most important member of the Church.

The third and last phase of Mary's mediatorial activity, enduring from her own assumption to the assumption of the whole Church into heaven, put an end to her temporary obscurity. Now, as at the beginning, she again precedes the Church, assists it with supernatural aid, and awaits its eventual triumph.

The mystery of Christ's resurrection and ascension is the glorious culmination of the mystery of redemption. The entire Church is implicated in this mystery and has inaugurated its own resurrection in its Head. Mary has actually arisen and has attained her total glorification. Her assumption is full of meaning for all of us. At the end of the world, the Church will arise in all its members at once. But this final resurrection of the collective Church is personified in Mary, whose resurrection is the prelude of the future bodily victory of the rest of us.

The Mother of God is now in heaven. The Church is also in heaven, in many of its members who are the saints. They all pray for us and our countless needs, thus continuing the divine plan of associating the creature with the Creator. Mary is not merely one intercessor among others. By the efficacy and universality of her activity she is first and above all others; her prayer is more powerful than the prayers of the whole Church.

Her activity in heaven is the prolongation of her function of representing and personifying the Church at the various stages of our redemption. Now, in the name of the Church, she shares in the mystery of the risen Christ and obtains for her children all the graces that sanctify them.

Her coredemptive activity, obviously, has no lacuna to fill in the redemptive work of her Son. All she has, she has received from Christ; yet her mission was never one of mere receptivity, for she was and is intensely productive. What she received was power to act and cooperate with the Redeemer for the salvation of mankind. She stands next to the Redeemer not as redemptress, but as coredemptress subordinate to him, and she can act only under his initiative and in dependence on him. But dependence does not exclude productivity. Her redemptive office, though wholly derived from Christ, is truly active and cooperative.

Accordingly, Mary's coredemptive mission was not simply passive, just as Christ's own mission was not wholly active.[66] Christ, too, received and consented. He received from his Father his office, his doctrine, his work and all the gifts he was to diffuse. If the incarnation is a mystical marriage, then consent is required not only from the bride (which is human nature, not Mary, even though Mary lent her voice to mankind), but also from the Bridegroom. According to Aquinas, no grace, not even the grace in which the first man was created, is conferred without the free acceptance of the recipient.[67] Christ's capital grace, of whose fullness we have all received, is no exception. The Son's first words addressed to the Father on entering the world: "Behold I come . . . it is written of me that I should do your will, O God" (Heb 10:7), have their echo in Mary's reply to the angel: "Behold the handmaid of the Lord; be it done to me according to your word."

The Son and the Mother both received, both consented and both acted.[68]

[66] See G. Philips, "Sommes-nous entrés dans une phase mariologique?" *Marianum* 14, 1952, 24.

[67] *Summa Theol.* I, q. 95, a. 1 ad 5.

[68] H. Barré C.S.Sp., "Le consentement à l'Incarnation rèdemptrice," *Marianum* 14, 1952, 223–266.

4

The Principle and the Analogy

AMONG theological disciplines, mariology occupies a distinguished position. What Mary is and what she means are defined by her relationship to Jesus Christ. She was called to her task and shaped for it by God. The incarnate Word took a definite form of life through this woman and set the course of her own life as in the case of no other creature. Because of her maternal association with the Redeemer, she pertains essentially to salvation history.

NB!

Hence mariology is a sort of corollary or complement of christology. Doctrine about Mary adds something to the doctrine about Christ—not, however, as coordinate with the latter, but as subordinate to it. Like ecclesiology or the theology of grace or the treatise on the sacraments, mariology contributes to the clarification of christology and soteriology. And because Mary is the perfect type and representative of the Church, there is also in mariology a definite ecclesiological dimension.

In this light, therefore, we shall review recent attempts to discern the fundamental principle of mariology in the perspective of ecclesiology, and to evaluate these attempts. Therefore, we shall first discuss the Mary-Church analogy itself, as viewed by different theologians, as the primary principle of mariology; then the analogy as the consequence of the fundamental principle; and lastly, the finality of the Mary-Church analogy.

1. The Mary–Church Analogy as the Primary Principle of Mariology

Mary as Prototype of the Church

In Semmelroth's judgment, marian theology, even in modern times, lacks the unity and harmony that ought to characterize it. Although the profound meaning of some aspects of the mystery of Mary has been plumbed, a compact and unified marian treatise has not yet been constructed, since the fundamental principle of mariology has not been correctly assigned. Until we transcend the limits of mariology itself and penetrate to the center of salvation history, we cannot apprehend the basic principle regulating marian theology. Accordingly, Semmelroth devotes the first part of *Mary, Archetype of the Church* to this problem in an endeavor to establish the supreme mariological principle, which he expresses in the proposition: "Mary is the prototype of the Church."

The solution Semmelroth proposes is not, he says, the product of arbitrary speculation, but derives from a constant tradition that seems to go back to divine revelation.[1] It is indicated in Gn 3:15, Jn 19:26f and Ap 12. Patristic teaching, as represented mainly by St. Irenaeus, St. Clement of Alexandria, St. Methodius of Olympus, St. Epiphanius, St. Ambrose and St. Augustine, explains and completes the scriptural witness. The Fathers passed the truth on to the medieval scholastics, who kept it alive in their interpretation of the Canticle of Canticles, namely that it refers to the union of Mary and the Church with Jesus Christ.[2]

Tradition does not, of course, explicitly identify the primary principle of mariology with the idea that Mary is the prototype of the Church. Yet reason perceives that the primary principle must be a mystery which cannot be reduced to any other in the

[1] O. Semmelroth S.J., *op. cit.* 36f.   [2] *Ibid.* 44–54.

field of mariology and which is the logical and theological source of all other marian mysteries.[3] Accordingly, if we examine the great mysteries in which the Blessed Virgin figures and compare them with her mission as archetype of the Church, we see that none is as fundamental as this one. And if we inquire which mystery of Mary or which of her prerogatives most closely links her with the central mystery of the redemptive economy, we again come to the same conclusion: Mary is the prototype of the Church.[4] Even the divine maternity has its ultimate basis in this truth; in the order of the divine intentions, Mary was called to be the Mother of God so that she might be the prototype of the Church.[5]

Semmelroth has no desire to depreciate the divine maternity; any attack seeking to dislodge this dignity from its rightful eminence would be a grave error. Nor, of course, does he contest Mary's mission as associate of her Son, the Redeemer. But the important thing is to know what is truly first in the finality of divine predestination. What, in God's wisdom, is the dominant notion relative to the Blessed Virgin? We correctly assert that, in the order of execution of the divine purpose, Mary is prototype of the Church because she is the Mother associated with her Son. But if we rise, as we ought, to the plane of God's intentional finality, we must admit that Mary became the Mother associated with the Redeemer in consequence of her destiny as prototype of the Church. This finality is primary and prevails over all other considerations. In God's design, the center of the economy of salvation is not the physical, historical Christ, but the whole Christ. Therefore, the supreme principle of marian theology is the mystery which brings Mary into closest contact with the Church. This mystery, according to Semmelroth, is the mystery of Mary as archetype of the Church, for—since the Church's essential function is to be the intermediary of salvation —it locates her in the very center of the economy of salvation.

[3] *Ibid.* 57. [4] *Ibid.* 65.
[5] *Ibid.* 58, 137.

As prototype of the Church, Mary is the epitome of the Church, the Church in germ; hence she possesses the fullness of the grace of the Church, and this grace she imparts to the Church as it expands on earth and in time.[6]

The value of this principle appears, Semmelroth thinks, when it is applied to the difficult question of Mary's cooperation in redemption. Christ alone, by his acts of oblation and satisfaction culminating in the sacrifice of Calvary, is the productive cause of our salvation. From him the Church receives grace and a share in his life. Each believer must accept God's offer of redemption, appropriating it to himself by faith and love.[7] Mary, as representative of mankind and prototype of the Church, consented to Christ's work in the name of the human race, and by this acceptance she appropriated the fruits of redemption not only for herself, but also for the universal Church. Thus she may be called coredemptress, in the sense that she contributed not to Christ's work, but to the application of its effect in the Church.[8] Her cooperation extended far beyond her own subjective redemption—understood as the application of the fruits of redemption to individuals—for this cooperation was at the same time the acceptance of redemption for the entire Church and, therefore, with regard to us, was objective redemption.[9]

Mary's title as prototype of the Church is justified and in line with patristic tradition; there is no quarrel with Semmelroth on this point. However, his hypothesis that it is the primary principle of mariology issues in frustration. The first principle of a theological discipline must be formally revealed, because the basic principles of theology are articles of faith. But the propo-

[6] *Ibid.* 59f.
[7] *Ibid.* 70f. See also Semmelroth's article, "Heilsgeschichtliche Sinnendeutung des Mariengeheimnisses und der Marienverehrung," *Geist und Leben* 23, 1950, 115f.
[8] *Mary, Archetype of the Church,* 73f.
[9] *Ibid.* 95f.

sition that Mary is the prototype of the Church is not formally revealed, although Scripture does contain some indications favorable to this idea. Even the Apocalypse, which brings Mary and the Church together in a single image, provides no more than a basis for deducing that the Blessed Virgin is the ideal of the Church and its most perfect realization.[10] And none of the Fathers has pushed the typology to the point of making Mary the representative of the Church in our supernatural restoration.[11]

Even apart from the fact that the typology extolled by Semmelroth is not a dogma of revelation, his thesis is marred by an enormous disadvantage, namely that it does not furnish a principle logically inducing an understanding of the divine maternity which, of all the great prerogatives of the Blessed Virgin, is the one most deeply rooted in the Christian consciousness. According to his reconstruction, in God's plan the divine maternity was subsequent to Mary's function as prototype of the Church; the truth is rather that she became so eminent a type because of her divine maternity. In other words, Mary is not the Mother of God because she was destined to be the archetype of the Church; but because she is the Mother of God, associated with the Redeemer in his saving work, she is endowed in her person and her mission with the qualities that make her the prototype of the Church.

In judging Semmelroth's proposal, we must also bear in mind that many Fathers are aware of other types of the Church in addition to Mary—for example, the entire Old Testament, the holy city of Jerusalem, the ark of Noah, the burning bush, the woman of Canaan, Mary Magdalen. Hence the Blessed Virgin is a type of the Church along with many other types. Mary is unquestionably a type of the Church in a unique way; but to

[10] D. Fernandez C.M.F., "Maria y la Iglesia en la moderna bibliografía alemana," *EM* 18, 1957, 89.

[11] C. Dillenschneider C.SS.R., *Le principe premier d'une théologie mariale organique,* Paris 1955, 58.

account for the special manner in which she is type of the Church, we have to have recourse to her divine maternity.[12]

Furthermore, a type, even a prototype, indicates a relation, an analogy which must be studied in the light of other, more fundamental principles. Mary's relation with the Church cannot be comprehended except in the light of her relation with Jesus Christ, Head of the Church. The most basic relation is the fact that she is his Mother.[13]

Lastly, Semmelroth's theory of Mary's part in our redemption, which he sets squarely upon his principle that she is the proto-type of the Church, is hardly in line with doctrinal development in this problem of marian theology. He attributes to Mary a true causality, but one that is purely receptive. However, the *acting not merely receptive.* tradition of many centuries and in particular the teachings of recent popes favor an activity for her that is far more than a simple acceptance of salvation that was wrought exclusively by Jesus. Mary on Calvary truly typifies and represents the Church, but precisely by her active cooperation in the very work of our redemption.

Mary as the Representative of the Church

In 1947 Heinrich Maria Köster published his *Die Magd des Herrn,* which was criticized widely, and for the most part un-favorably, in theological circles. Three years later, in his *Unus Mediator,* he undertook to answer his critics as well as to defend and consolidate his first position. Then, in 1954, he issued *Die Magd des Herrn* in a second, greatly improved edition. The master idea remains unchanged, but is more accurately expressed and more carefully worked out.

Köster stresses the importance of Mary in the history of sal-vation, in which Christian consciousness attributes to her a real

[12] M. Schmaus, *Katholische Dogmatik,* vol. 5, *Mariologie,* Munich 1955, 261.
[13] Basilio de San Pablo C.P., "Momentos de la maternidad de Maria sobre la Iglesia," *EM* 18, 1957, 323.

cooperation in objective redemption. But what is the nature of this collaboration? Is there a place for our Lady which is not already occupied and which in no way encroaches on Christ's redemptive work that is marred by no defect or lacuna? Such a place does exist. To discover it we need only have recourse to the great covenant or alliance which characterizes the history of our redemption from its earliest origins. This saving alliance cannot be a strictly bilateral contract between God who saves and man whom he wishes to save. It is gratuitously offered to us by God, yet it implies some reciprocity between the two parties. God invites man to a sacred partnership; man must respond to this call and set forth to meet God.[14]

The New Testament presents God the Father who offers the alliance, sinful humanity to which it is offered, and Jesus Christ, the one Mediator, who alone carries out the covenant in the mystery of redemption. But the representation of sinful mankind by the incarnate Son of God seems to require from mankind an acceptance of the substitution; on our part, some declaration of solidarity with our Mediator seems necessary.[15]

Who is qualified to make this acceptance if not Mary, in whom the meeting of the Son of God with mankind is accomplished at the moment of the incarnation? In the name of mankind she pronounced her *fiat* and received the Savior by a true maternal conception; through her lifelong prolongation of this same consent she entered, still in the name of mankind, into the whole redemptive mystery of her Son and received from it the fruits of salvation for all of us. Thus everything is accounted for: the unique office of Jesus the Mediator in his redemptive work and Mary's ecumenical office in the redemptive work of her Son.

After devoting more than half of his book to the develop-

14 H. M. Köster, *Die Magd des Herrn,* 2nd. ed., Limburg an der Lahn 1954, 59–62, 76–81, 97f.
15 *Ibid.* 151.

162

ment of this thesis, Köster raises the question whether this idea of Mary's role in salvation possesses all the properties that ought to be found in the fundamental principle of marian theology. He is inclined to answer in the affirmative, provided that the proposition is carefully worded. He puts it thus: "Mary, as a member, is the representative and personal summit of mankind which is to be saved and actually is saved; that is, confronting the one Mediator, the incarnate Son of God, she represents the Church in its salvific alliance with God."[16] Or, more simply and briefly, with Köster's meticulous nuances in mind, we may say that the fundamental principle is Mary's function of representing the Church for the reception of salvation.

NB

This principle enables us to perceive that Mary is one of us, since she belongs to mankind which is in need of redemption and has been redeemed. At the same time, she is set apart from us by her rank and her mission, for she is the personal summit and the representative of all the redeemed. She is likewise distinguished from Christ in rank and mission, for she is not, like him, Head of mankind, but is the representative of mankind for the purpose of receiving the fruits of redemption from him. At the moment of the incarnation, when the Son of God first laid hold of humanity, the representative of mankind could be no other than his Mother, for only she could furnish him with his human nature for the hypostatic union. And when Christ again laid hold of mankind on Calvary, the representative of mankind became coredemptress. Finally, this same representative of mankind became the mediatress of all graces by making the salvific alliance effective for redeemed individuals.[17] In like manner, starting with this basic principle, all the other privileges of Mary become intelligible.

critique

But Köster's valiant attempt to establish his fundamental principle does not turn out successfully. He himself seems to harbor a suspicion that the absence of divine maternity from his

[16] *Ibid.* 296.   [17] *Ibid.* 300f.

163

formulation of the principle is a defect.[18] We rightly expect the primary principle of marian theology to promote an understanding of everything else in the treatise. But the idea that Mary is the representative of mankind in need of redemption can scarcely be regarded as the principle which facilitates our grasp of the divine maternity. On the contrary, Mary's divine maternity is the principle permitting us to grasp her role as representative of mankind that is to be saved. The very fact that our humanity, in the person of Mary, generates Christ our Head explains why this same humanity is fittingly represented by her before Christ.[19]

Köster asserts that his principle safeguards Mary's superiority over all the others who have been redeemed on the score that she alone, as the personal summit and representative not only of individuals, but of the human race as such, enters into the order of objective redemption. However, the principle of intelligibility of this matchless rank is precisely her dignity as pre-redeemed Mother of the Redeemer. Although she pertains to the order of those who have been redeemed by her Son, she incomparably surpasses them by her maternity which inaugurated objective redemption and which, at the climax of objective redemption on Calvary, equipped her to cooperate with the Redeemer in his sacrifice. Therefore, Mary's divine maternity is the principle aiding us in understanding what Köster proposes as the primary principle of marian theology, and it accounts for her role of universal representative of the human race not only for the reception of the fruits of redemption, but also for an active collaboration in the very work of Christ that accomplished our salvation on the cross.

Accordingly, Köster's theory is no more acceptable than that of Semmelroth. The Mary-Church analogy is not capable of yielding the fundamental principle of mariology. Yet some relationship must exist between the principle and the analogy.

[18] *Ibid.* 299.
[19] See Dillenschneider, *Le principe d'une théologie mariale organique*, 70.

164

2. THE MARY-CHURCH ANALOGY AS THE CONSEQUENCE OF THE FUNDAMENTAL PRINCIPLE

The analogy between Mary and the Church supposes some resemblances and dissimilarities between the two. Among the basic differences is the fact that the Church is a society, an institution designed to celebrate and perpetuate the mysteries of the passion and resurrection of Jesus Christ from generation to generation. The Church distributes the supernatural gifts of Christ by the exercise of its hierarchical and sacerdotal offices. Mary does not possess any hierarchical or sacerdotal power, although she contributes mightily to the union of the supreme High Priest with his people. Mary is completely preserved from sin; the Church must, because of the imperfection of its members, unremittingly combat sin within itself. Mary has arrived at the term of glorification, while the Church is on the way; the community must still await in its other members the goal already reached in its most eminent member.

Despite such differences, Mary and the Church resemble each other in many respects. In fact, there is more than a series of parallels between them; Mary is the prototype, the basic figure of the Church, embodying within herself what is best in the Church, so that from her we can come to a clearer knowledge of the Church. What is written about the Church can be read also in reference to Mary, just as what is written about Mary can in many essential points be understood also in reference to the Church. The mystery of Mary and the mystery of the Church are interwoven in many details.[20]

As we saw in the third chapter, Mary, Mother of Christ, is also the mother of the Church and of Christians; the Church, too, is mother of Christians. The Church is the spouse of Christ; Mary is the Mother of Christ, associated with him in his redemptive mission in a union that eminently verifies, while it

[20] See M. Schmaus, *op. cit.* 271.

165

vastly surpasses, all that the biblical imagery of spouse suggests. The Church is the new Eve, mother of all the supernaturally living; Mary is also the new Eve, mother of all who live the new life brought by Christ. Mary is the Virgin of virgins, in the most literal and exalted sense; the Church is likewise virginal, in the sense that it has never adulterated the faith, but has always been true to Christ's doctrine. Mary is supremely holy and full of grace, with a sanctity which from the instant of her conception and through her entire life kept all sin remote from her, and which progressed every day of her sojourn on earth until it flowered into her glory and resurrection. The Church is likewise holy and full of grace in the measure of its capacity and confidently awaits the resurrection of its members. Mary had a coredemptive mission in association with the redemptive mission of Christ at its inception and achievement. The Church is likewise associated with this mission by its office of applying the merits and atonement of Calvary successively in space and time.

What connection links these resemblances, at every point of which Mary surpasses the Church, with the fundamental principle of mariology? This principle is not some synthetic formula or axiom from which all the truths about the Blessed Virgin can be deduced by the rational procedures of human logic, for her sublime graces and offices were imparted to her in accord with God's free choice, which we can know only through revelation. Rather, as theologians have increasingly insisted during the past thirty years, it is a primary revealed truth that serves as a principle of intelligibility shedding light over all the teachings of revelation concerning Mary and empowering us to apprehend their profound unity. Viewed thus, the fundamental principle of mariology is the dogma which Pius XII approves as "the principle, the key, and the center of all the privileges of Mary,"[21]

[21] Radio Message, *Por un Designio, AAS* 43, 1951, 123. Concerning the teaching of modern popes on the primary principle of mariology, along with a theological vindication of their position, see above, 99–103.

that is, the divine maternity, understood not in some arbitrary, abstract sense, but in its concrete, revealed reality, as her relationship to the divine Word arising from the fact that she conceived and gave birth to him in his human nature; Mary is the Mother of the second Person of the Trinity who became incarnate for the redemption of mankind.[22]

This primary principle clarifies all the great prerogatives, graces and offices of Mary, including the place she occupies and the functions she exercises in the Church. As the Redeemer's Mother who provided him with his human nature, she stands closest to the source of grace and receives grace in plenitude from him. That is why she is "full of grace."[23] Her fullness of grace entails her immaculate conception and her freedom from all sin throughout her life. These magnificent gifts are easily intelligible in the light of the divine maternity. The same is true of her perpetual virginity. With revelation of this fact before us, we can readily understand why God's Mother, made fruitful by the action of the Holy Spirit, should preserve her virginity intact at Christ's birth and ever after.

Mary's mediatorial office is likewise intelligible. Her divine maternity draws her near to God, who employs the most perfect beings, the ones closest to him, as intermediaries between him and less perfect beings. The mediatorial character of Mary's motherhood is manifested in the ancient theme of the new Eve. Because she is the Savior's Mother, she is associated with him in most intimate community of life for the propagation of the life of grace. The divine Word, who existed eternally before she was born, personally invited her to be his Mother, and by becoming incarnate in her on reception of her free consent, he entered into a union with her which has no counterpart in ordinary motherhood and which recalls, while it goes far beyond,

[22] See P. Mahoney O.P., "The Unitive Principle of Marian Theology," *The Thomist* 18, 1955, 462.
[23] *Summa Theol.* III, q. 27, a. 5; see q. 7, aa. 1, 9, 13.

167

the union between spouses. Thus Mary's salvific association with Christ stems from her divine maternity.

She who cooperated with her Son in the redemptive act of sacrifice further cooperates with him in heaven for distributing the graces of salvation that were merited on Calvary. As on the cross, Christ has the main causality in this action; but in association with him and dependence on him, the Mother dispenses all supernatural graces to the children of men that they may be transformed into the children of God.

Finally, Mary is the universal Mother. Her motherhood did not end with the birth of Christ, for the temporal generation of the Word is not the term, but the beginning. The Virgin's Son is the Head to which many members are to be joined. They make up his mystical body, the Church, and form with their Head a single mystical person, the whole Christ. Therefore, she who gave birth to the Head necessarily gives birth to the members. At the incarnation she conceived us spiritually, for her maternal action inaugurated the generation of the mystical Christ. On Calvary she bore us spiritually, for there she cooperated maternally to bring about our rebirth in Christ by gaining for us, in subordination to him, the graces of our incorporation into his body. Her mediatorial activity in heaven is likewise maternal not only by the motherly love animating it, but by its effect, which is the supernatural birth of men century after century and their growth in divine life.

Therefore, the revealed truth that Mary is the Mother of God is, in the ordering of God's wisdom, the basic reason underlying all the perfections which account for her resemblance to the Church or, more accurately, elevate her to be the supreme exemplar, ideal image and perfect realization of the Church. Because of her divine maternity, she is the one full of grace, the new Eve, the most pure Virgin, the associate of the Redeemer, the coredemptress and mediatress of all graces, mother of Christians and prototype of the Church. The divine maternity is the foundation of Mary's relationship to Christ; consequently, it is

168

the foundation of her relationship to the work of Christ, to the whole Christ, and to the mystical body of Christ.

3. The Finality of the Mary-Church Analogy

The relationship thus accounted for seems clear enough, and most theologians who have thought about the Blessed Virgin's connection with the Church would come to the same conclusion. Even Semmelroth admits that, in the order of execution, Mary's typology with reference to the Church is a result of the divine maternity. However, as we observed above, he contends that, in the order of God's intentional finality which dominates all other considerations, the divine maternity is a consequence of Mary's destiny to be the prototype of the Church. Accordingly, the primary principle of marian theology, viewed from the high level of God's designs, is no other than Mary's vocation to be the prototype of the Church.

This position receives support from A. Patfoort who, in a critique of C. Dillenschneider's *Le principe premier d'une théologie mariale organique,* believes that it is possible to integrate the opinions seeking the unity of marian theology in an ecclesiological perspective (according to which Mary is prototype or representative of the Church) and to recognize the primacy assigned to this view without sacrificing the cardinal prerogative of the divine maternity.[24] If we start from Mary's quality as prototype or representative of the Church and acknowledge that in the finality of God's providence this quality is supreme, we can clarify the totality of the mystery of Mary. At the same time, the eminent dignity of the divine maternity is not compromised, for it, too, in its own sphere, is supreme and retains its primacy. In fact, a real, organic unity reigns among all the basic principles that have been proposed for marian theology, but they

[24] A. Patfoort O.P., "Le principe premier de la mariologie?" *RSPT* 41, 1957, 450.

169

are situated at various depths or are assigned to different registers. In the concrete order, God's decree places the divine maternity itself at the service of sinners, and in this line of finality the ecclesiological role is primary. A simple distinction well accounts for all the data. "Mother of God" is the ultimate principle in the order of formal causality, whereas "prototype of the Church" is the ultimate principle in the order of finality.[25]

Proposals of this sort are defective in that they fall short of true ultimates in the domain of finality. Reduced to essential terms, they state that the Mother of God exists for the ultimate purpose of being the prototype of the Church. Such a contention cannot be justified, either within the limited sphere of mariology regarded as a branch of theology or in the universal sphere of the hierarchy of ends. As the Trinity is the origin and end of all divine activity and as the God-man Jesus Christ is the origin and end of the redemptive economy, so "Mother of God" is, under the incarnate Word, the source and end of all the truths of mariology. All of Mary's privileges, prerogatives and offices have their finality in her divine motherhood.[26] This is true also of her quality as prototype of the Church, which joins all her other perfections in converging on the divine maternity; for the perfection of her maternity, involving and elevating all her other perfections, is the end which the Church aspires to attain.

A clarification of Mary's own finality is furnished by the doctrine that the Mother of God pertains to the hypostatic order. Order is a union of elements internally dependent among themselves and finalized by a common end. The universe of creatures is divided into three great orders, according to their relationship with God.[27] The order of nature comprises creatures regarded as effects of God, made to his image and gathered together in a harmonious world the better to resemble him. The order of

25 *Ibid.* 452.

26 For an able exposition of the divine maternity as the end of mariology, see P. Mahoney O.P., *art. cit.* 463–478.

27 See M. J. Nicolas O.P., *art. cit.* 707–741.

grace consists of spiritual creatures who are united to God by supernatural knowledge and charity. At the summit is the hypostatic order, in which a created nature is taken into personal union with God; it is the order of the incarnate Word and draws to itself the orders of nature and of grace.

God's election of Mary to be the Mother of his Son is the basis for the doctrine, common among theologians as a definitive acquisition of modern mariology, that the Blessed Virgin belongs intrinsically to the hypostatic order, whose elements are finalized by the hypostatic union, God's greatest communication to created nature. From all eternity she is joined to the incarnate Word in one and the same decree of predestination.[28] She is not substantially united to a divine Person; yet the hypostatic union between Christ's human nature and the Person of the Word was accomplished through her and in her. The Son of God is her Son; she has a relationship of real affinity with the second Person of the Trinity.[29] Accordingly, her divine motherhood elevates her to the hypostatic order, along with the human nature of the Word, above the entire universe of nature and the world of grace.

Since the order of nature is wholly orientated to the order of grace, and since the order of grace is wholly orientated to the hypostatic order, these two orders must have their summit and find their end in those who occupy the hypostatic order, that is, in Jesus Christ and his Mother. The hypostatic order is indeed for the redemption of the human race, in the sense that all men are its beneficiaries, but it is also the end of redemption. Therefore, the Blessed Virgin, who belongs to this order, has a redemptive causality, although she also shares in redemptive finality. In a very true sense the universe, and particularly the

[28] *Munificentissimus Deus* 768, repeats the teaching of Pius IX in the bull *Ineffabilis Deus* that the Mother of God and Jesus Christ are connected in "one and the same decree of predestination."

[29] *Summa Theol.* III, q. 27, a. 4.

Church of the redeemed, which are ordained to Christ, are like-wise ordained to Mary.[30]

Because of her supernatural perfections which her divine maternity modifies and sublimates, Mary is set up by God as the totally successful example of what the reception of the incarnate Word can be in the human race. Her unreserved compliance with the divine initiative, her integration into all the phases of the redemption, her assumption and her very motherhood are signs, directed to us in our sluggish acceptance of God, of what the incarnation proposes and achieves. She prefigures and sums up the response of mankind to the supernatural enrichment offered to us by the God-man. She is, we may say, the very incarnation of the reception of divinity which radiates from the hypostatic union.

Hence she is the perfect model of the children of God, the ideal of redeemed mankind. Redemption has been completely triumphant in her alone, for she alone of all the redeemed was utterly taken over by God in such a way that his grace never encountered any reluctance or resistance on her part and the blood of the Savior could exert all its power in her soul and body. She is the masterpiece of the Redeemer, the fullest realization of God's own idea of a perfect human being.

Rightly, then, Mary is honored as the archetype of the Church. She is the ideal personification of the Church, the embodiment of the supernatural perfection to which the Church aspires, the resplendent image in which the Church can clearly see what Christ requires of it and what he desires it to be. In her the Church can discern its own objectives: to be immaculate and sinless, like Mary; to be holy, like Mary; to be virginal, like Mary, with undivided loyalty to Christ; to cooperate on its level with the work of Christ, as Mary did on an essentially higher level; to be a perfect mother in bearing and rearing other Christs, as Mary bore and fostered Jesus Christ. Mary received

[30] See J. M. Cascante, "Replanteo e inicios de solución al problema de las relaciones entre María y la Iglesia," *EM* 18, 1957, 277.

God perfectly in every sense, to the point of conceiving him by maternal generation. Her flawless reception of God shows forth the aim of all the striving of the Church—the reception of Christ and therefore of God.

In the eternal divine plan, Mary is undoubtedly for the Church. She collaborated with Christ in objective redemption and still collaborates with him for the salvation of mankind. But the Church is not the ultimate goal of Mary's maternity or activity, any more than it is the ultimate goal of the hypostatic union or of Christ's activity. The Savior and his Mother work for the incorporation of the human race into Christ, that in Christ the men who have been redeemed may at last attain God, their final end.

Thus by God's appointment, the universe, disrupted by the sins of Adam and Eve and all their progeny, is recapitulated in the God-man and his Mother, the Redeemer and coredemptress, that mankind assembled in the Church, mystical body of Christ, may return through the new Eve and the new Adam in ascending order to the primordial source and ultimate end of all divine communications to creatures, God himself.

Discussion of the relationship between Mary and the Church opens up a further question. In two of his great encyclicals, *Mystici corporis Christi* and *Humani generis,* Pius XII stressed the truth that the Church and the mystical body of Christ are identical. A consideration of this point of view can add much to our understanding of Mary's importance in our Christian lives and apostolic activity. Therefore, we shall next devote our attention to Mary's position and function in Christ's mystical body. As we noted in our first chapter, this is one of the most important issues in mariology, and likewise one of the most controversial.

173

5

Mary in the Mystical Body

THE devotion which many Catholics have to the Blessed Virgin remains on a subtheological level. They understand that their spiritual life requires filial love of the Mother of God, who is also their mother. But their theological knowledge is likely to be unequal to their piety and apostolic activity. They rightly regard Mary as the ideal of purity, humility and union with God. They are also aware that her matchless prerogatives flow from her divine maternity. But what is sensed confusedly by all Christians ought to be brought out clearly by theologians. If Mary is to occupy in Christian life the eminent place that is her due, and if Christians, and especially Catholics, are to accord that place to her with all their hearts, she must be situated in the rich doctrine of the mystical body of Christ. That devotedness to the Blessed Virgin may be something more than personal piety, that it may be a powerful drive in our lives of productive Christian social action, we must aspire to a keener perception of the absolutely unique position she has in the Church. By stressing the social aspect of Mary's eminence, we shall appreciate more adequately her importance in the Church's dogma and theology, and consequently we shall discern more distinctly the place she ought to have in our spiritual life and our apostolate: hers is the first place after that of her Son.

174

1. MOTHER OF THE MYSTICAL BODY
AND OF THE WORLD

The supernatural order is not an imitation of the natural order; on the contrary, the natural order is fashioned on the model of the supernatural order. "The order of nature was created and established for the order of grace . . . The order of grace, the heights of which are occupied by Christ and the Blessed Virgin, is the idea and model according to which God created and arranged the order of nature and of the whole universe."[1] It is because the natural order is an image of the supernatural order that we can gain some understanding, by the natural things we see, of the existence, character or propriety of the supernatural things we do not see. Natural life is an image of supernatural life that is incomparably more excellent. The qualities of father, mother, husband and wife which we observe in the natural order are images of titles, properties and qualities, all analogous but vastly superior, found in the supernatural order. In this supernatural order, God is our Father who begets us to supernatural life, and we are his children; Jesus Christ is the spouse of our souls, and our souls are his spouses; he is also our brother, and we are brothers and sisters to him. All this is said in a true sense. Accordingly, we ought to have, in a sense that is likewise true, a mother in the supernatural order. And this mother of ours, for our life of grace, is Mary.

Mary is our mother more excellently and perfectly than our mothers in the natural order are. Supernatural life is what the Church has in mind when it invites all nations to rejoice in the life that is conferred on them by the Blessed Virgin: "Redeemed peoples, exult in the life bestowed by the Virgin."[2] This supernatural life is true life and is more perfect than natural life, for

[1] Cornelius a Lapide S.J., *Commentarium in Ecclesiasticum*, in *Commentaria in Scripturam sacram*, Paris 1859, vol. 9, chapter 24, 618.
[2] Hymn for Lauds, *Officium Sanctae Mariae in Sabbato*.

it is a participation in God's life, which is life par excellence. From this point of view natural life, which is assuredly real life, is an imitation of supernatural life. Nature is for the supernatural; the things that make up the natural order are images of those of the supernatural order and serve to acquaint us with that order so far as we can grasp it during the present time of faith. Supernatural and divine things are always above natural and human things, for they are closer to God and therefore share more abundantly of God who is being and truth in essence. "The closer a thing is to its principle in any order, the greater the share it has in the effect of that principle."[3]

By the grace of God, we have been taken up supernaturally into God's family. By the indwelling of the Holy Spirit in our souls, divine life floods us, Christ is our brother, and the heavenly Father is our father. In this family there is also a mother; she is the Mother of the only begotten Son of God and is likewise the mother of all who have Christ for a brother. Mary is the mother of the whole Christ, Head and members. The fact that we owe human existence to a human mother is not compromised. But in the supernatural order, our nature is not an independent entity. As all reality reaches its climax in Christ, the Head of mankind, so all motherhood reaches its climax in the motherhood of God's Mother. Human motherhood is not thereby less precious, but on the contrary has its ultimate meaning and value from the idea of motherhood in the supernatural economy. Furthermore, if Mary is the mother of the mystical body, she is also the mother of all men, because all men are for the mystical body. In that case, she is situated at the center of the history of salvation, and therefore at the center of universal history. And this is the first truth we ought to grasp about the place of Mary in the mystical body.

[3] *Summa Theol.* III, q. 27, a. 5.

176

2. Scriptural Analogies of Union with Christ

God has raised to the supernatural order not individual men, but the human race. This truth commands the doctrines of original sin and redemption. Yet the social character of our supernatural elevation does not slight the individual person; still less does it imply that individual persons are only means for achieving a social end. Rather, individual persons are regarded in the eternal plan as parts of a whole. Each person is envisaged by God as a stone in an edifice, a cell in an organism, a member of the body of Christ. But if the members of Christ's body compose with him an organic whole, the human being who is indispensably and personally necessary for the existence and career of the incarnate Word, Mary the Mother of God, must straightway take her station next to the Head, in the first place, with a role that is shared with no other. She is God's masterpiece, and in his eternal thought he lovingly contemplates her as the one creature who has perfectly carried out his designs.

That is what Mary is for God. What is she for us? In our egoism we sometimes tend to cherish an individualist point of view, to see Mary as the mediatress who, after her Son, is concerned in her motherly way about our personal welfare. Such a view is not wrong, for the mystical body of Christ is an organism made up of persons, each of whom is beyond price and has personal relations with God. But it is an inadequate representation of Mary's activity in our sanctification. Mary cannot wish to sanctify us otherwise than Christ does, and Christ wishes his mystical body to develop harmoniously. Mary's maternity of grace is not exercised first on individuals and then only by way of consequence or afterthought on the body; it is exercised on the body and the members simultaneously and on the members as integrating the body. Whatever comes to us in the economy of salvation comes to us

NB!

NB!

177

socially; grace is given to us not as isolated individuals, but as members of Christ's body. We grow in supernatural life by growing in union with Christ; the grace we receive is the grace of Christ our Head, flowing into us. Mary is the new Eve, whose activity in our behalf has to correspond to that of the new Adam. Our natural life comes to us ultimately from Adam and Eve; our supernatural life comes to us from Jesus through Mary. The Mother of Christ is the mother of each of Christ's members because she is the mother of the whole Christ.

This is still a somewhat general way of setting forth Mary's activity in our sanctification. To make it more specific, we may turn to the comparisons and analogies which revelation suggests to us. Since grace is given to us as members of the mystical body, can we not enhance our knowledge about Mary's position in the mystical body by considering the various details we are taught about that supernatural organism? In proceeding thus, to be sure, we immediately encounter the difficulty which characterizes all theological investigation, that is, the fact that supernatural mysteries exceed the powers of our human minds. However, since nature is an image of the supernatural, a study of the metaphors, figures and analogies we are able to gather from Scripture will convey to us some insight into the divine truths God has revealed. In this way, by exploiting inspired analogies, we can hope to gain a glimpse of the treasures contained in God's message to us. This is what St. Paul and St. John have taught us with regard to the mystery of our incorporation into Christ. The Church is represented as the temple of the Holy Spirit, and our souls, too, are temples fashioned to the likeness of the first temple. The Church is also the field in which the good seed has been sown, and the vine of which Christ is the trunk. It is also the ideal spouse acquired by Christ and purified by his blood. It is also an immense body whose soul is the Holy Spirit. All these images are informative and suggestive; and although they are undoubtedly deficient, they complement and mutually correct one another, thus en-

178

abling us to enter more deeply into a reality which, because it is divine, passes beyond our human processes of thinking.

3. MARY'S PLACE IN THE MYSTICAL BODY SOUGHT THROUGH THESE ANALOGIES

1. *The Comparison of the Temple.* "You are fellow citizens with the saints, and are of the family of God, built upon the foundation of the apostles and prophets, the *corner foundation-stone* being Christ Jesus himself. In him the whole building, accurately fitted together, rises into a holy temple in the Lord; in him you are also being built together into a spiritual dwelling place of God" (Eph 2:19–22).[4]   Mт. 16

The comparison of the building erected on the cornerstone that is Christ teaches us that the Church is not a formless entity, but that it has a well-defined structure and is so stable as to defy time. In this temple of God, Christ is the cornerstone and the faithful are the living stones which, resting on him, constitute the superstructure of the building.

What place belongs to the Blessed Virgin in this edifice? The building rests on the apostles and prophets, with Christ as the cornerstone that sustains the whole temple. Is Mary excluded from the function of the cornerstone and relegated to the role played by the simple faithful? Such an interpretation is intolerable. St. Paul's mention of prophets and apostles stresses the hierarchical order in the Church, with reference to the preaching of the faith and the spreading of the reign of Christ. He had no reason to speak of Mary, whose function is quite different. Mary is indeed a stone in this mighty building,   NB!
but a unique one. She is not the cornerstone in the same sense as Christ: "Other foundation no man can lay, but that which is laid: which is Christ Jesus" (1 Cor 3:11). Yet she is, after Christ, the main stone that gives consistency to the edifice; not only does she, as Christ's Mother, furnish this stone which is

4 Spencer's translation.

179

the foundation of the structure, but as universal mediatress she lends vigor, solidity and stability to the great temple of the Church. Thus the Blessed Virgin is the first stone laid after the cornerstone, that on which rests the whole edifice of our salvation, that which transmits to Christ, foundation on which everything has to be built, the immense weight of the living temple.[5] Although Mary has no jurisdictional authority, she acts with true supremacy in directing men to their destiny. The temple of Christ is still in process of construction: "In him you also are being built together." Since each of these living stones must fit into the structure, they have to be shaped, smoothed, polished. And that is the work of Mary, whose motherly activity fashions in souls the dispositions needed to fit them into Christ.

2. *The Comparison of the Cultivated Field.* "You are a field of God's tilling, a structure of God's design" (1 Cor 3:9). A like process may be discerned in the figure of the cultivated field, an analogy that brings out the activity of grace and stresses the unity produced in the mystical body by the cause which operates in the interior and communicates life. St. Paul rounds out his beautiful allegory by associating the image of the field with that of the building under construction. Many activities in this work of spiritual cultivation cooperate toward the end sought by God: the labor of preachers who sow the seed, the cares of God's servants who tend its growth, the higher causality of Christ, the vital coursing of the inner sap, and at the summit the action of God who gives life and growth to the seed planted in the field of the Church. A wide region here opens up for Mary's motherly activity. Working along with Christ, the divine "Gardener," who makes the garden of the Church fertile with his blood, Mary the universal mediatress has her indispensable part in causing a bountiful crop of virtues to take root and flower healthily in our souls.

3. *The Comparison of the Vine.* "I am the vine, you are the

[5] See H. Rondet S.J., "De la place de la Très Sainte Vierge dans l'Église corps mystique du Christ," *BSFEM* 3, 1937, 216.

branches; he who abides in me and I in him will bear much fruit: for without me you can do nothing "(Jn 15:5).

When we pass from the figure of the cultivated field to that of the vine and the branches, which is the most beautiful expression Jesus gave of our supernatural union with him, we find similar reasons for application to Mary. This comparison has the advantage of impressing on us the truth that the Church does not appear suddenly on the scene in its ultimate maturity, but that it grows little by little and is still in process of becoming. If Christ is the vine on which we are the branches, Mary is the primary branch, that which unites the tendrils to the trunk, that through which all the sap must pass to carry life and develop the leaves and ripen the grapes. The apostles, too, are main branches, but under Mary; for her causality, though not hierarchical, is far superior to theirs in its universality and mode of operation. Without encroaching on Christ's unique mediation, we can say of Mary as we say of her Son, to the exclusion of every other saint: without her we can do nothing.

4. *The Comparison of Mystical Matrimony.* "Husbands, love your wives, as Christ also loved the Church, and delivered himself up for it . . . No man ever hated his own flesh, but nourishes and cherishes it, as also Christ does the Church: because we are members of his body, of his flesh, and of his bones . . . This is a great sacrament: but I speak in Christ and in the Church" (Eph 5:25–32).

We mount still higher when we express the relations between Christ and the Church by means of a comparison drawn from the union of man and woman in marriage. This image of mystical matrimony between Christ and the Church stresses the union of supernatural charity, a bond even stronger than the conjugal union of husband and wife. Christ is the divine Spouse, the Church is his bride. The analogy shows that the preëminence of Christ the Head belongs to the spiritual and social order, and that the body of Christ is a collective person-

181

ality which is the complement of the individual person of Christ. The Church is nothing without Christ; but we may also say that Christ has need of his Church, because the Church is his mystical body and the Son of God has assumed a body of flesh to find in his members the fullness of his humanity. The Church is a sort of expansion or prolongation of the person of the incarnate Word in an organized multitude of other persons united to him by a bond as strong as that between husband and wife. But of all these persons Mary is the first. "It is commonly said that the bride of Christ is threefold: that is, the whole universal Church militant which is called the general spouse of Christ, and each faithful and loving soul which is called the particular spouse of Christ, and finally the Blessed Virgin Mary, who bore Christ, is regarded as the singular spouse of Christ."[6] In a subordinate capacity, Mary is associated with her Son in the work of redemption; but if we subordinate Mary to her divine Son, we immediately subordinate all the rest of mankind to her. She is the mother of men because she is the first link between the Head of the mystical body and the mystical body itself.

The basis of Christ's union with his Mother is far superior to ours in every respect. Scheeben tried to bring out the difference by calling Mary the maternal bride of Christ or the bridal Mother of God.[7] Such formulas and the concept underlying them have been rejected by most theologians. A more accurate expression of the truth is that Mary is the chosen woman through whom the divine espousals between the Son of God and redeemed mankind have been celebrated. But to state the truth fairly we must add that all the perfection contained in the idea of nuptial relationship is verified in Mary in a sense that exceeds the matrimonial metaphor. What raises her above

NB!

[6] Dionysius the Carthusian, *In Cantica Canticorum prooemium*, in *Opera* 7, 291. For a more exact description of Mary's relationship to Christ, see 121–126.

[7] *Handbuch der katholischen Dogmatik*, Freiburg im Breisgau 1882, vol. 3, 491, no. 1590, and frequently elsewhere.

all the children of men and places her next to her divine Son is the fact that she is his Mother. This is what makes her the new Eve to the new Adam.

Not only to adorn her did the God-man shower his love-gifts on Mary, from the immaculate conception to the assumption. The first Eve had supported and concurred in Adam's sin; the new Eve takes her station at the side of the new Adam to rescue us from that sin. Her maternal activity is a cooperation for the work of mankind's redemption. This activity is based on her free consent; Mary is the Eve of the new covenant, responding in the name of the entire race to God's invitation that summons us to salvation and to the divine nuptials.[8] And her consent was a consent to the sacrificial death of her divine Son; that is why the Christian world, seeing the Mother of God standing under the cross, can think of her as a kind of co-offerer of the sacrifice. In her Son and through her Son she yields the fruit of her own body for the saving of the world. She stands there indomitably as the representative of mankind that is to be redeemed, cooperating in the name of her race, that from our side too the highpriestly oblation may be a truly human offering.

5. *The Comparison of the Body.* "As the body is one, and has many members, and all the members of the body, whereas they are many, yet are one body, so also is Christ. For in one Spirit were we all baptized into one body ... You are the body of Christ, and members of member" (1 Cor 12:12f, 27).

The Church is like a human body composed of many members, organs and cells, each having its own functions, yet all contributing to the unity of the composite that grows under the action of an identical vital principle in the same divine life, the same sanctifying grace. We learn from this comparison that the divine life comes to us socially, that we are not sanctified independently of one another, and that there is no wholesome

---

[8] See *Summa Theol.* III, q. 30, a. 1: "In the name of the whole human race" Mary gave her consent for a "spiritual marriage between the Son of God and human nature."

and durable growth for the body unless each member, each organ, even each cell develops harmoniously until the body shall reach its full stature. And we are told what this stature is: it is that of Christ himself: "Until we all attain to . . . a fully developed manhood, to the full measure of the stature of Christ" (Eph 4:13).[9] This clarification corrects what is excessively physiological in the comparison of the vine. The growth of the mystical body is that of an organism at once visible and invisible, sensible and spiritual, that of a body made up of rational creatures who are both flesh and spirit and whose lifework and perfection consist in reproducing Christ, their model and Head.

If Mary has some essential function to perform in this great organism of the mystical body whose Head is Christ, she must exercise an activity analogous to that of some supremely important organ of the human body. The soul of the mystical body is the Holy Spirit; its Head is Christ. Which member or organ most accurately represents the maternal function exercised by the Blessed Virgin?

In the human body, some members are active and dynamic, others are more passive, receiving vital impulses from other members rather than transmitting them. Some are more closely connected with the head, others are more remote from the head. Some contribute more decisively and extensively to the life and growth of the organism, others remain on a lower level, so that their operations count for little in the activity of the composite.

The supernatural organism of the mystical body exhibits a similar variety of members and diversity of vital functions. Some members are more important than others because they perform operations that are more valuable for the good of the whole, toward which all the members should cooperate. "As in one body we have many members, but all the members have not the same office, so we, being many, are one body in Christ, and

[9] Spencer's translation.

every one members of one another; and having different gifts, according to the grace that is given us" (Rom 12:4f).

In this great variety of functions, the most eminent and essential are those of Christ and his Mother. As far as Christ is concerned, the question is settled: God "has made him Head over all the Church which is his body" (Eph 1:22). But Scripture gives us no such information about Mary. And tradition is not much clearer. What, then, is the solution? Before engaging in this discussion, we should be on our guard against ascribing to a metaphor the same doctrinal value as that contained in the clear formulas which condense the truths of our faith without the obscurity of type or figure. Otherwise we run the risk of violating metaphorical language by assigning to it doctrinal values not within its competency. In applying to the Blessed Virgin a metaphor that may characterize her mission in the supernatural order of grace, we can do no more than transfer to this order a comparison or likeness suggesting that Mary exercises functions analogous to those which the word signifies in its literal sense.[10]

The metaphor of the heart best brings out Mary's place in the mystical body relative to the Holy Spirit as the soul and Christ as the Head of this supernatural organism. As the heart is animated by the soul, Mary's person and activity are completely sustained and animated by the Holy Spirit. Having conceived Christ by the power of the Holy Spirit, the Blessed Virgin nourished him, the Head of the mystical body, in her womb with her maternal blood and drew him into blood relationship with the human race. But the heart, which nourishes the head by the blood it sends throughout the whole organism, is also dependent on the head, which regulates all movement. Even in affective life the heart contracts or dilates according as objects are presented by the mind. This is an apt figure of the

[10] For an account of Mary as the "neck" of the mystical body, see my article, "The Place of Our Lady in the Mystical Body," *Marian Studies* 3, 1952, 186–188.

subordinate and dependent role represented by Mary with respect to Christ in the supernatural economy. All that Mary has she owes to Christ, source of her incomparable greatness. Even her immaculate conception, the point of departure (in the order of time) of all her privileges, is a fruit of the redemption effected by Christ; and her fullness of grace is but a participation in Christ's fullness. Thus the location of the heart under the head and the connection of the heart with the head by the nerves equipping it for its service express Mary's full dependence on Christ and her subordination to him.

The figure of the heart further indicates Mary's position relative to the rest of the members of the mystical body. A beautiful parallel emerges from the common view that the heart is the second noblest part of the body. For after Christ, the Head, Mary is the most excellent member in his body. The life that courses through the whole body is strikingly manifest in her.

But the superiority of the heart over the other members rests mainly on the life-giving activity by which the heart causes the circulation of the blood and thus supplies the whole organism with constantly renewed nourishment. The vital activity of the heart is not limited to some of the body's members; it reaches them all and transmits to all the life and vigor that sustain them. Similar is the action of the Blessed Virgin relative to all the other members of the mystical body. An image of Mary's universal motherhood and mediation is easily discerned. As the body's members receive blood from the heart and are nourished by its circulation, so we receive every grace through her mediatorial activity. By cooperating in the work of salvation, she has received the whole merit of the redemptive sacrifice and thereby all graces of salvation for mankind. If God has enriched her with such a wealth of divine favors that no created mind can comprehend them, his purpose is that we may all receive a share in that fullness. Mary was made the Mother of God with a view to our redemption; her great mission in our economy is to transmit to all the world the treasures of grace her soul abounds in. Hence in God's redemptive program our supernatural life is no less dependent on Mary's maternal and mediatorial activity than our natural life is dependent on the functioning of the heart. And as the heart does its work whether we think of it or not, so Mary works for our salvation whether we are conscious of her cooperation or whether, because of spiritual sluggishness or defective religious knowledge, we omit recourse to her.

In this connection, another parallel may be noted: as long as the heart of a sick person is sound and capable of performing its functions, we do not give up hope of that person's recovery. Similarly, when we call Mary the heart of the mystical body, we exalt her intercessory power, in which mankind puts its unconditional and boundless trust.

The figure of the heart is likewise justified when we consider the Blessed Virgin's position in the whole of the mystical body. Like the heart in the body, Mary has a central and hidden place in the Church. Otherwise than the head, which governs man's activity and presides over his operations by issuing its orders from a position of visible command, the heart exercises its beneficent influence through the body's arteries by an invisible and hidden action. Mary, physical mother of Christ and spiritual mother of all the faithful, holds no office in the hierarchical, social organization of the Church. No sacrament is administered in her name, no bishop rules in the Church in virtue of a commission received from her. Her cooperation is silent, hidden; yet she has her indispensable part in the more intimate activity of the Head, in the communication of life itself to the members.

But especially the heart as symbol of love brings out Mary's position in the mystical body. We are all aware that the brain, not the heart, is the seat of sensible affections, but that does not diminish the value of the figure. All peoples, with the exception of some oriental nations, regard the heart as a symbol of love. And in fact, although the heart is not properly the organ of

187

affective life, it is, in addition to being a natural symbol of love, the organ in which are felt the repercussions and are manifested the effects of love as in no other organ of the body. The father is head of the family and represents the importance of authority and justice; but the mother, as heart of the family, has the special task of being prodigal in love and of binding together the members of the family in warm affection. Mary has a similiar task in the Church; she was designed by God to be the heart of his family in her capacity as mother of all the faithful, as comforter of the afflicted and refuge of sinners.

In an exchange of comments during the "Second Week of Theology" held in Madrid in 1942, J. M. Bover suggested that Mary's role cannot be symbolized by any part of the body, for the simple reason that she is not in the mystical body, but outside it. She is the Mother of the whole Christ, Head and members. And the mother does not form part of the bodies of her children, but is quite distinct from them. This objection, at first sight, seems to have some cogency. But when it is scrutinized more closely, it is seen to lack foundation. For all who in any way receive influence from Christ, the Head, are in some sense members of the mystical body. And theologians assert confidently that Mary is thus a member. As an example, we may quote Roschini: "The head, in its order, denotes absolute priority over all the other members, among whom is also the Mother of God. This absolute priority belongs to Christ alone, from whom, as primary source and universal mover, all supernatural influence flows forth to all the members of his mystical body, not excluding the Blessed Virgin."[11] For Mary to be outside the mystical body, it would be necessary that no supernatural influence should flow to her from her Son. And that would in truth be an enormity in dogma.

Carl Feckes contributes to a clarification of the issue by distinguishing the several senses and therefore comprehensions of the term "Church": "This organic whole, Mary *and* the Church,

[11] *Mariologia*, Milan 1942, vol. 3, 426.

is in turn called the Church. It is the Church in the fuller sense. In this concept of the Church, Mary is included as the noblest and most perfect part, the heart of the mystical body. The Church in the *fullest* sense includes Christ himself, its Head that sanctifies and vivifies the whole."[12] In any case, we should not push any bodily metaphor too far; rather, as H. Rondet reminds us, we should advance from the figure to the reality it suggests: "If we stress the fact that in the mystical body Christ is the Head, we shall immediately assign to Mary the role of an essential organ: the neck, said St. Bernardine of Siena; the heart, repeat many modern authors, after Scheeben. Whether static [neck] or dynamic [heart], the image is but an image, and we must go beyond it."[13] Emile Mersch S.J. adds that supernatural life flows through Mary into the whole body, and that "her role is not partial but total, although secondary. As the Mother of God, she is in her way what the God-man is in his way: both have a universal function."[14]

Conclusion

Precious for us are the lessons disengaged from our considera-tion of the social aspects of Mary's motherhood of men. Among the members of the mystical body, there is an incessant circula-tion of life; no one can live the life of Christ without being grafted onto the mystic vine, no one can grow in grace without being a living cell or member of the body of Christ. The more vigorous each one's supernatural life is, the more will life de-velop throughout the entire organism. But the very perfection of this life requires a perfect docility to the action of the Holy Spirit, the docility of Mary herself. The same docility must

[12] *Das Mysterium der heiligen Kirche,* 277.
[13] "De la place de la Très Sainte Vierge dans l'Église corps mystique du Christ," *BSFEM* 3, 1937, 217.
[14] *The Theology of the Mystical Body,* trans. by C. Vollert S.J., St. Louis 1951, 173.

prevail on the level of the apostolate. To be effective, any form of the apostolate must be soundly organized, and it cannot be soundly organized without fidelity to the hierarchy, such as Mary had with regard to Jesus and later toward his apostles.[15]

A truth we may never forget is that the Mother of God was not merely associated with the beginning of the human life of the Redeemer, but that she shared in his whole career and office and still continues to do so. She was adorned with so many outstanding graces and privileges not only on account of her exalted dignity, but because she has an essential place in the saving work of conferring grace. Unless we perceive this, we remain far short of the full truth and do not rise to the heights of mariology. Mary, mother of the whole Christ, must influence every phase of Christian life. The common motherhood of the Blessed Virgin involves a new relation toward men, to which on the side of men a definite religious attitude toward her corresponds, differing from every other. Mary is the mother, we are her children. We have such a relation toward no other saint. And this is the conviction of the Catholic people: Mary is active with a mother's love in behalf of her children. Therefore, we must entrust our lives to her; and as for our eternal salvation, to whom, under God, shall we turn if not to Mary, mother of the whole Christ?

[15] See H. Rondet S.J., *art. cit.* 223.

6

The Holiness of Mary

MARY'S eminence as Mother of God, involving her unique position and functions in the mystical body of Christ, quite naturally suggests an inquiry into her grace and holiness.

Scriptural accounts of the Blessed Virgin's saintly life, though not abundant, are striking. The New Testament displays her unwavering faith in God's mysteries, her entire conformity with God's will, her perfect virginity, her deep humility, her valiancy in suffering. It also reveals something of God's extraordinary gifts of grace to Mary. Yet the description presents few details. Theological reflection and elaboration are needed. Investigation of the question over many hundreds of years has issued in considerable success.

The study of grace is always difficult, partly because of the very nature of the theme, partly because of God's sovereign freedom in conferring his gifts, "which he distributes just as he wishes" (1 Cor 12:11). The difficulty increases when the theologian turns to Mary's grace, for in the supernatural world she occupies a unique position and performs a unique function. Her relationship with the Blessed Trinity is without parallel in the universe. In the words of Pius XII, Mary, raised up to the very order of the hypostatic union, is the first-born daughter of the Father, the devoted Mother of the Son, and the beloved spouse of the Holy Spirit.[1] How conceive, to say nothing of calculating, the perfection of grace in one who is daughter of God, mother of God, bride of God?

1. GUIDING PRINCIPLES

The divine maternity, Mary's supreme glory, is the norm and criterion for the study of all her perfections. It determines the orientation of the whole science of mariology.[2] It must, however, be understood not in some sterile, abstract sense, but in its true existential perspective. We cannot gain an intelligence of Mary's exceptional career in the history of salvation unless we perceive that she is the Mother of God's Son who became incarnate to redeem the sinful race of Adam by a life of expiatory renouncement and by associating mankind, beginning with his very Mother, in his own redemptive renouncements. The divine maternity is essentially ordered to the ends of our economy of salvation, the redemptive finalities to which the life of Christ himself was ordered.[3] The divine maternity, taken in this concrete, historical sense, offers four guiding lights that illuminate the question of Mary's grace and holiness. These are: 1) the requisite preparation and equipment for the divine motherhood; 2) the Mother's close connection with her Son, source of all grace; 3) her mission is salvation; and 4) the ardent love between Mother and Child.

God never assigns an office to anyone without giving to that

[1] *Bendito seia o Senhor, AAS* 38, 1946, 266. On Mary and the hypostatic order, see the basic article by M. J. Nicolas O.P., "L'appartenance de la Mère de Dieu à l'ordre hypostatique," *BSFEM* 3, 1937, 145–181, also M. Dionne, "La grâce de Marie est d'ordre hypostatique," *Laval Théologique et Philosophique* 10, 1954, 141–145.

[2] See G. de Yurre, "La maternidad divina y la gracia santificante," *EM* 5, 1946, 111.

[3] See G. de Broglie S.J., "Le 'principe fondamental' de la théologie mariale," *Maria: Études sur la Sainte Vierge,* vol. 6, 1961, 297–365.

192

person the graces needed for carrying out his appointed duties. St. Paul grasped this clearly when he wrote: "Our competency is from God. He it is who has made us competent ministers of a new covenant" (1 Cor 3:5f). St. Thomas repeats the same truth in his own way: "God so prepares and endows those whom he chooses for an office that they are made capable of discharging the office to which they are chosen."[4] Theologians have often adapted this thought to bring out the supernatural perfections of Christ's human nature. The same norm must hold for everyone who is called to high office in the economy of salvation; most certainly it must avail in the case of her who was called to be the Mother of God and was invested with tremendous responsibility in the work of redemption. As St. Thomas points out: "The Blessed Virgin was chosen by God to be his Mother. Hence there can be no doubt that God by his grace fitted her for this office."[5] Application of this principle opens up one way leading to a more precise knowledge of the graces Mary received from God.

2) The second guiding thought is Mary's close connection with the source of grace. St. Thomas applies this idea to Christ's sacred humanity: "Christ had the fullness of grace . . . because he had grace in its highest degree, in the most perfect way it can be possessed. This appears from the nearness of Christ's soul to the cause of grace. For the nearer a recipient is to an inflowing cause, the more copiously it receives. And therefore the soul of Christ, which is more closely joined to God than all other rational creatures, receives the greatest possible outpouring of his grace."[6] An obvious transition is made to the case of the Mother: "The nearer a thing is to its principle in any order, the more it shares in the effect of that principle. . . . But the Blessed Virgin Mary was nearest to Christ in his humanity, because he derived his human nature from her. And that is why

[4] *Summa Theol.* III, q. 27, a. 4.   [5] *Ibid.*
[6] *Summa Theol.* III, q. 7, a. 9.

she had to receive a greater fullness of grace from Christ than all others."[7]

Thus the divine maternity is the reason why God was so lavish with the grace he gave to Mary. Supreme holiness was required by the noble maternal function of rearing her Child and of contributing to the formation of his mind and character. To exert the maternal influence she ought to exert on her young Son, she had to possess an unparalleled fullness of grace. The example of her life had to be perfect, so that her Son could receive without misgivings all that his Mother could propose for his human education.

For once on this earth God wished to bring about a perfect supernatural accord between two beings, a perfect union of a soul with Christ. The intimacy between the Child and his Mother, never to be troubled by any fault or imperfection, goes far to account for the fullness of grace bestowed on Mary. Particularly, however, God inundated her with his richest graces that she might accomplish the task he had allotted to her in his salvific plan. One of her greatest services is that she brought up her Son in a family environment of unfailing sanctity, where his own sanctity could flower harmoniously in a human way.

Reflection on the divine maternity opens up limitless horizons in the study of Mary's grace. Her maternity permeates her whole person and throws light on her dignity, her supernatural perfections, her mission in life, her natural qualities, her very existence.[8] Everything in Mary, and unquestionably her sanctity, is dominated by the divine maternity. The designation "capital grace" which is occasionally used in her regard seems incongruous; for not she, but Christ, is the Head. But we can with propriety refer to her supernatural endowment as "maternal grace,"

[7] *Ibid.* q. 27, a. 5.
[8] See N. di S. Brocardo O.C.D., "La grazia di Maria e i suoi problemi," *Alma Socia Christi* 11, 1953, 30f.

which equips her for her universal function of Mother of the whole Christ, Head and members, and for all mankind.[9]

The third guiding principle is Mary's mission in the history of salvation. This mission, embracing her functions of core-demptress and of mediatress in the dispensing of graces, is thoroughly maternal, since she was made the associate of the Redeemer precisely because she was his Mother. Such is the teaching of Leo XIII: "The Virgin was chosen to be the Mother of God, and by this very fact was made his associate [consors] in saving the human race."[10] Accordingly, the divine maternity has a functional aspect that involves Mary's collaboration in the process of redemption. As associate of the Redeemer on Calvary, she had to be perfect in grace. To be able to offer, along with her Son, a sacrifice agreeable to the Father, she had to be completely worthy in the eyes of God.

The Blessed Virgin's activity as coredemptress contributes greatly to our understanding of her fullness of grace. The redemptive sacrifice requires holiness in the person who offers it, as well as holiness in the act of offering. Christ, all-holy in his human nature, offered his sacrifice with consummate obedience and love. Associated with Christ in this sacrifice, Mary had to have all the holiness possible in a created person, and she had to make her maternal oblation with perfect obedience and love.

Consequently, Mary's grace may not be isolated from her official mission. Grace was apportioned to her to enable her to accomplish that mission. Certainly, all the grace she received is first of all hers; it sanctified her beyond all angels and men and transfigured her whole life. But in God's providence it was meant to redound to the benefit of all mankind; Mary's grace was designed for her exalted position as Mother of the Savior and as coredemptress of the race.

<hr />

[9] See S. Gutierrez O.S.A., "La plenitud de gracia de la Santísima Virgen," EM 5, 1946, 181.

[10] Supremi Apostolatus, September 1, 1883, ASS 16, 1883–1884, 114.

It goes without saying that, as Mary's grace is derived from her Son, so too the entire value of her coredemption comes from him. Therefore, both her grace and her coredemptive power attest that Jesus Christ is the one Mediator between God and men, the Mediator on whom the grace and the mediatorial activity of all others totally depend.

④ The fourth guiding thought is the intimate love between the Son and his Mother. Unlike our love, which derives personal integration or at least some passing satisfaction from what is loved, divine love receives no advantage from any quarter but only gives and enriches. It is the measure of all perfection in creatures. "God's love infuses and creates goodness in things."[11] It extends to the whole universe and is everywhere operative, though more in some parts than in others. In the unique world of Mary it is operative more than anywhere else. It is the love of him who possesses infinite goods to bestow. In the case of adorning and enriching his Mother, Christ's love cannot but vie with his wealth.

Contemplation of these guiding principles, which have their origin in the divine maternity, will do much to bring out and clarify for us the perfection of Mary's grace, holiness and life of virtue.

2. ASPECTS OF MARY'S GRACE

Holiness in the created order is a supernatural perfection that proceeds from grace and includes all virtues. If we examine Mary's holiness and virtuous life, we can come to some appreciation of her grace.

What precisely is holiness? We may answer, in a general way, that holiness is the separation of a creature from profane usage by its consecration to God, that is, to his service and to divine worship. Whatever is devoted to God and belongs to him is sacred and holy. Therefore, God himself is necessarily

[11] *Summa Theol.* I, q. 20, a. 2.

holy by his very nature, since all that is dedicated to him, whether intelligent being or inanimate thing, becomes holy by pertaining to him. He is the sole source from whom all holiness is derived.[12] In a rational creature, consequently, holiness is union with God, a participation in divinity. A man is holy because he is admitted into the life of God; only union with him who is holy by nature can make us holy by grace.

A more comprehensive notion of holiness requires a distinction between its two essential aspects. In the first place, there is an objective holiness, or consecration, which is brought about by an action that dedicates a man or a thing to God. Such an object is definitively God's property. The purpose of the consecration is to render the object fit for divine worship and for any mission or service God may prescribe. In itself, consecration does not necessarily require the collaboration of human freedom.

Subjective holiness, which can exist only in an intelligent being, is the effect of grace; it is caused, sustained and nourished by grace. This grace, in itself, never fails, although it is submitted to the fluctuations of man's free response. The divine influence cannot be entirely effective unless it obtains such cooperation. God cannot take complete possession of a person unless the latter freely consents. Without this consent, the ultimate depth of the free being would elude God; but by the unreserved gift of the human will, the person wholly passes over to God.

Mary was called to be the physical mother of God the Savior. She was called to share actively in the events of Christ's life, to cooperate in the mysteries of the incarnation and redemption. To carry out this mission, the most important ever confided to a human being, she was invested with objective holiness; God consecrated her with a consecration that corresponds to her vocation. She also has subjective holiness; impelled by her intense personal love of God, itself the fruit of grace, she freely ac-

[12] See F. Bourassa S.J., "Verum sacrificium," *Sciences Ecclésiastiques* 3, 1950, 149f.

197

cepted the divine gift. Her high vocation required fullness of grace, and to the offered grace she presented a perfect receptivity.

The distinction between the two aspects of holiness, objective and subjective, suggests a solution to the problem whether the divine maternity was formally sanctifying for Mary.[13] On the one hand, the divine maternity must have been a source of holiness for Mary. On the other hand, holiness is formally caused by habitual grace—that is why this grace is called sanctifying. The perplexity is dissipated once we consider that the divine maternity involved a new and deeper consecration of Mary's person; the sanctification is objective. When Mary became Mother of the divine Word, she was raised to a higher nobility, to an exceptional dignity. She received the highest consecration possible for a human person, and yet this new consecration did not formally sanctify her. Over and above this objective sanctification, a subjective sanctification inevitably ensued by reason of the free acceptance Mary offered to the divine maternity.

Such seems to be the meaning of Christ's reply to the woman who had cried out in praise of his Mother: "Blessed the womb that has borne you; blessed the breasts that have suckled you!" Our Lord answered: "Blessed, rather, are those that hear the word of God and observe it!" (Lk 11:27f). This declaration is applicable to Mary's attitude at the time of the angel's announcement. The sole fact of her motherhood could not take the place of hearing and keeping God's word. Mary is blessed because she accepted the divine message and conformed to it with an assent that held nothing back. The merit of the assent was reinforced by the free act of faith that presided over it. Earlier Elizabeth, under inspiration, had exclaimed: "Happy is

[13] Here I follow J. Galot S.J., "La sainteté de Marie," *Maria: Études sur la Sainte Vierge,* vol. 6, 432–434. On this controverted question, see G. Van Ackeren S.J., "Does the Divine Maternity Formally Sanctify Mary's Soul?" *MS* 6, 1955, 63–101.

she who believed that what was told her in behalf of the Lord would be fulfilled!" (Lk 1:45). Mary received the Lord's word with faith and entire submission. That is why her subjective holiness increased at that time, and that also, according to these two testimonies of the Gospel, is why she is blessed.

Therefore, the two aspects of holiness must be kept distinct. Yet they are closely connected. Objective consecration furnishes the foundation for subjective holiness, the life of grace. It is a point of departure that needs to be completed by a holiness which implies the free will's cooperation. Mary's first consecration took place at the first instant of her existence—at her immaculate conception. It dominated the whole development of her life of grace that followed. Her initial consecration was heightened by a new consecration when the Holy Spirit came upon her to bring about in her the incarnation of the Son of God. The consecration of the divine maternity equipped Mary to fulfill her maternal mission along with all the demands it involved in the sphere of collaboration with the work of redemption, and it was the basis of an enormous augmentation of her subjective holiness.

Mary was conceived with a fullness of grace. With still greater fullness, she reached the highpoint of her earthly life when she became the Mother of Christ. With the greatest fullness of all, she was assumed into heaven. We need not attempt here to define the genuine meaning of the Greek text that is rendered in many versions as "Hail, full of grace" (Lk 1:28). We can be content to reflect on the office deputed to Mary at this sacred moment—the office of God's Mother and associate for the world's salvation. She could not be worthy of such a commission or fit for it without a wealth of grace. St. Thomas is loyal to tradition when, after noting that Christ in his human nature had a fullness of grace so copious that it could overflow from him into all men, he continues: "The Blessed Virgin Mary received such a fullness of grace that she was nearest of all to the Author of grace; for she received within herself him

199

who is full of all grace."[14] Pius IX, in the document containing
the solemn definition of the immaculate conception, expresses
a firm Catholic conviction: "In this unique and majestic greet-
ing, that had never been heard before, it is plain that the Mother
of God was the repository of all graces, that she was adorned
with all the gifts of the Holy Spirit, indeed that she was the almost measureless treasury and inexhaustible abyss of all these
gifts."[15]

Fullness of grace is, of course, relative to the person of
whom it is predicated. Mary's fullness of grace must correspond
to the greatness and functions of the divine maternity.[16] Only
God can gauge its perfection. Yet we may confidently assert
that her fullness of grace transcended the fullness of grace of
all others. Pius IX sums up tradition in this matter: "Far beyond all angelic spirits and saints, Mary has been wondrously
endowed by God with an abundance of all heavenly gifts so that
she, forever free from all stain of sin, in her beauty and perfection possessed a fullness of purity and holiness which, outside
God, cannot be conceived, and which no one except God can
grasp."[17]

If Mary's fullness of grace is beyond comparison with that
of other saints, perhaps it may be defined by comparison with
that of Christ. The words of Pius IX suggest such a comparison.
If we look up from below we behold Christ's and Mary's fullness of grace on the unscalable height of the hypostatic order.
That is not surprising, for the Mother stands in the circle of
her Son. To be sure, the gap between the grace of Son and
Mother cannot be spanned. Yet Christ's absolutely highest full-

---

[14] *Summa Theol.* III, q. 27, a. 5 ad 1.

[15] *Ineffabilis Deus,* in H. Marin, S.J., *Doctrina Pontificia,* vol. 4, *Docu-
mentos Marianos,* Madrid 1954, no. 288.

[16] See St. Thomas, *loc. cit.*

[17] *Ineffabilis Deus,* no. 269. See Frank Calkins O.S.M., "Mary's Fullness of
Grace," *Mariology,* vol. 2, 297–312.

ness of grace is the model whose best image is found in the fullness of grace of his Mother.

3. Growth of Grace in Mary

Nothing, perhaps, so clearly points up the difference between
Christ's and Mary's fullness of grace as the progressive development of her holiness. Christ's grace could not increase, for grace
is proportionate to the beatific vision which he possessed in
consummate form all during his terrestrial life, even though
some of its effects were for a time inoperative. But Mary was a
wayfarer toward eternal life, advancing from perfection to perfection, from one fullness of grace to another, until the moment
of her departure from earth.

The divine maternity was decisive in the sanctification of the
Blessed Virgin. Tradition is explicit on the truth that when
Mary became the Mother of Christ she received an immeasur-
able increase in her fullness of grace. Other times of outstanding importance in the maturing of her grace were the day of
Calvary, when she offered her greatest sacrifice and became definitively the mother of the children of God, and the day of
Pentecost, when the Holy Spirit took firmer possession of her
who had always been His dearly beloved spouse. On such days
her fullness of grace expanded sharply by immense bounds. But
it also grew from day to day, for every day was rich in the
virtuous acts of routine life.

Scripture tells us very little about Mary's history, but that
little sets her before us in the practice of many virtues. She is
praised by Elizabeth for the greatness of her faith. She has un-
abated confidence in God at the time of Joseph's bewilderment.
Her love for God is expressed by her simple statement that she
is the little slave girl of the Lord and by her complete conformity with his will. Prudence and modesty mark her conver-
sation with the angel. With zeal for God's law she meticulously
observes the Mosaic prescriptions at the time of her purifica-

tion. As a young mother, she takes devoted care of her infant Child. Her love for others is illustrated by her concern at the wedding feast in Cana. She remains steadfast at the foot of the cross in her unbreakable sacrificial will. These are only a few items in her life, but they indicate her constancy in acts that are worthy of the Mother of God.

In the divine plan, Mary's life and grace, united to those of Christ, were oriented toward Calvary. During the many years she had to plod the weary way of lowliness and toil, she was being educated by God and for her most dreadful hour, for her appointment with the Cross, the hour of the collapse of all human hopes. Inexorably, the hour approached and struck. At last she stood there, mother of a Man condemned to the gallows by verdict of the highest judge in the land. How far off, now, that joyful cry she had uttered in her youth: "Behold, from this hour onward age after age will call me blessed" (Lk 1:48). How niggardly that prophecy had been fulfilled for her during her whole life up to this time! The pitiful little crib in Bethlehem, the escape into Egypt, the obscurity of despised Nazareth, the neglect of her during her Son's public life—all this was the hollow echo of the blessedness foretold for her. In the offering she was now called upon to make, Mary had to gather together all that her previous life had amassed of grace, faith, hope and love, and she had to carry them to the extreme limit. Her love for God reached its highest point, and she offered her Son to death. At the same time her love for all men achieved its maximum intensity, not only in the forgiveness she accorded to all her Son's enemies, which in the circumstances was heroic, but in her will to contribute by her sacrifice to the salvation of mankind. At the hour of the redemptive sacrifice Mary's grace and holiness soared to new, unimaginable heights.

On Calvary the mother's faith, hope and love were subjected to their severest test, but triumphed all the more at her Son's resurrection. And now her grace entered a new phase, for neither the resurrection nor Pentecost halted its development. But this development was no longer in the order of objective redemption, for that was accomplished. It was a development in the new mission assigned to Mary as mother of Christians, for her cooperation in subjective redemption. Mary's grace and her virtues continued to flower evermore during the latter years of her sojourn on earth.

4. THE GIFTS OF GRACE AND MYSTICAL LIFE

When we speak of the Blessed Virgin's grace, we mean first of all her sanctifying grace. All other graces have their root and their finality in sanctifying grace, and without it they are of little profit to the possessor. But we should not overlook the glorious retinue that accompanies sanctifying grace: the infused virtues of faith, hope and charity, the infused moral virtues, the gifts of the Holy Spirit. As the years lengthened, her faith in the divine mysteries deepened, her hope in God became stronger, her love for the Blessed Trinity intensified, and all her other virtues and gifts developed for an ever richer supernatural life.

Mary's fullness of grace does not entail a host of extraordinary marvels not required by her position and mission. For instance, she did not have the use of reason from the first instant of her life. This idea has been proposed in the past as well as more recently.[18] It is at best a gratuitous assumption. To receive the initial grace destined for her, Mary did not have to be conscious of it or straightway to give her free consent to it, any more than an infant has to be conscious and free in order to receive truly the grace of baptism. The argument that she could thus begin to merit immediately is feeble in the extreme. Length of time is not requisite for greatness of merit; if more time were needed, why should God not have prolonged her life for a decade or a

[18] Among others, by L. Colomer O.F.M., "El primer momento de la Virgen," *EM* 14, 1955, 271f.

century, or even up to and beyond the nine hundred and sixty-nine years of Methuselah? The purpose of the immaculate conception was not a sudden elevation of Mary's intellect and consciousness to adulthood. It was a privilege accorded to a newly conceived infant in the human conditions of her life's inception, when she was incapable of knowing and willing. The grace conferred on Mary at her first instant would later influence her consciousness and would invite, and abundantly obtain, the full cooperation of her will; it was bestowed for a whole lifetime, not just for the first moment. It developed in her harmoniously with her physical growth.[19]

The correct concern to recognize all the supernatural perfection God lavished on Mary ought not to issue in the contention that she possessed unusual gifts which are not in line with her particular state. Some theologians have attributed to her fullness of grace certain charisms attending other missions than the one entrusted to Mary. They seem to fear that they would be failing in proper love for her if they denied to her graces that pertain to the priestly office, the apostolic office of government, and yet others. They feel obliged to include in her holiness all the supernatural gifts that have ever been granted to any or all the other saints.

What should be our attitude in this regard?[20] We do well to follow the lead of St. Thomas. He lays down his principle: "She who brought forth 'the Father's only-begotten Son, full of grace and truth' (Jn 1:14), received greater privileges of grace than all others."[21] Then he draws an inference: "There is no doubt that the Blessed Virgin received in high degree the gift

[19] This point and some others to be considered in this section are well presented by J. Galot S.J., "La sainteté de Marie," *Maria: Etudes sur la Sainte Vierge,* vol. 6, 442–447.

[20] C. Feckes, "Die Gnadenausstattung Mariens," in P. Sträter S.J., ed., *Katholische Marienkunde,* vol. 2, *Maria in der Glaubenswissenschaft,* Paderborn 1947, 156ff., answers this question fairly and reasonably.

[21] *Summa Theol.* III, q. 27, a. 1.

of wisdom and the grace of miracles, and also the grace of prophecy." But at once he adds a prudent restriction: "She did not, however, receive these graces and others like them so as to put them to every use . . . but only as befitted her condition of life." With the finality of the divine maternity in mind, as well as the fact that Mary was a woman and a wayfarer, St. Thomas applies his principle: "She had the use of wisdom in contemplation . . . but not for the purpose of teaching, because that was not suitable for the female sex. . . . The working of miracles was not for her during her lifetime, because at that period the teaching of Christ was to be confirmed by miracles, and so it was fitting that only Christ and his disciples, who were the bearers of his doctrine, should work miracles."[22]

On the basis of such sound reasoning, we should be slow to ascribe to Mary gifts of grace that are not in accord with the purpose of the divine maternity or that are proper to authoritative officials in the Church. We do no hurt to Mary if we say that she did not possess this or that particular gift which God has conferred on some saint for some special mission. Rising high above all such charisms is the grace of the divine motherhood. Mary received in great abundance all the graces that empowered her to discharge the task that was hers in the work of salvation and, since she brought to these graces a cooperation that knew no reluctance, she carried out her function perfectly and in it was sanctified to the maximum degree. We do not have to suppose that in her mission as Mother of Christ, as coredemptress, and subsequently as mother of Christians, she possessed the special gifts of apostles such as St. Paul or of doctors of the Church such as St. Augustine. Her greatness is attuned to her own mission. She was not meant by God to be a supernatural warehouse of all possible charisms and graces. She did not have to perform every kind of task, but only the one to which she had been appointed.

[22] *Ibid.* a. 5 ad 3.

If we consider Mary's grace in the perspective of her mission, we can readily discern the relation between her divine maternity and her grace. Although the divine maternity did not formally sanctify her, it thoroughly consecrated her entire person. It also placed her in ideal conditions for the greatest development of her life of grace and for the greatest intensification of her love for God. As she progressed in knowledge of her Son, her love for God tended to blend more and more with her love for Jesus; thus she loved God with all the ardor of maternal love. In the intimacy of the family circle at Nazareth, Mary's advance in grace was powerfully promoted by her close association with Christ over the long years.

This maternal environment helps to clarify Mary's mystical life. Her experience of God was primarily the fruit of her maternal contact with Jesus. We have no solid basis for projecting her mystical life beyond her life of faith. A number of theologians have wished to attribute to her the beatific vision during her sojourn on earth, at least on certain occasions, such as during the birth of Christ.[23] This position, which is not backed up by evidence, seems to be hardly compatible with the state of faith that is one of the prominent marks of her greatness. When Elizabeth extolled her, she proclaimed that Mary was blessed for having believed. The moment of the annunciation was a moment of ardent faith, not of vision.

Nor can we discern in the career of Mary any extraordinary mystical phenomena, such as ecstasies or revelations never before or since heard of and unknown to the Church. The message delivered by the angel Gabriel and the prophecy of Simeon were indeed special revelations. But Jesus was for her a living teaching and her greatest revelation. And her ecstasy was not the kind that involves loss of consciousness, but the ever deepening wonder she experienced as she progressively discovered all that her Son was. The very simplicity of Mary's words and conduct

[23] See F. J. Connell C.SS.R., "Our Lady's Knowledge," *Mariology*, vol. 2, 314–317, and the references there given.

in the few scenes recorded by the evangelists invites us to sobriety when we turn our thoughts to the mystical life of God's Mother.

Perhaps we do not stray from truth when we say that Mary's mystical life was simply her life of faith and charity pervaded by the fire of maternal love and thereby reaching the deepest recesses of her soul. It was a life supernaturally vitalized by graces of enlightenment, spiritual energy and love, which enabled Mary to penetrate more and more into the mystery of Christ. We detect in it no traces of exotic marvels which so easily stir the imagination and lead people to gather in crowds to slake their thirst for sensationalism. The authentic marvel of Mary's mystical life was its perfect conformity to God within the ambit of faith that is at once luminous and obscure, and the astounding phenomenon of a mother's love that focused on her Son who was her Creator, her Savior and her God.

When we review the Blessed Virgin's supernatural endowment, we see that her grace, from its beginning in the immaculate conception to its consummation at the assumption, is not an indiscriminate piling up of gifts from God, but an harmonious masterpiece of divine power and love.

This unity is clear in its negative aspects—her immunity from sin and from subjection to the devil. Although Mary was a child of Adam, she did not inherit his sin; that was her first victory. Although she had to lead her life in the darkness of faith, in poverty, lowliness and suffering, yet she remained completely pure and stainless; that was her daily victory. Although she may have passed through the somber gate of death, yet death could not hold her captive; and that was her final victory.

However, we gain a more adequate notion of Mary's grace if we view it more positively in the light of her close union with God and her deep sharing in God's life. From the first instant of her existence she was God's dearest and most precious daughter through the grace of the immaculate conception. Uninterruptedly, she grew up toward God during a long life that

207

was rich in blessings, virtuous acts and heroic accomplishment of the momentous mission confided to her. When at length her earthly course was run, she was taken up, glorified in soul and body, into God's eternal life. The verse of her song turned out to be wonderfully true: "How sublime is what he has done for me—the Mighty One, whose name is 'Holy'!" (Lk 1:49).

7

Mary and Salvation

PHILOSOPHERS of history have set themselves the task of discovering and formulating an explanation of the universe. Their efforts are confined to the level of the natural world. Since all nature is orientated toward a supernatural end, the theology of history must take over where the philosophy of history is obliged to leave off. The theology of history, in turn, is based on the sources of revelation, which sums up the record of the universe in two words, or rather two persons: Adam and Jesus Christ. The material world is for man, and man himself is for Christ, the foundation,[1] the model[2] and the end, under God, of the human race and of all reality.[3] But in fidelity to revelation, especially as clarified by tradition, we must bring forward a second parallel, that between Eve and Mary. At the side of the first man stands the first woman, mother of all the living; at the side of Christ stands Mary, mother of all the redeemed. And that introduces yet a third parallel, between mankind and the Church, the mystical body of Christ. At the origin of the race,

[1] "Other foundation no man can lay, but that which is laid, which is Christ Jesus" (1 Cor 3:11).
[2] "Whom he foreknew, he also predestinated to be made conformable to the image of his Son" (Rom 8:29).
[3] "You are Christ's, and Christ is God's" (1 Cor 3:23). "And when all things shall be subdued unto him, then the Son also himself shall be subject to him that put all things under him, that God may be all in all" (1 Cor 15:28).

Eve was the associate and wife of Adam; these two are the parents of all men whom God, in his divine goodness, destined for eternal life. But what Adam and Eve could not distinctly foresee was that the race which was to spring from them would not reach its sublime goal without the conjoined action of a new Adam and a new Eve, who were to impart to the first pair's posterity the life of grace.

Where Christ is, there is Mary; and where Christ acts, there Mary acts too, not by title of equality with him, but as assistant providentially assigned. This truth stands forth clearly if we pass in review a number of striking incidents in the lives of Jesus and his Mother. Even a summary examination discloses the enduring union between Christ and Mary, and by way of consequence, the continuous influence Mary had in conferring grace. A survey of the activity Mary shared with Christ leads to an inevitable conclusion: therefore now too, and for all time, the supernatural life of the mystical body depends, of course in a subsidiary way, on Mary, our mother.

The vision of salvation to come began to emerge dimly from the mists of the future shortly after the fateful sin of our first parents. "I will put enmities between you and the woman, and your seed and her seed," God said to the tempter.[4] From the very outset Christ and his Mother are contrasted, in veiled terms, with the ancient Adam and Eve. The contrast is also between the two races—the fallen race and the redeemed race, mankind enslaved under the tyranny of sin and death and the mystical body living the life of grace. "Two parents have generated us for death, two parents have generated us for life."[5]

Whatever the literal interpretation of the text in Genesis may be and notwithstanding the fact that the Fathers saw no specific marian reference in it, Mary would seem to be the woman ultimately meant, for the seed of the woman certainly includes

[4] See Gn 3:15.
[5] St. Augustine, Serm. 22, 10, PL 38, 154.

Christ,[6] Son of Mary. And the conflict between the woman and the serpent stems from the latter's hideous success in inducing Eve to fall, so that the eventual defeat of the serpent, indicated by the crushing of his head, cannot be anything else than the annulling of the effects wrought by his crafty attack. The immediate effect of the seduction was the loss of sanctifying grace in the souls of our first ancestors and the disastrous introduction of sin, death of the soul. Accordingly, the crushing of the tempter's head must signify the destruction of his evil triumph. As sin is essentially the privation of the life of grace, the vanquishing of this privation must be a fresh production of life, in which Mary cooperates. Her function in the causing of this new, supernatural life is that of a woman doing her part for the generation of a new living being; it is a maternal function. Already in the protogospel, therefore, Mary would seem to be proclaimed, at least in the broader sense of the prophecy, the Mother of divine grace.

The antithesis between Eve and Mary is a favorite theme of the Fathers, who exploit the contrast to bring to light the Blessed Virgin's spiritual motherhood. St. Jerome sums up patristic thought when he writes: "After the Virgin conceived in her womb and bore her Son for us . . . the curse was dissolved: death through Eve, life through Mary."[7] The author of a sermon formerly ascribed to St. Augustine has the same idea of Mary: "She alone deserves to be called Mother and spouse; she repaired the damage caused by the first mother; she brought redemption to man who was lost. For the mother of our race brought down punishment on the world; but the Mother of our Lord brought forth salvation for the world. The author of sin was Eve; the author of merit is Mary. Eve harmed us by killing

[6] See J. M. Bover S.J., "Universalis B. Virginis mediatio," *Gregorianum* 5, 1924, 572: "That Christ is . . . the promised seed of the woman is held by the whole Christian religion, by all the Fathers without exception, and by all theologians."

[7] Epist. 22, 21, PL 22, 408.

211

us; Mary helped us by restoring life to us."[8] The spiritual nature of the Blessed Virgin's motherhood is stressed by St. Augustine in a passage that has become classical: "Mary is not the Mother, according to the spirit, of our Head, the Savior; for she is spiritually born of him . . . But she is truly the mother of us, his members, because she cooperated with Christ by her charity to give birth to the faithful in the Church, who are members of the head."[9] To be our mother, Mary must communicate life to us and the life she communicates is sanctifying grace, true life in the supernatural order. Because she is Mother of Christ physically, she is mother according to grace of all who are incorporated into Christ.

When the time drew near for carrying out the promise of the protogospel, God prepared Mary for her divine and spiritual motherhood by sanctifying her in fullness. She was conceived immaculate and was perfected, to a degree never duplicated in any creature, by sanctifying grace and its accompaniment of infused virtues and gifts of the Holy Spirit. Before a woman can be a mother in the natural order, she must have attained the physical perfection that enables her to do her part in conferring life on a new human being. Before Mary could be our mother in the supernatural economy, she had to have the supernatural life of grace in such abundance that it not only perfected her individually, but equipped her to share that life with her future children. "God so prepares and endows those whom he chooses for a particular office that they are made capable of discharging it."[10] More specifically, "God gives grace according to the purpose for which he has chosen a person . . . The Blessed Virgin Mary received such a fullness of grace that she was nearest of all to the Author of grace, because she received within herself him who is full of all grace; and then, by bring-

[8] Serm. 208, *PL* 39, 2130f.
[9] *De sancta virginitate* 5, *PL* 40, 399.
[10] *Summa Theol.* III, q. 27, a. 4.

ing him forth, she did her part in conveying grace to all."[11]
St. Thomas does not limit Mary's causality in the bestowal of
grace to the indirect function of giving birth to Christ; for the
Blessed Virgin "was full of grace . . . with a view to diffusing
grace among all men. It is a great thing in any saint that he
has grace enough to procure the salvation of many; but to have
grace enough for the salvation of all men in the world, that is
indeed the supreme perfection; and that is the case with Christ
and the Blessed Virgin."[12] This plenitude of grace which belongs
to Mary as the most exalted of God's creatures has been aptly
called, by analogy with Christ's capital grace, the Blessed
Virgin's "maternal grace," because it not only sanctified her
incomparably beyond all other saints, but empowered her to be
the mother of grace with regard to the whole human family.[13]

Yet Mary's fullness of grace did not actually make her our
spiritual mother; it only prepared her for that office. Spiritual
motherhood implies the actual production of grace in us, for
motherhood consists in the communication of life. How is this
verified in the relationship between the Blessed Virgin and us?

The initial phase of Mary's actual motherhood over us was
inaugurated at the incarnation when, in the little room at
Nazareth, the Son of God took to himself a human nature in
the womb of the Blessed Virgin. Relations between Mary and
the mystical body are discerned even at this scene of the annunciation, because then, as Pius XII teaches in the epilogue to
his encyclical *Mystici corporis*,[14] "her sinless soul was filled
with the divine Spirit of Jesus more than all other created souls
taken together; and 'in the name of the whole human race'
she gave her consent for a 'spiritual marriage between the Son
of God and human nature'."[15] Mary gave the bridal consent to

[11] *Ibid.* a. 5 ad 1.
[12] *Expositio in Ave Maria*, ed. Parm., 16, 134.
[13] See M. Llamera O.P., "La Maternidad espiritual de María," *EM* 3,
1943, 153f.; "María, madre corredentora," *EM* 7, 1947, 165.
[14] *AAS* 35, 1943, 247f.   [15] *Summa Theol.* III, q. 30, a. 1.

213

this divine marriage union as mankind's representative. By that act she made it possible for the eternal Word of God to acquire a mystical body from his brethren according to the flesh. As the Pope goes on to say: "within her virginal womb Christ our Lord was already crowned with the exalted title of Head of the Church." For nine months, Mary was the actual temple of God, and then in Bethlehem she brought forth her first-born Son: "she brought him forth in a marvelous birth as the source of all supernatural life." By her maternity she gave to the mystical body its head, its source of life; the Word became incarnate to be the first-born of many brethren.

We begin to see Mary's place in the divine plan. She is the Mother of God. That is her matchless dignity, her proper activity. Her motherly relation to us, her causality in grace flows from this activity. We should not unduly press the distinction between the divine maternity and the maternity of grace, necessary though it is for a correct grasp of the mystery; otherwise we may run the risk of losing sight of a concrete truth: God never thought of a Mother for his Son who is not also our mother. The redemptive incarnation was to be effected with the concurrence of the Mother of the whole Christ.

Pope Pius XII proclaimed this doctrine in a broadcast to the Marian Congress held at Ottawa in 1947:

> When the little maid of Nazareth uttered her *fiat* to the message of the Angel and the Word was made flesh in her womb, she became not only the Mother of God in the physical order of nature, but also in the supernatural order of grace she became the mother of all who through the Holy Spirit would be made one under the headship of her divine Son. The Mother of the Head would be the mother of the members. The Mother of the Vine would be the mother of the branches.[16]

That is why St. Leo the Great could say: "The birthday of the Head is the birthday of the body."[17] For "Mary gave birth to Christ, and in Christ she gave birth to Christians."[18] The Head

---

[16] *AAS* 39, 1947, 271.　　　　[17] Serm. 26, 2, *PL* 54, 213.
[18] Geoffrey of Vendôme, Serm. 7, *PL* 157, 265.

214

and the body cannot be separated, and therefore Mary "bore in her womb the whole mystical body, along with the physical body of Christ."[19]

Thus Mary's spiritual motherhood is a prolongation of her divine motherhood; she could not give birth to Jesus without becoming at the same time mother of his members. We can and must make a distinction between Christ the physical person and Christ the mystical person,[20] but we ought not to divide them. Jesus came on earth to be the first-born among many brethren, to incorporate them into his person, and in that way to make them sons of the heavenly Father.

This furnishes us with an explanation of the Blessed Virgin's motherhood of grace. When she became Mother of Christ, Head of the mystical body, she thereby became Mother of Christ in his members, mother of all those who have supernatural life by being one with Christ. We cannot separate in Mary the Mother of God and the mother of men. By consenting to be the Mother of Jesus, she consented by the same act to be the mother of all who would be members of the mystical body. The Mother of the One is the mother of all. And Mary, vaguely perhaps yet truly, understood all this when she replied to the angel: "Be it done to me according to your word."

Mary's active cooperation in bestowing grace is indicated in a number of Gospel scenes which show that Christ, beginning to distribute grace during the time of his mortal life, willed to associate his Mother with him. The first sanctification Jesus accomplished in this world was, according to the inspired narrative, that of St. John the Baptist; and this sanctification was

---

[19] Dionysius the Carthusian, *De dignitate et laudibus B.V.M.* 4, 16.

[20] Such is the bold language of St. Thomas: "Christ and his members are one mystical person" (*De veritate,* q. 29, a. 7 ad 11). "The head and members are as one mystic person" (*Summa Theol.* III, q. 48, a. 2 ad 1). "As the natural body is one, though made up of various members, so the whole Church, which is the mystical body of Christ, is accounted as one person with its head, which is Christ" (*ibid.* q. 49, a. 1). "Christ and the Church are one mystical person, whose head is Christ, and the body is all the just" (*Ad Col.* lect. 1, cap. vi).

wrought through the presence and word of Mary, on the occasion of her visit to Elizabeth. Filled with the Holy Spirit, John's mother cried out: "As soon as the voice of your salutation sounded in my ears, the babe in my womb leaped for joy" (Lk 1:44). This was the fulfillment of the angel's prediction about St. John: "He shall be filled with the Holy Ghost even from his mother's womb" (Lk 1:15).[21] The passage has universally been understood by theologians as referring to a true sanctification, cleansing the precursor's soul of original sin before his birth.[22] Some time after the nativity of Christ, Mary "presented him, newly born, as Prophet, King and Priest to those who were the first of the Jews and Gentiles coming to adore him."[23] The mother took her Child in her arms and held him out to the shepherds, and later to the Magi, for their homage. Since the first days of Christ on earth, she has fostered the adoration which men come to offer to her divine Son. She was never to be deprived of that privilege; until the end of the world she would always instill in men a love and reverence for the Church and its Head.

The Blessed Virgin's care and concern for the mystical body reached out to the public life of our Lord. The miracle at Cana took place at the instigation of Mary, and the witnesses of the event gave glory to the Master and believed in him. "Her only Son, heeding a mother's prayer in Cana of Galilee, performed the miracle by which 'his disciples believed in him' (Jn 2:11)."[24] Her activity in spreading the faith was clearly manifested. In thus marking her place in the first miracle worked by Christ, that which resulted in the act of faith of the apostles,

[21] See M. J. Lagrange O.P., *Évangile selon Saint-Luc,* 7th ed., Paris 1948, 42.

[22] See Lagrange, *ibid.* 17. St. Thomas, *Compendium of Theology,* St. Louis 1948, chapter 224, states: "Some men . . . have been sanctified in the wombs of their mothers, in virtue of an extraordinary privilege of grace. Thus . . . the angel says of St. John the Baptist: 'He shall be filled with the Holy Ghost even from his mother's womb'."

[23] *Mystici corporis* 247.   [24] *Ibid.*

God unmistakably wishes us to perceive the influence that would always be hers; the Mother of God has lost none of the power that was hers at the beginning.

On Calvary, the mystical Christ was born in pain; then it was that the Church was drawn from the side of her crucified Spouse, as Eve had been drawn from the side of Adam. "Eve from the side of the sleeper, the Church from the side of the Sufferer."[25] The soldier pierced the heart of the executed Christ and there flowed forth blood and water, images of the Christian sacraments, of that baptism and that Eucharist which owe all their efficacy to the passion. In that passion, Mary had her destined part: "Now there stood by the cross of Jesus his Mother" (Jn 19:25). Made ready by her fullness of grace to be the mother of grace, she then, intimately associated with her Son in the work of redemption, actually became the spiritual mother of mankind. Long ago, at the angel's visit, in her love she had begun to carry us in her heart as soon as she began to carry her Child in her womb. In this same love she brought us forth on Calvary with indescribable sufferings. The bequest of the dying Christ: "Behold your son," had prepared her for the ultimate renouncement. "Surely she is our mother, the mother of compassion and grace, to whom Christ entrusted us, expiring on the cross."[26] Her co-suffering with the death of the Redeemer regenerated the world; for Mary at the foot of the cross was more than ever the mother of our race to cooperate in gaining pardon for us and to procure for us the life of grace. Finishing the act begun at the annunciation, she offered the bloody sacrifice with her Son. While those events were taking place on Calvary, at a time when the Christian priesthood had not yet started to function, the Blessed Virgin shared, even more than at the incarnation, in the unique priesthood of the Redeemer.

---

[25] St. Augustine, *Enarr. in Psalm.* 138, 2, *PL* 37, 1785. See H. Rondet S.J., *art. cit.* 210.

[26] Pius VIII, *Praesentissimum sane, Bullarium Romanum* 18, 96.

Mary's maternal activity in the economy of grace at the hour when her Son was at the climax of his saving mission on the cross is so momentous and so stuns natural reason that the voice of the official teachers in the Church ought to be heard. Leo XIII tells us clearly: "The most holy Virgin, Mother of Jesus Christ, is also the mother of all Christians, for she gave birth to us on Mount Calvary in the midst of the Redeemer's excruciating torments."[27] Pius XII is no less explicit: "She became our mother when the divine Redeemer was accomplishing his sacrifice of himself."[28] In his great encyclical *Mystici corporis,* the same Pontiff says of Mary: "As another Eve she offered him on Golgotha to the eternal Father for all the children of Adam who were so wretchedly defiled by his fall, and her mother's rights and mother's love were included in the holocaust." At that decisive hour in the history of mankind Mary was not merely a private person, a mother suffering with her tortured Son, but was there officially as the new Eve. She was already the representative of her race when she became the Mother of Christ at the annunciation; on Calvary she performed her greatest act in that capacity. By divine appointment, she exercised, in accord with God's redemptive plan, a critical role in the Savior's sacrifice on the cross: renouncing her mother's rights and giving supreme expression to her mother's love, she offered her Son to the eternal Father. With full power of her will she united herself with Christ as the Eve of the New Testament, cooperating in the immolation of the divine Victim, the new Adam. We may not overlook the important fact that Pius XII draws Mary into the sacerdotal sacrifice of Jesus Christ. And the scope of her cooperation is clearly set forth: it extends as far as the sacrifice of her Son, reaching out to all the children of Adam.

The logical result of the Blessed Virgin's co-sacrifice is

[27] *Quamquam pluries, ASS* 22, 1889–1890, 67.
[28] *Mediator Dei, AAS* 39, 1947, 58.

brought to light in the same encyclical: "Thus she, who corporally was the Mother of our Head, through the added title of suffering and glory became spiritually the mother of all his members." Even at the moment of conceiving Christ, Mary was united with the members of the mystical body; but on Calvary, through her bitter sufferings with him, she acquired inviolable maternal rights over us and was charged with maternal duties toward us. She could hardly be called our mother in a full and proper sense unless she had a causal activity in our redemption. But such activity was hers; the consequence is that we owe the eternally momentous grace of our divine sonship to the wounds and death of her Son and to her own maternal agony.

Thus was the Church born, holy and sanctifying, drawn from the Savior's side. Yet we do not properly live by the Redeemer's death. This death is the life of our souls in the sense that it is its cause. By dying for us, by offering his death as the awful price of our salvation, Christ merited for us our supernatural life of grace. In the same sense, Mary gave us life by giving us the Savior's death. Supernatural life is the gift of divine grace and charity diffused in our souls by the Holy Spirit who comes to dwell in us: "The charity of God is poured forth in our hearts by the Holy Ghost who is given to us" (Rom 5:5). Dwelling thus in us, the Holy Spirit divinely and supernaturally vivifies our souls. Each person actually possesses this life through the application to him of the power of Christ's death and resurrection, and this application is made in the unfolding of time by the means established and left by the Savior to the Church. And so on the fiftieth day after the resurrection, the tenth day after the ascension, on the day of Pentecost, when the hearts of the disciples had been well prepared by prayer and contemplation in the Cenacle, the heavens were opened to let down the Holy Spirit; and the fruit of the sacrifice offered by the Redeemer and his Mother on Calvary was given in fullness and thereafter would continue to be given for all time.

The Mother of God had a function to perform in this application. She had surrendered up for us him who is the cause and source of our spiritual life. But beyond that, she had part in the actual bestowal of the Holy Spirit which completes the redemption; for it was her prayers that opened heaven for the descent of the Giver of Life. That and no less is what Pius XII, summing up the mind of tradition, tells us: "She it was who by her powerful prayers obtained the grace that the Spirit of our divine Redeemer, already conferred on the cross, should be given through miraculous gifts to the newly founded Church on Pentecost." The apostles closed ranks around their dear mother, united in a common spirit of recollection and love.

The chief activity responsible for the growth of the primitive Church is that of God and is ascribed by appropriation to the Holy Spirit. "The Paraclete, the Holy Ghost, whom the Father will send in my name, he will teach you all things and bring all things to your mind, whatsoever I shall have said to you" (Jn 14:26). But to organize the Church, the apostles had to draw on their own resources. They had to pray, reflect and consult with one another. They had to assemble their memories, revive the years passed in the company of Jesus, reproduce faithfully his doctrinal instructions and moral teachings. The light of the Holy Spirit was in them, but that light supposed human experience and knowledge which it would illuminate with new brilliance. In this work, Mary was with them. She had received the Holy Spirit in fullness and was therefore able to counsel, advise and remind them. Tradition assures us with many testimonies that the Blessed Virgin had such an office. Eadmer's voice is one of the clearest:

Her stay on earth among the apostles after the Lord's ascension was useful and even necessary for our faith. Although they were taught all truth by the revelation of the Holy Spirit, she, enlightened by the same Spirit, understood the depth of this truth incomparably more perfectly and clearly, and therefore many things were made known to them by her, for she had learned about the mysteries of our Lord Jesus Christ not only by way of simple knowledge, but by way of personal experience.[29]

Eight centuries later, Leo XIII echoes the same thought: after the ascension of her Son, the Blessed Virgin, "although worthy of heaven, was detained on earth to be the most excellent consoler and teacher of the newborn Church, for she had penetrated into the abyss of divine wisdom more deeply than anyone could have thought."[30]

Mary did not, of course, preside at the assemblies of the apostles, as though she had been invested with an authority superior to theirs. Peter, visible head of the visible Church, alone had the primacy over the young society. But in the taxing labor of organizing the Church conformably to the Master's intentions, Peter and his companions had to go over all they had learned from Christ and about Christ in the few years they had spent with him. In this enterprise, Mary assisted by recounting for them her rich experience that had lasted over thirty years. The Mother never forgot a detail of that marvelous period. "Mary kept all these words, pondering them in her heart" (Lk 2:19). The lowly routine and the striking events of that blessed life were originally her own treasure, and that treasure she gave to the Church.

Thus Mary remained on earth after the ascension, not for her own sake, surely, but for the sake of the mystical body. As in former days she had watched over the crib of Jesus, she later watched over the cradle of the nascent Church. The Church was teeming with the life and power that guaranteed its eventual triumph, but its members were still weak and its organization was rudimentary. It was a delicate organism, like a newborn infant. The dangers menacing its first steps were terrifying; the mystical Christ had to grow up in a hostile environment bristling with hatred, ill will and murderous persecutions. But under

---

[29] *De excellentia Virginis Mariae* 7, *PL* 159, 571. This work was once thought to be a sermon by St. Anselm; see *DTC* 4, col. 1977.
[30] *Iucunda semper, ASS* 27, 1895–1896, 179.

the guidance of the Holy Spirit, Mary and the apostles faithfully carried out their respective functions that were providentially assigned to them, and were successful in their efforts to conduct the infant Church through those first anxious years.

Our birth to the life of grace and our supernatural growth require the continued action of the mother who bears us and who bears Christ in us. And that is the way the Catholic populace understands Mary's spiritual motherhood: it not only was a past act whose effects continue to be operative in us, but is also a present and unceasing intervention in our birth to grace and our faltering progress toward heaven, in the gradual forming of Jesus Christ in us.

8

Development in Marian Dogma

ALTHOUGH many Christians firmly believe in the defined dogmas of the immaculate conception and the assumption, there are some, especially those of an inquiring mind, who occasionally experience perplexity. Where do we find these truths in revelation? Scripture seems to be silent about them; the Church of the early centuries seems to know nothing about them. This situation brings us face to face with one of the most difficult problems concerning the development of marian dogma.

Particularly, the solemn definition of Mary's assumption into heaven has focused the attention of contemporary theologians on this problem of doctrinal development. Prior to the proclamation, during the debate whether the assumption could be defined, voices were raised in demand for a renewed examination of the entire subject of dogmatic progress. Even the proposal to proclaim Mary as Mother of the Church at the Second Vatican Council caused considerable debate, though in this instance concern centered more on emphasis than on the actuality of Mary's motherhood of the mystical body of Christ: should Mary be proclaimed as Mother of the Church in the schema *De Ecclesia*, or should this proclamation be made separately? As it turned out, this proclamation was made both ways, in the schema, and by Paul VI separately in his promulgation of the schema.

All who refuse to rest content with mere marian formulas and who crave a real solution are confronted with the task of determining how the explicit dogma of today is contained in the implicit faith of yesterday. At this point, views begin to diverge.

Engrossing though the problem is, no solution acceptable to all theologians has been found. Yet we cannot doubt that there is a solution. Uncertainty in this domain arises not from a neglect or violation of logic, but from the inherent difficulty of following the higher logic that governs the development. Our own day has witnessed an event that has complicated the problem and made the quest for a solution more imperative; the definition of the assumption in 1950 did not rely either on historical evidence from the first Christian centuries or on theological conclusions. Theories framed along such lines have to be reëxamined in the light of the apostolic constitution *Munificentissimus Deus*.[1]

This document has furnished theologians with an incentive to reconsider the entire question of the nature and factors of doctrinal development. Many difficulties surrounding the problem stem from excessively rigid theories forged by some authors; when applied to certain dogmas that have been defined, these theories have to be acknowledged as insufficient. The situation invites us to face the possible necessity of revising previously held positions.

1. PRELIMINARY NOTIONS

If we ask how the dogma of the assumption or any newly defined dogma is contained in the deposit of revelation, we cannot expect a reply until we come to an understanding of the term "deposit of revelation."

Revelation is God's word, to which man is bound to yield the

[1] See M. Flick S.J., "Il problema dello sviluppo del dogma nella teologia contemporanea," in *Lo Sviluppo del Dogma secondo la Dottrina Cattolica* (*SDDC*), Rome 1953, 8. This volume contains a series of articles by various authors, previously published in *Gregorianum* 33, 1952 and 34, 1953.

commitment of faith because of the authority of God who reveals. Faith and revelation imply an affirmation, a proposition with its subject, its predicate, and a nexus asserted between both. According to traditional Catholic teaching, revelation is the speech of God who attests a truth, *locutio Dei attestans*. Every attestation made to men in words is an expressed judgment in which the subject represents a definite thing, and the predicate affirms an aspect or quality of that thing. Hence revelation is made to us through words perceived by the senses or directly formed by God in the mind of a prophet. Such revelation has no other content than what is expressed by concepts and judgments. The thing revealed is not the same as the concepts and judgments, but is represented by them and is revealed so far as it is thus represented.[2]

The truths of revelation are formulated in human language. By assenting to them, the believer is joined to God and adheres to him. Of course, faith does not stop with formulas, but reaches the things themselves. Yet revelation is not directly a person or a thing but is a truth uttered in human language by God, a body of truths expressed in our ideas and our words.

In the technical and current sense, a dogma is a truth revealed by God and proposed as such to our belief by the magisterium of the Church. The question of dogmatic development concerns mainly the original revelation considered in its sources; theologians undertake to study its leisurely elaboration in the course of centuries and the expression of it in precise formulas by the teaching Church. This is progress from the initial revelation toward dogma. However, there is also progress from one dogma that was defined earlier to another that is defined later—for example, from the dogma of Mary's immaculate conception toward that of her bodily assumption.[3]

---

[2] See C. Boyer S.J., "Relazione tra il progresso filosofico, teologico, dogmatico," *SDDC* 220f; G. Filograssi S.J., "Tradizione divino-apostolica e magistero della chiesa," *ibid.* 139f.

[3] *Munificentissimus Deus* 754: "*Arctissime enim haec duo privilegia inter se conectuntur.*"

225

To fix the exact notion of development, we first must distinguish the object of the dogma, that is, the revealed reality to which faith adheres and which is unchangeable; secondly, the human concept of the dogma by which we grasp this reality; and thirdly, the dogmatic formula which expresses this concept and this reality. All theologians agree that doctrinal development does not stop with the mere dogmatic formulation, but extends to the concept itself, that is, the understanding of the revealed reality.[4]

The term "deposit" is scriptural: "*O Timothe, depositum custodi*" (1 Tim 6:20); "*Bonum depositum custodi per Spiritum Sanctum qui habitat in nobis*" (2 Tim 1:14). "Deposit" may signify the realities that surpass the expressions we can formulate about them, such as God, Christ, the indwelling Holy Spirit, redemption, the Mass, the Church, grace, the sacraments. "Deposit" can also refer to the sense of these realities, our intellectual grasp of them by means of judgments and propositions. St. Thomas explains that the act of faith terminates in revealed realities or things, but so far as they are attained by revealed enunciations, without which these realities would be unknown to us or even nonexistent (*Summa*, II-II, q. 1, a. 2). The deposit of revelation comprises the entire mystery of salvation, with all the divinely guaranteed truths which open up its meaning to us. From a first divine light clarifying the facts, institutions and rites of the mystery of salvation, subsequent evolution disengages and brings out other and more explicit divine communications about these facts, institutions and rites. Thus, because the rite of baptism was viewed by the early Church with a clarity corresponding to the divine significance with which it was initially charged, it was administered even to infants and was never repeated. From these two usages we can conclude, by way of an authentic development, to the presence of original sin in infants and to

[4] See C. Dillenschneider C.SS.R., *Le sens de la Foi et le Progrès Dogmatique du Mystère Marial*, Rome 1954, 5.

the existence of an indelible character imprinted in the soul by the sacrament.[5]

This sacred deposit is a living thing. It is living in the Church, which is aided by the Holy Spirit to keep it pure from all alloy, to become more and more aware of it, and to propose it according to the dimensions it takes progressively by bringing into the open truths that were at first implicit in it.

The development is not tied down to the sole powers of reason, but takes place under the influence of the Holy Spirit. Pius XII in *Munificentissimus Deus* insists that the Spirit of Truth infallibly guides the Church toward a more perfect knowledge of revealed truths: "*eam [Ecclesiam] ad revelatarum perficiendam veritatum cognitionem infallibiliter dirigit.*"[6] Divine enlightenment is needed because the order of faith surpasses the order of natural knowledge both by the elevation of its mysteries and by the manner of its development. Faith comes from hearing, and hearing from the word of Christ (Rom 10:17). Hence it employs human words and rational concepts to attain revealed truths, but it attains them in a way that transcends the power of mere concepts and is capable of a development proportionate to the high range of its mysteries. Therefore, we should expect development to proceed by an unfolding of the implications inherent in the concepts; but we should also expect to be in need of supernatural reinforcement in our endeavor to perceive the implications.[7]

To preserve publicly the deposit of revelation throughout the centuries, God chose to endow his Church with an infallible teaching authority; a deposit infallibly revealed deserves to be infallibly interpreted. The Holy Spirit, who revealed in the apostles, ever afterward assists in the Church, that the Church

---

[5] C. Journet, *Esquisse du développement du dogme marial,* Paris 1954, 14f.
[6] *AAS* 42, 1950, 769.
[7] E. Dhanis S.J., "Révélation explicite et implicite," *Gregorianum* 34, 1953, 229.

may remember the truth in entirety, penetrate it deeply, and teach it alone.

2. THE CONSENSUS OF THE CHURCH AND THE JUDGMENT OF THE MAGISTERIUM

Tradition is equally a source of revelation as Scripture. At times, it may even be clearer and more complete than Scripture. Yet from one point of view, Scripture has an incontestable advantage: Scripture is inspired. Therefore, the question whether what it tells us is the word of God and hence whether it is revealed to us does not arise. Tradition, however, does not have consigned to it writings that are inspired, and so the question whether what it transmits to us is revealed is always in order, but the answer is not always easy to give.

Our main means of knowing whether the truths conveyed to us by tradition are revealed is the constant consensus of the living Church, particularly of its living magisterium. Pius XII recalls this fact in *Munificentissimus Deus*. The greater part of the document is given over to the task of recording the agreement of the Church on the doctrine of the assumption; such agreement imparts assurance that this truth is included in the deposit of revelation. The basic theme governing all other considerations and shedding light on them is the consensus of the ordinary magisterium, although great importance is attributed to the belief of the faithful, who were found to be in remarkable accord on this subject.

This unusual agreement among Catholic bishops and the faithful, who express their minds that the bodily assumption of God's Mother into heaven is definable as a dogma of faith, exhibits the concordant teaching of the ordinary magisterium of the Church and the unanimous faith of the Christian populace, as sustained and directed by this same doctrinal authority. By itself, therefore, and in a manner that is altogether certain and free from all error, it makes clear that Mary's privilege is a truth revealed by God and contained in the divine deposit

228

which Christ delivered to his spouse to be guarded faithfully and proclaimed infallibly. . . . Accordingly, the universal consent of the ordinary teaching authority of the Church furnishes a certain and solid
argument to demonstrate that the bodily assumption of the Blessed
Virgin Mary into heaven . . . is a truth revealed by God.[8]

The consent of the Church regarding the revealed character   *NB !*
of a truth may appear more plainly than the manner in which
the truth is included in the deposit. The Church advances in
time according to the good pleasure of the Holy Spirit, without
always being able to select the paths of its own progress. If he
wills to summon his faithful to a common belief before mani-
festing to them how the truth has been revealed, we have but
to follow his leadership.

Catholic schools generally teach that the magisterium of the   *NB !*
Church is the proximate norm and rule of faith. The encyclical
Humani generis has made this teaching its own, now for the
first time inserted into so important a document issued directly
by the Supreme Pontiff.[9] "In matters of faith and morals, this
sacred magisterium must be the proximate and universal norm
of truth for every theologian, since to it Christ our Lord has
entrusted the whole deposit of faith—Sacred Scripture and
divine tradition—to be preserved, guarded and interpreted."[10]

Authentic interpretation of the deposit, like the deposit itself,
has been confided by Christ not to individuals among the faithful nor to historians nor even to theologians, but to the official
teaching authority of the Church. The formula adopted in the
encyclical is precise, perhaps as in no previous papal document.
"This deposit of faith the divine Redeemer has given for authentic interpretation not to each of the faithful, nor even to
theologians, but only to the magisterium of the Church."[11]
When the question comes up, whether it is found there explicitly

[8] *AAS* 42, 1950, 765f.
[9] G. Filograssi S.J., "Tradizione divino-apostolica e magistero della chiesa,"
SDDC 147.
[10] *AAS* 42, 1950, 567.   [11] *Ibid.* 569.

or implicitly, the definitive judgment pertains solely to the Church.

Therefore, the main and indispensable organ of dogmatic tradition is the living magisterium of the Church. Apart from it, no authentic tradition is possible, for it alone is the authorized guardian and interpreter of tradition. Nevertheless, the conclusion does not follow that the magisterium is simply the same thing as tradition. The authoritative proclamation of the revealed message pertains to the magisterium alone and requires the obedience of the whole believing Church. However, not only the official witnesses and protectors of the deposit, but also, in dependence on and under the leadership of the magisterium, theologians, saints, preachers and the faithful generally collaborate in the transmission of revealed doctrine.[12]

When Pius XII sought the views of the bishops concerning belief in the assumption in 1946, he interrogated them not only about their own faith, but also about that of the people confided to their pastoral care. "We earnestly request you to indicate to us the devotion which the clergy and people committed to your charge, in accord with each one's faith and piety, have toward the assumption of the Most Blessed Virgin Mary."[13] In the consistorial allocution of October 30, 1950, he explains his mind clearly: "We sent letters to all the bishops, asking them to communicate to us not only their own views on the matter, but also to inform us about the views of the clergy and people entrusted to their charge." And because the voices of the pastors and the Christian populace professed the same faith "with a remarkable and practically unanimous accord,"[14] the Pope was convinced that he did not have to delay in pronouncing the solemn definition.

If the Pope thought that the magisterium was simply identi-

[12] See Dillenschneider, *op. cit.* 113ff.
[13] *Deiparae Virginis, AAS* 1950, 783.
[14] *Ibid.* 775.

fied with dogmatic tradition, inquiry about the belief of the lay faithful would have been superfluous. To testify to tradition, consequently, is to testify to the present and living faith of the entire Church of Christ, teachers and taught.

3. SCRUTINY OF THE DEPOSIT

Such consensus is based on some sort of perception that a truth of faith is contained in the deposit of revelation. *How* is it perceived?

The Way of Analytical Reasoning

To be believed with divine faith, a truth must be revealed in itself, not merely deduced from revelation. If a syllogism is really deductive and presents in its conclusion a concept that is in no way contained in a revealed premise, the conclusion cannot be said to be revealed. If, however, analysis of a revealed truth issues in the discovery of an essential property included in it, the syllogism is not simply deductive, and the concept that is found to be contained formally, even though not explicitly, in the revealed truth is not simply new.[15]

In other words, a syllogism that is employed to ascertain what a revealed truth actually involves serves the purpose of explaining. Its function is to lay open what is found to be formally implicit in the revealed concept. If an explicative (as distinguished from a truly deductive) syllogism leads to the discovery that one truth is contained in another, the newly apprehended truth is properly to be regarded as implicitly revealed, and the conclusion is to be believed solely on God's authority. But it is believed with divine faith because it is formally though im-

15 See M. F. Jiménez, "Un paso más hacia la solución del problema de la evolución del dogma: Existe el llamado virtual revelado?" *Rivista Española de Teología* 16, 1956, 325.

plicitly included in the revealed deposit, rather than because it is concluded from what is revealed.

Conclusions of this kind are implicitly revealed whether they enter into the extension of the subject or into the comprehension of the predicate of the revealed proposition. Into the extension of an idea enter all the individuals to whom or to which the idea applies. Into its comprehension enter all the notes that proximately or remotely pertain to its definition. In an affirmative judgment, all that enters into the comprehension of its predicate is affirmed of all the individuals that enter into the extension of its subject.

Consequently, when God expresses his revelation in a judgment, both the subject and the predicate are revealed. The comprehension of the predicate is as much revealed as the extension of the subject. God reveals of each individual entering into the extension of the subject all that enters into the comprehension of the predicate. In the same way as we analyze the extension of the subject to see which individuals are embraced in it, we can analyze the comprehension of the predicate to detect what is contained in it. As long as our reasoning proceeds by way of analysis, not synthesis, we do not emerge outside the revealed concept or judgment.[16] God reveals not mere words, but realities represented by concepts and expressed in judgments, and he is therefore responsible for all that the concepts and judgments formally state, whether explicitly or implicitly. When the analysis of the subject and predicate of the revealed proposition reaches its term, nothing is found to be new except that a truth which was previously present implicitly has been brought out explicitly and is now clearly perceived.

In the course of the history of dogmas, many truths have been uncovered solely in consequence of such reasoning and are today held as dogmas of faith. Therefore, they were revealed formally, though only implicitly; that is, they were formally implicit in other truths that were explicitly revealed.

[16] *Ibid.* 326.

However, although the development of dogma can take place by way of logical analysis or conclusion, such theories cannot satisfactorily explain all the dogmatic progress that has occurred, especially in the domain of marian theology.

When the Church defines a truth, it does not canonize human logic. It defines because, under the guidance of the Spirit of Truth, it discerns the truth by a higher methodology than is possible for our human inferences.

Passage from the implicit to the explicit cannot always be effected by procedures of pure logic. Thus theologians have never succeeded in demonstrating by sheer logic that the immaculate conception and the assumption are formally or even virtually implicit in the deposit of revelation. Yet these truths have been defined. Theologians of today, attentive to these two dogmas, have recognized the necessity of recourse to another way than that of human logic to account for the definability of certain truths.

Therefore, the whole task is not finished when we have analyzed the inspired text. The process of human reasoning is unquestionably valuable, for if God has spoken to men he has wished them to use their own powers for understanding his message. But he may have said more than the human letter is capable of conveying, for this human letter is unable by itself to carry the entire vast mystery which God has willed to make known. The basis of doctrinal development is not alone what God has said outright, but also what he has intended to communicate to us by the human language he has employed.[17]

The supernatural economy is a matter of God's free choice. Therefore, an insistent desire to deduce from the simple principle of Mary's divine maternity all sorts of privileges which do not clash with her condition as a creature hardly makes for good theology, because it overlooks God's sovereign liberty in the bestowal of his bounty. Every supernatural gift depends on God's free donation. A first gift does not necessarily demand a

[17] C. Dillenschneider, *op. cit.* 39f.

second, even if the second one seems to us to be perfectly in line with the first. The second is not inevitably connected with the first unless the first cannot exist without the second. No logical or dialectical method is capable of demonstrating with certitude that the divine maternity strictly demands the privileges of the immaculate conception or the assumption, which nevertheless are defined dogmas.

Therefore, other ways of detecting in the deposit of revelation the presence of implicitly revealed truths have been attempted. To supply for the inadequacies of logical procedures, recourse is made to the Christian sense as a means which God has made available to his Church for bringing out explicitly his profound designs in the supernatural order.

The Way of the Christian Sense

The way of the Christian sense is highly important; it is also difficult and requires delicacy in treatment. It goes by various names, such as sense of the faith, sense of the faithful, and social consciousness of the Church. It has nothing in common with the religious sentiment of the modernists, for "sense" as it is used in the term "Christian sense" connotes intellectual perception and supposes an intelligible object. Further, it has nothing to do with the "appetitive and affective faculties" reprobated in *Humani generis*.[18] Without implying a critical, systematic, scientifically elaborated knowledge, it is the voice or testimony of the consciousness of truth possessed. It involves discernment, intellectual appreciation, a power of discrimination. It supposes a supernatural illumination proceeding from faith, grace and the gifts of the Holy Spirit, a supernatural insight enabling the believer to discern, in fellowship with the Church, the implications of the revelation proposed to him by the magisterium.[19]

[18] *AAS* 42, 1950, 574.

[19] A discussion of the Christian sense and its functions in doctrinal development is presented by C. Balić O.F.M., "Il senso cristiano e il progresso del dogma," *SDDC* 106–134.

The Christian's supernatural power of comprehension is stressed by Pius XII in *Mystici corporis Christi:*

Our Savior endows his Church with power in order that the faithful may understand divine things more clearly and desire them more eagerly. From him comes into the body of the Church all the light that supernaturally illuminates those who believe. . . . Christ infuses the light of faith into believers. He divinely enriches the pastors and teachers, and especially his Vicar on earth, with the supernatural gifts of knowledge, understanding and wisdom, that they may faithfully preserve the treasury of faith, valiantly defend it, and with reverence and care explain it.[20]

In the apostolic constitution *Munificentissimus Deus,* the Christian sense that is common to pastors and the faithful is highly extolled. The decisive argument on which the Pope bases his stand is the general conviction shared by the Church teaching and taught. The faithful, "enlightened by divine grace and full of reverence toward her who is the Mother of God and our dear Mother, have recognized with daily increasing clarity the marvelous order and harmony of the privileges which God has providentially bestowed on the Redeemer's loving associate."[21] Not only have the faithful rejected the idea that Mary's virginal body could have fallen prey to corruption, but they even came to perceive her bodily glorification in heaven. For the truth of the assumption is "deeply rooted in the minds of Christ's faithful."[22]

The genesis of such conviction is not hard to explain. Every day the Christian people repeat the angel's salutation: "full of grace," and Elizabeth's exclamation: "you are blessed among women." They often have before their minds Mary's own words: "He that is mighty has done great things to me," and "all generations shall call me blessed." In their contemplation of the close bond uniting Mother and Son, they readily, by a sort of spontaneous intuition, apprehend her various great perfections.

[20] *AAS* 35, 1943, 215f.   [21] *AAS* 42, 1950, 758.
[22] *Ibid.* 769.

Further nourished by the Mass and other liturgical services, and by the preaching of their pastors, their Christian sense flowers into a knowledge of truths obscurely or implicitly contained in the deposit of revelation.

Other ages witnessed the same phenomenon for other truths. About the year 1332 John XXII mentioned in a sermon his personal view that the souls of the just would not see the essence of God until after the general resurrection and the last judgment. His discourse troubled many of his auditors; when the same doctrine was preached at the University of Paris, "a great murmuring arose among the students." The question was warmly discussed in various places and sees; finally the University of Paris along with the King petitioned the Pope to define "the truth in the sense in which it had always been held by the piety of the Christian people."[23] Thus in a question to which neither Scripture nor the early Fathers give a favorable testimony that is clear and explicit, the Christian sense turned out to be a witness of tradition.

That the Christian sense may be an effective factor in promoting the development of dogma, certain conditions must be fulfilled.[24] In the first place, the Christian sense must maintain contact with truths that have been explicitly revealed. There is no such thing as an autonomous Christian sense. For the simple believer as well as for the learned theologian, the source of all doctrinal evolution is the deposit of revelation proposed by the magisterium.

Secondly, the value of the Christian sense in doctrinal development is restricted to truths that directly touch or interest the greater part of the faithful. No help is to be expected from popular belief in subtle questions which are the province of erudite and scientific men. But the Christian people, enlightened by faith, are able to see the connection between Mary's divine maternity and the immaculate conception. The faithful possess

[23] X. Le Bachelet, "Benoit XII," *DTC* 2. 1, col. 665ff.
[24] See Dillenschnieder, *op. cit.* 327–341.

a similar insight with regard to the Blessed Virgin's assumption or her intercessory mediation in heaven. Truths such as these do not surmount the level of popular belief.

Thirdly and most important, the Christian sense must be (3) universal. The Christian sense of an individual believer is of itself lacking in dogmatic value, for individuals are not sheltered from error or prejudice. The situation changes when this sense is universal, when it is on the point of becoming unanimous among the clergy and the faithful. Then it has an indisputable value as a criterion of revealed truth. For the infallibility of the entire Church governed by the magisterium and guided by the Holy Spirit is implicated when the Christian sense is truly universal. This infallibility is on a plane different from that of the magisterium, for it is an infallibility not of official teaching and authoritative judgment, but of living and active testimony.[25] Even prior to the authoritative judgment of the teaching Church, therefore, the universal Christian sense is a real factor in doctrinal progress.

That a causality of supreme importance is exercised by the Holy Spirit not only in the definition of dogmas, but in the slow elaboration of them down the ages, is an acknowledged fact that does not have to be stressed. This Spirit of the seven gifts who dwells in us is the Spirit of Pentecost, the Spirit of Truth, who has a special mission to make known to the world the full message of Christ and his plans for our salvation. This special task is indicated in the words: "The Paraclete, the Holy Ghost, whom the Father will send in my name, he will teach you all things and bring all things to your mind, whatever I shall have said to you" (Jn 14:26). "When he, the Spirit of Truth, is come, he will teach you all truth . . . and the things that are to come, he shall show you" (Jn 16:13). Up to the death of the last apostle, the Spirit could enrich the deposit by revealing new truths; after that moment, he guides the Church toward a more comprehensive understanding by illuminating the

25 *Ibid.* 340.

mind, to dissipate the clouds still hiding the revealed mysteries.

In addition to the limitations of the Christian sense set by conditions like those outlined above, proper precautions in controlling it must be taken by the official teaching authority.[26] Faithful to its charge, the magisterium keeps the deposit intact, "adding nothing, subtracting nothing,"[27] always vigilant to see that the process of bringing out truths that were originally implicit is in conformity and continuity with revelation. Thus all doctrinal development remains under the management of the teaching Church. The Holy Spirit, whose infallible assistance is promised to the universal magisterium, will never permit a defection.

A further duty incumbent on the magisterium is that of investigating the sense of the faith. The Christian sense is by no means a norm for the magisterium to follow, but it is something for the magisterium to know about. The Church must inquire into its own living tradition, and in practice, before defining certain truths, takes the common sense of the faithful into account. Excellent instances of such investigation are the inquiries that were made prior to the definitions of the immaculate conception and the assumption. The profession of faith made by the Christian people certainly derives its force from the official teachers. Yet, since the Holy Spirit directly and immediately influences also the faithful, their belief possesses its own weight, and, as it precedes the definition, can give a certain orientation to the magisterium.[28] That is why the magisterium, when it is on the point of defining a truth that interests the devotion and life of the whole Church, interrogates the living faith of the Catholic populace.

This present, living tradition in the Church is precisely the universal Christian sense, through which the Holy Spirit gives testimony of the truth. When Mary's prerogatives that are de-

---

[26] *Ibid.* 343–360.   [27] *Munificentissimus Deus* 757.
[28] C. Balić, O.F.M., *art. cit.* 126, 133.

pendent on God's free selection are in question, theological reasoning is unable, of its own resources, to demonstrate with an evidence capable of convincing all theologians their inclusion in the deposit of faith. No theologian has succeeded in devising such a proof for the two marian dogmas proclaimed within a century.

Therefore, the magisterium did not think that it ought to wait until a fully conclusive demonstration was forthcoming. Although the Supreme Pontiffs inserted into *Ineffabilis* and *Munificentissimus* the arguments worked out by theology, they did not thereby issue any pronouncement on the value of those arguments. What they found important to know was not whether Mary's prerogatives were correctly deduced from revealed principles, but whether they are contained in revelation. To satisfy themselves on this point, they inquired into the *conscientia fidei* of the whole Church, of the teachers as well as of the taught.[29]

Most essential among the magisterium's relations to the Christian sense is the duty of interpreting and judging it, for the official teaching authority alone has the ability to determine without error its dogmatic value and universal character.

This predominant role of the magisterium is emphasized by Pius XII. The judgment of the bishops is what particularly interests him. "Especially we desire most earnestly to know whether you ... think that the bodily assumption of the Blessed Virgin can be proposed and defined as a dogma of faith."[30] In the harmonious teaching of the magisterium and the corresponding faith of the Christian populace that is sustained and directed by the magisterium, the Pope recognizes the sure sign that this privilege is a truth revealed by God and contained in the sacred deposit.[31] Doctrinal agreement among members of the hierarchy possesses a power not alone of authentic testimony which

---

29 C. Dillenschneider, *op. cit.* 371.
30 *Deiparae Virginis, AAS* 42, 1950, 783.
31 *Munificentissimus Deus* 756.

is within the capacity of the lay faithful, but of authentic teaching. "The universal consent of the ordinary teaching authority of the Church furnishes a certain and solid argument to demonstrate that the bodily assumption of the Blessed Virgin Mary into heaven . . . is a truth revealed by God."[32]

Therefore, in evaluating the Christian sense, the first and the last words belong to the magisterium, because from it the faithful receive the knowledge of the deposit which is the basis of their insights, and because it judges the dogmatic weight of their perceptions. Thus the Christian sense, as a factor in doctrinal development, and the magisterium are not on a par; the former is subordinate to the latter.

Accordingly, when zones of uncertainty remain on the side of the Christian sense, the teaching authority of the Church alone can resolve them. Properly to discharge its mission of faithfully guarding and expounding the deposit, the magisterium requires an infallible charism of penetration and discernment enabling it to perceive clearly and surely all that is involved in the great truths of revelation.[33] Hence the magisterium is a momentous factor in doctrinal development. It is divinely equipped for its task by a power that is superior both to the natural capacities of reason and to the intuitions of the Christian sense.

Ultimate recourse to the magisterium is not a desperate expedient contrived to solve the problem of doctrinal development when the efforts of theologians are deficient or when the witness of the Christian sense proves inconclusive. It is in the nature of things. It does not imply any degradation of the theologian's function or depreciation of the value of the Christian sense. It merely takes into account the power conferred on the teaching Church which surpasses both our human logic and the vigor of the sense of the faith.

[32] *Ibid.* 757.   [33] C. Dillenschneider, *op. cit.* 359f.

4. From Implicit to Explicit

Yet our minds remain unsatisfied as long as we do not clearly see how the truths proposed for our belief are contained in the deposit of revelation. In our endeavor to approach such perception, we must distinguish two steps in the delivery of the deposit to the early Church.[34]

The first step ended when the deposit was received in the collective intelligence of the apostles. The apostles came to their knowledge of the Christian mysteries by way of revelation that was proposed to them through the channels of sight and hearing and was clarified by a prophetic light. This light emanated from Christ and from the Holy Spirit whom Christ sent to them after his ascent to the Father. It reached each apostle directly; it is the light of revelation.

In the second step, the deposit issued from the apostles to be received in the intelligence of the primitive Church. Since the prophetic light that clarified revelation in the minds of the apostles did not pass over to the communities of the faithful, the latter could not penetrate its meaning as deeply or know it as comprehensively as did the apostles. For the apostles, as foundations of the Church (Eph 2:20), had to understand the economy of grace with a perfection that was proper for masters sent out with the heavy commission of teaching all the nations.

This does not mean that they carried in their minds the explicit formulation, automatically elaborated, of all the dogmas that would be promulgated during the coming centuries; the hypothesis seems highly improbable. If the apostles possessed such knowledge, how are we to explain their negligence or refusal to transmit it to us? And if they did so, what are we to think of the deluge of oblivion suddenly inundating the second generation of Christians?[35] Nevertheless, personally formed by

[34] C. Journet, *Esquisse du développement du dogme marial*, Paris 1954, 20ff.

[35] H. de Lubac S.J., "Bulletin de théologie fondamentale: Le problème du développement du dogme," *RSR* 35, 1948, 152.

Christ and illuminated by the Holy Spirit, they had an exceptional grasp of revealed truth, which they understood in the clarity of an infused prophetic light they could not share with their fellow men. They had to translate their knowledge into formulas which their contemporaries could comprehend. The deposit of revelation as thus expressed in their words, their writings, and their institutions is the point of departure for doctrinal development.[36]

To deliver the deposit, the apostles employed both the oral and the written word, as occasion warranted. The truth received from them by way of writing is Scripture; the truth received by way of oral speech is tradition, taken in the restricted sense as distinct from Scripture. To account for belief in revealed truths that are not expressly formulated in Scripture, we need not in all cases conclude that they emanate from oral preaching never put down in writing. The first Christian generations read Scripture as explained by the apostles and their immediate disciples and so were in a position to understand the written word in the sense intended by the authors. Thus with regard to *kecharitomene* in Luke, chapter 1: since Greek verbs ending in *oo* imply a plenitude, the verb can well be translated as "full of grace." Any uncertainty about its real force was easily resolved by oral clarification of the text, and this understanding was never lost in the ages that followed. Therefore, we are quite justified in taking *kecharitomene* as a basis of theology about the Blessed Virgin.

For another example, we may consider the doctrine on the necessity of baptism for infants. No text of Scripture expressly mentions children in this connection. Does this mean that we have to appeal to an oral source? Perhaps not. This teaching may well be comprised in texts such as the following: "Going, therefore, make disciples of all nations, baptizing them" (Mt 28:19); "Unless a man be born again of water and the Holy Ghost, he cannot enter into the kingdom of God" (Jn 3:5);

[36] C. Journet, *op. cit.* 28.

"Know you not that all we who are baptized in Christ Jesus are baptized in his death? For we are buried together with him in baptism into death, that as Christ is risen from the dead by the glory of the Father, so we also may walk in newness of life" (Rom 6:3f). What is needed here is less a recourse to an accessory, extra-scriptural revelation, than a light on the meaning intended by the apostles. And if the Church is divinely assisted to declare this meaning it has no need, in cases such as this, to appeal to an oral tradition parallel to Scripture—of which there is no early record.[37]

Accordingly, the point of departure for doctrinal progress is furnished by the apostolic formulas as they came from the mouth or pen of those who framed them and as they were grasped by the Church which was still under the direct magisterium of the apostles. Yet, however loyally the primitive Church adhered to these announcements, it was incapable of reading in them all their content that was still implicit. Many events and much time were required to exploit all the wealth stored in them. Such development would no longer be, as in the ages before Christ, a progress stemming from new revelations; it would be effected by new explicitations of the revelation that had been completed. To guide this progress a magisterium infallibly assisted by the Holy Spirit would be enough.

Transmission of the deposit necessitates its development. An inert deposit, such as a chest of jewels, is preserved without change. But a living deposit, as a plant or a child, is preserved by cherishing it and permitting it to evolve. If the deposit of revelation is living in the minds of those who possess it, they who have the duty of preserving it carry out their commission by fostering its development. Under the watchful care of the living magisterium, the deposit slowly and progressively flowers into "new dogmas": new not in their substance, but in their explicitation; not in their root, but in their development; not by

[37] *Ibid.* 38.

way of accretion from without, but by way of vital unfolding from within.

Since God wished the genuine sense of the revealed deposit, both oral and written, to be maintained for all time in integrity, he endowed the successors of the apostles with the light necessary for understanding and developing it infallibly, unceasingly and publicly. Without this rule of faith, we could not know with certainty the meaning of many revealed truths whose sense has been controverted, such as: "The Word was made flesh"; "This is my body"; "Depart from me, ye cursed, into everlasting fire"; "The charity of God is poured forth in our hearts by the Holy Ghost who is given to us." We would not know the real import of such truths except in a human and even conjectural fashion, and so they could never be objects of divine faith.[38]

Passage of a truth from an implicit to an explicit state is effected according to logic, yet requires the enlightening action of the Holy Spirit. For the process by which a newly defined dogma issues from the deposit of revelation unfolds entirely in the murky night of faith. It starts from a mystery, first grasped indistinctly and obscurely, to emerge in the same mystery grasped distinctly and clearly. To guide and guarantee this development, the sole light of human reason is not enough. The infallible assistance of the Holy Spirit must supplement man's intellectual deficiencies. Undoubtedly the theologian, beginning with a revealed principle, can obtain a conclusion by way of careful deduction. But apart from the magisterium divinely aided, he cannot be sure that the truth of faith standing at the head of his discourse has been apprehended without admixture of error or limitation and has been sufficiently penetrated to its depths.[39]

It is quite certain, as proponents of the theory of an intrinsic, metaphysical connection between the virtually implicit and the deposit of faith maintain, that if revelation came to a close when the last apostle died, the truth that has developed must be log-

[38] *Ibid.* 52.   [39] *Ibid.* 54f.

244

ically attached to the primitive revealed truth. For, as they point out, if there is no line of objective identity between the original revelation and the dogma of today, and if no logical connection exists between the statement of the initial truth and that of the evolved truth, we are in presence of a new revelation.

But a logical connection may exist between a truth explicitly revealed and an aspect or implication of this truth not yet recognized, and nevertheless our minds left to themselves cannot clearly discern it. A divine light is needed to make it evident. Human logic, working necessarily on the inadequate concepts in which the revealed reality is conveyed to us, cannot bring forth all the wealth of the mystery. In such a situation the Holy Spirit, who has informed us about this truth through the medium of deficient formulas, does not communicate to us a new truth —for then we would have a new revelation—but makes visible an aspect of the same truth that we did not distinctly grasp before.

Therefore, logic connects our evolved belief with the original revelation. But this is a divine logic that elevates and perfects our human logic by supplying for its shortcomings. Through the formulas in which revealed realities are expressed, God teaches us not simply what these formulas of themselves communicate to us, but what he intends to make known by them. The Spirit of God leads us to the whole truth implicit in the formulas.

Thus a logical connection links Mary's immaculate conception and her assumption into heaven with the revealed truth of her divine maternity. Our intellect, left to its own resources, is not powerless, for it is able to appreciate the seemliness of these two privileges; but it cannot fully establish the connection. An increase of divine light must shine into our minds. That is the work of the Holy Spirit who, without revealing anything new, sharpens the perceptiveness of the Church in order that it may discern this connection which human reason by itself is incapable of completely vindicating. The truth of Mary's perfect maternity is not augmented by the new dogmas; the only thing new is the clear idea of the immaculate conception or the assumption that was inadequately expressed in the human enunciation of her divine motherhood. What emerges at the term of the evolution is not a new truth, but the same truth more adequately manifested in some of its aspects.[40] We know, this time infallibly, by the increase of light which the illuminating activity of the Holy Spirit sheds on his Church, that the connection exists.

The histories of dogmas bear out these views. To define the immaculate conception and the assumption, the Church did not wait until theologians came to an agreement on the means of proving their definability. By its action in defining, the Church did not exactly "consecrate the theological speculation about these themes which implicitly contained the truth defined today."[41] Directed by the Holy Spirit, the Church placed the weight of its authority on the side of true logic—which is here the "logic" of God. This divine logic is by no means opposed to human logic, but surpasses and elevates it. The Church can define infallibly a truth contained implicitly in the deposit of revelation because it has its ear attuned to this higher logic which it exercises in response to the impulse received from the Spirit of Truth.[42]

Before proclaiming a dogma, the Church, of course, consults theologians, but it also judges them carefully. It takes cognizance of the theological reasons they propose, but does not pronounce on the demonstrative value of their deductions. It does not confer on their arguments a logic that was previously lacking. It simply attests that the conclusions of these arguments correctly express the living faith of the Church which cannot err

40 See C. Dillenschneider, *op. cit.* 102ff.
41 C. Boyer S.J., "Qu'-est-ce la théologie?" *Gregorianum* 21, 1940, 264.
42 C. Dillenschneider, *op. cit.* 104. See K. Rahner, "The Development of Dogma," *Theological Investigations,* Baltimore 1961, vol. 1, 39–77. "The Church has the organ to hear whether what is perceived by us as the consequent of theological elaboration . . . is in fact the word of God himself."

in interpreting revelation. The Church defines as a dogma only the truth it has discovered, with the Holy Spirit's assistance, to be implicitly contained in some mystery of faith that has been formally and explicitly revealed.

As is exemplified in the dogma of the assumption, a truth that was at first regarded as a theological opinion and became universal little by little, may end up by being recognized as revealed. Because of its affinity with other truths of faith and the lines of argumentation designed to set forth its connection with the deposit, the idea dawns that this truth may be included in divine revelation. The Holy Spirit's influence will tend to insinuate into the mind an assurance quietly cooperating with the inferential procedures that have already shown how this truth may be integrated into the aggregate of Christian knowledge. The opinion, still hesitant, will emerge that there is question of a truth which the Church may some day define. This view will be reinforced in the measure that believers discover that they possess it in common. At the same time its fruitfulness and its harmony with the whole of Christian faith and activity will clearly appear. If the Holy Spirit continues to direct minds along these channels, the persuasion may be widely propagated in the teaching and taught Church, until it becomes a quite general conviction.[43]

The very fact that such a truth gains credit in Christian circles, among theologians and the faithful, is a presumption in its favor. The presumption gathers strength if the magisterium positively promotes the doctrine. Thus in our own day the magisterium has not only not disavowed the doctrinal current proclaiming Mary's coredemptive office, but is openly sympathetic toward it.[44] Recognition by the Church becomes more manifest when a traditional teaching is embodied in the liturgy. This kind

[43] E. Dhanis S.J., Révélation explicite et implicite," *Gregorianum* 34, 1953, 233f.
[44] See C. Dillenschneider, *op. cit.* 112.

247

of recognition was given rather early to the Blessed Virgin's assumption, later to her immaculate conception.

In response to the promptings of the Holy Spirit, who infallibly guides the Church toward a more perfect knowledge of revealed truth,[45] conviction about the revealed character of the doctrine may continue to grow, to the point of inducing the official teaching authority to take a definitive position. Finally, if the Pope and the bishops of the world display a unanimous belief on this doctrine, the infallibility of the Church is engaged. Then nothing remains but a solemn definition.

Assurance that the immaculate conception and the assumption are included implicitly in the deposit of revelation was gained along these lines. In a similar way the magisterium may propose other truths for our belief in the future.

The arguments which have been so carefully and lovingly drawn up to demonstrate the credibility of such dogmas have notably failed to win a unanimous verdict of approval. Confronted with the argumentation, some theologians speak of rigorously logical reasoning, of strictly scientific, fully convincing deduction. Others speak of reasons of appropriateness, of analogies, of considerations calculated to court the mind's assent. Accordingly, these proofs do not seem to lead to the desired goal if they are appraised solely in themselves, apart from the living tradition of the Church. In the dogmas of the immaculate conception and the assumption, what is involved is less the logic of syllogistic deduction than the logic of the will of Christ, who freely decided that his mother should share completely in his own triumphant victory over the devil, sin and death.

5. Statement of a Theory

In all doctrinal development logic is at work, for newly defined dogmas must be logically connected with the original revelation

---

[45] *Munificentissimus Deus* 769: *"Veritatis Spiritus . . . eam [Ecclesiam] ad revelatarum perficiendam veritatum cognitionem infallibiliter dirigit."*

that was completed with the apostolic era. If this is not always human logic with its perceptions of metaphysical necessity arrived at by inferential procedures, it is certainly divine logic, the wisdom of God's free dispositions, entailing consequent necessity. God, if he so judges, with sovereign liberty wills a thing, an office, a function, a prerogative, an institution in the supernatural economy. Consequent on his willing, what he has willed is necessary. But how are we to discover this, since there may be no connection that is metaphysically imperative? In many cases such discovery is impossible without the Holy Spirit's enlightenment, which operates not by revealing new truths, but by illuminating the minds of Christian men and their supreme teachers to discern all that is intended in truths that have been explicitly revealed, conformably with God's free appointing.

When confronted by diverging theories of doctrinal development, the theologian does not have to single out one of them and repudiate the rest. All of them may have some part of the truth. The danger is to confine oneself within a narrow exclusivism. Thus, denial of all efficacy to the process of theological reasoning in the evolution of dogma would be reckless.

An adequate solution must await an adequate and detailed history of the development that has taken place. That history has not yet been written; problems still exist, and they are many. "Who could flatter himself that he has solved all the problems? Would such a claim even make sense?"[46] Even if the desired history were at hand, the full solution would still elude us. "The complete law of dogmatic development cannot be established until the entire process has reached its term. . . . The attempt to draw up an adequate formula to account for all development, with the aim of controlling the course of its history and of rejecting deviations from it as false development, is doomed beforehand to failure."[47] The future reserves its own problems.

With such warnings in mind, and with a deep conviction

[46] H. de Lubac S.J., *art. cit.* 132.　　[47] K. Rahner, *art. cit.*

that the underlying factors in dogmatic progress are, on the one hand, the Holy Spirit, inspirer and supreme illuminator of the deposit of revelation, and on the other, the Church with its divinely enlightened magisterium, we venture the following statement, which must be regarded as merely tentative.[48] The basic theory accounting for all doctrinal developments and capable even of shedding light on the vicissitudes that have marked a dogma's history seems to be this: the Church, and especially its collegial magisterium culminating in the Pope, is empowered by divine illumination to read progressively in the initial deposit the full truth which God the Revealer meant to include in the concepts, propositions and formulas in which his message to mankind is expressed—particularly in the case of those implicitly revealed truths, such as the immaculate conception and the assumption, that are not connected with what is explicitly revealed by intrinsic, antecedent, metaphysical necessity.

[48] H. Holstein S.J., "Le développement du dogme marial," *Maria: Études sur la Sainte Vierge,* ed. H. du Manoir S.J., Paris 1961, accounts for the development of the dogmas of the immaculate conception and the assumption in a way that is in substantial agreement with the theory here proposed.

Index of Names

251

1. In 200-300 words state the relations of Mariology to other parts of theology, bringing out the moderate position of the author (pp. 42-48)

2. Pros + Cons of Divine maternity as fundamental principle.
   (pp. 57-64)

3. Fundamental Principles of any science + theology in particular.
   (chap. 2, section 1).

4. Explain + Criticize Kesten's Theory of Receptive Co-redemption.
   (143-150

5. How do logic, faith and authority conduce to the development of dogma (231-240